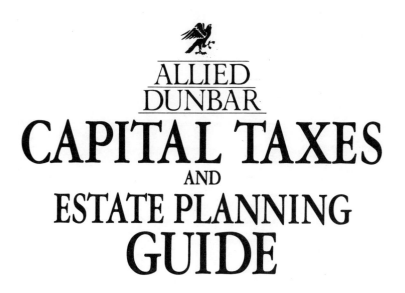

ALLIED DUNBAR
CAPITAL TAXES
AND
ESTATE PLANNING
GUIDE

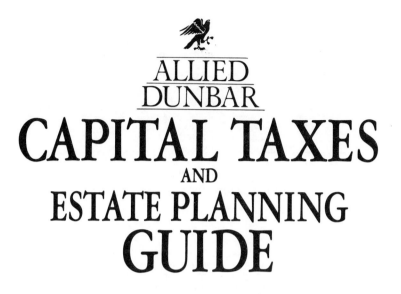

ALLIED DUNBAR
CAPITAL TAXES
AND
ESTATE PLANNING
GUIDE

By

W I Sinclair, FCA
A partner in Kidsons Impey

and

P D Silke, B Phil, M Soc Sc
Solicitor

LONGMAN

© Allied Dunbar Financial Services Ltd 1990

ISBN 0 85121 6412

Published by

Longman Law, Tax and Finance
Longman Group UK Limited
21–27 Lamb's Conduit Street, London WC1N 3NJ

Associated Offices

Australia, Hong Kong, Malaysia, Singapore, USA

A CIP catalogue record for this book is available from the British Library.

Printed in Great Britain by Mackays of Chatham PLC

Abbreviations

AEA	Administration of Estates Act 1925
AJA	Administration of Justice Act 1982
CAA	Capital Allowances Act 1990
CGT	Capital gains tax
CGTA	Capital Gains Tax Act 1979
CTT	Capital transfer tax
CTTA	Capital Transfer Tax Act 1984
DLT	Development land tax
DLTA	Development Land Tax Act 1976
FA	Finance Act
F2A	Finance (No 2) Act
FLRA	Family Law Reform Act 1969
FPA	Family Provisions Act 1966
ICTA	Income and Corporation Taxes Act
IEA	Intestates' Estates Act 1952
IHT	Inheritance tax
ITA	Inheritance Tax Act 1984
IPFDA	Inheritance (Provision for Family and Dependants) Act 1975
JTA	Judicial Trustee Act 1896
MFPA	Matrimonial and Family Proceedings Act 1984
NCPR	Non-Contentious Probate 1987 Rules
PA	Partnership Act 1890
PTA	Public Trustees Act 1906
S	Section (of Income and Corporation Taxes Act 1988 unless otherwise stated)
Sch	Schedule (of Income and Corporation Taxes Act 1988 unless otherwise stated)
TA	Trustee Act 1925
TIA	Trustee Investments Act 1961
TMA	Taxes Management Act 1970
WA	Wills Act 1968
WA 1837	Wills Act 1837
WSSA	Wills (Soldiers and Sailors) Act 1918
SSA	Succession (Scotland) Act 1964
TSA	Trusts (Scotland) Act 1921 & 1961
ESA	Executors (Scotland) Act

Introduction

This is the fifth edition of a book which was originally published as the *Hambro Capital Taxes and Estate Planning Guide* in 1982. The fourth edition appeared in 1988 and it has now been revised to reflect the many changes to the legislation which have taken place in the fields of capital taxes, trusts and estates.

During the past two years, sweeping changes have been made, both to inheritance tax and capital gains tax. Of particular importance to tax planning are the changes to capital gains tax gifts relief and the introduction of the independent taxation of husband and wife. The rules are covered in this edition, together with details of the other changes.

We are most grateful to those who have written to us with kind and helpful comments regarding previous editions, some of which have been taken into account in the preparation of this volume.

As a broad generalisation, tax planning covers two main areas. The first concerns taxes on income and the second taxes on capital. The book is concerned with the area of capital taxation and gives both a guide to the actual taxes as well as planning points. In addition, separate chapters outline the law involved in such matters as drawing up your will and forming trusts; also administering trusts and the estates of deceased persons. In other words, the book takes a comprehensive look at the taxes on capital and practical ways in which savings are possible, with an eye on the most important legal aspects of estate and trust planning and administration.

The book does not deal with the field of taxes on income. Naturally, you should always bear in mind that specific transactions may involve taxes on both income and capital. However, there is a logical dividing line in most cases. What is certain is that capital taxes often inter-relate one with another, which is one reason for including within a single book capital gains tax, inheritance tax and stamp duty.

Another reason for grouping together within one volume the various taxes on capital is that changes to the legislation sometimes cover more than one tax at the same time. Perhaps more important, a relief from one capital tax may raise planning considerations concerning another. For example, if you avail yourself of the capital gains tax rollover rules regarding certain gifts, you may well still ultimately be liable to inheritance tax in that respect.

The present Government stated its intention to carry out widespread reforms in the field of capital taxation. Many of these have been made. Capital gains tax reforms and the introduction of inheritance tax, together with capital gains tax rebasing and the revised rate structures have in general produced a more lenient capital tax system. However, should a different government be elected, sweeping changes are inevitable. It is our intention to bring out further editions to reflect major changes to the legislation, although not necessarily on a regular annual basis. This fifth edition is based on the law at 30 September 1990, including the Finance Act 1990.

Now, just a word about the way in which the book is organised. Each of the taxation chapters explains the basic rules, sometimes illustrating these with examples. Planning points are given where appropriate in the text. These will be found in contrasting italic type. A comprehensive table of contents at the front of the book makes it easy to refer to the appropriate subject matter and hence any related planning points. (In addition, an index is provided at the back of the book). A further feature is a section called *Tax Planning Signposts* which will help you locate tax planning points regarding selected situations.

This book is a companion volume to the *Allied Dunbar Tax Guide*, like which it has been designed as a general guide for both the professional and non-professional user. Because the book concisely covers a very wide field, it has been necessary to omit some of the exemptions and qualifications with which the law abounds. This does have the positive advantage of increased clarity. However, if a particular problem is not solved by this book, the time has come to look at one of the multi-volume text books or consult a specialist. Certainly reference to a solicitor will normally be necessary in matters concerning wills and trusts.

We acknowledge with thanks the very valuable assistance given to us in connection with this edition by our respective colleagues, including Messrs E B Lipkin, LLB, FCA, ATII and K G S Stockings, ATII of Kidsons Impey; and by Simon Arnot, BA, LLB, Barrister; M D Davies, BA, Solicitor; Wallace Dobbin, BA, Barrister; V J Jerrard, LLB, ACII, Solicitor; S G Reynolds, LLB; D C Vessey, BSc and C M Green (all of Allied Dunbar Assurance plc).

Our special thanks are extended to Vince Jerrard for contributing the chapter on capital taxes and life assurance and to Messrs Neill Clerk & Plant Hill, Solicitors, Glasgow and Greenock, for their most helpful advice concerning the chapter on Scottish law.

1 October 1990   W I Sinclair

P D Silke

Contents

6 Capital gains tax — companies 81

7 Inheritance tax 91

13 The law of wills, succession and trusts in Scotland 231

14 Capital taxes and life assurance 245

by Vince Jerrard

16 Capital tax planning signposts   279

1 The basis of liability to capital taxes

1.1 Who pays capital taxes?

Tax on capital gains arising in the UK is payable by individuals, partnerships, estates, trusts, companies and certain other organisations which are resident and/or ordinarily resident here (1.7). They are also liable to tax on capital gains arising abroad, subject to the rules outlined later in this book (2.21). Non-resident individuals etc, may be liable to capital gains tax on assets realised in the UK in certain circumstances, for example if they were used in a trade here (2.21).

Inheritance tax normally only applies to individuals and trusts (occasionally close companies). UK domiciled individuals (1.6) are liable on their worldwide assets but, in general, those not domiciled (or deemed domiciled — 7.5) in the UK are only liable on their assets situated in the UK.

In general, stamp duty is charged on documents (instruments) and may be payable by any of those listed earlier. However, if the instruments are executed overseas and relate to foreign property, no UK stamp duty is likely to be due. Reference should be made to the more detailed treatment of this subject in Chapter 15.

1.2 What capital taxes are payable?

In certain circumstances (see below) income tax may be chargeable on capital profits but this book is concerned chiefly with capital taxes. In particular, three main taxes apply in the UK to capital realisations and transfers. These are capital gains tax, inheritance tax and stamp duty.

Capital gains tax applies to chargeable gains (2.1). In the case of companies, corporation tax is charged on the gains.

The percentage rates at which stamp duty applies vary but are seldom more than 1%. Thus, in percentage terms, this tax is not likely to be as important as the others but could be highly significant in large cases.

One feature of the capital taxes listed above is that they are not mutually exclusive. In fact they could all apply at once. For example, if a father sold to his son a valuable property, for less than its full value, he could be assessed to capital gains tax, and inheritance tax might be payable if he died within seven years. Also, the son might need to pay stamp duty. Thus it is necessary to keep in mind all the capital taxes in appropriate situations.

1.3   Income tax on capital transactions

As mentioned earlier, income tax might be charged on capital transactions, instead of capital gains tax. In the case of a company, corporation tax could be charged as if the gains were revenue profits. This could normally happen in one of two ways: either certain anti-avoidance legislation would take effect, or the taxpayer would be treated as trading in the assets concerned.

In general, prior to 6 April 1988, the tax on capital gains was likely to be no more than on trading and in many cases less. It was therefore normally desirable to have purchases and sales of assets treated as *capital* rather than *trading,* if possible. However, from 6 April 1988, capital gains are generally taxed at the same rates as for income tax.

As well as your regular business, certain other activities might constitute *trading,* depending on the circumstances. The following are some general guidelines:

(1)   Regular buying and selling normally constitutes trading, although this does not usually apply to share dealings by an individual.

(2)   An isolated transaction might still be held to be trading if it is by its very nature commercial. For instance, a single purchase and sale of unmatured whisky would normally be treated as a trading transaction, because unmatured whisky is mainly owned for commercial purposes.

(3)   Isolated purchases and sales of works of art are not normally

trading. Here, the items are owned to be admired, rather than for commercial purposes. Capital gains tax, however, might be payable on sales of works of art for over £6,000 each (4.2).

(4) Isolated transactions in income-producing assets are not usually treated as trading. Capital gains tax would normally apply.

(5) What you do to something that you purchase before selling it could indicate that you are trading. For example, if you buy a ship, convert it and then sell it you would be treated as trading.

(6) Repetition of the same transaction is evidence of trading.

(7) Dealing in property is likely to be treated as trading.

(8) The possession of expert business knowledge regarding a transaction that you carry out will increase the chances of this being treated as trading.

1.4 Anti-avoidance legislation

Certain provisions counter the avoidance of capital gains tax itself. These impose capital gains tax and are considered later (2.20).

Certain other provisions impose income tax on otherwise capital transactions. The main ones are Sections 703 and 776 ICTA 1988. Section 703 deals with the avoidance of taxes on income by means of transactions in securities, Section 776 with so-called artificial transactions in land and applies to land in the UK owned by residents or non-residents. There are procedures for applying to the Revenue for clearance for both sections.

Another section of the Taxes Act 1988 which could result in such transactions as making and repaying loans giving rise to income tax is Section 677, which relates to trusts (9.3).

In general, the above provisions are beyond the scope of this book but Section 703 should be considered particularly in larger cases involving company reconstructions. It is advisable to seek clearance from the Revenue in advance. Note that for the Revenue to invoke Section 703 there must be some avoidance of taxes on income (either income tax or corporation tax), but not only capital gains tax. Fortunately, now that the income and capital gains of an individual are broadly charged at the same rates, the various anti-avoidance provisions mentioned above are generally no longer so penal.

- *The main requisite for Section 776 to bite is that a capital gain is realised on land which was purchased or developed with a view to selling at a profit. It helps a lot in contesting an assessment under this section to have documentary evidence, such as minutes of meetings and correspondence, to the effect that when you bought the land, you did so for investment purposes, etc, and not for quick sale.*

1.5 Domicile and residence

As indicated earlier, the incidence of the main capital taxes is greatly affected by the domicile and residence of the potential taxpayer. The rest of this chapter therefore deals with this important subject. The position is summarised in the following table and dealt with in more detail on the next pages. (Domicile is defined in para 1.6 and residence in para 1.7.)

1.5.1 Table: The effect of domicile and residence on capital taxes

Tax	Situation of assets	Taxed on arising basis	Taxed on remittance basis (2.35)	Tax free
Capital gains tax	UK or Abroad	UK domiciled and resident or ordinarily resident	Non-domiciled but resident or ordinarily resident (assets abroad)	Neither resident nor ordinarily resident
Inheritance tax (residence is normally immaterial)	UK	UK domiciled or non-domiciled		
	Abroad	UK domiciled or deemed domiciled (7.5)		Non-domiciled

Tax treatment depending on taxpayers' residence and domicile

1.6 Domicile

Your domicile is the country which you regard as your natural home. It is your place of abode to which you intend to return in the event of your going abroad. For most people it is their country of birth. Everyone has one domicile only. Unlike dual nationality, it is not possible to have two domiciles under English law. There are three main categories of domicile:

(1) Domicile of origin.
(2) Domicile of choice.
(3) Domicile of dependency.

You receive a *domicile of origin* at birth; it is normally that of your father at the date of your birth. In the case, however, of an illegitimate child or one born after the death of his father his domicile of origin is that of his mother. Your domicile of origin can be abandoned and you can take on a domicile of choice (see below). You will quickly revert to your domicile of origin, however, if you take up permanent residence again in that country.

If you abandon your domicile of origin and go and live in another country with the intention of permanently living there, the new country will become your *domicile of choice*. You will normally have to abandon most of your links with your original country of domicile (1.8). If you lose or abandon your domicile of choice, your domicile of origin automatically applies once again, unless you establish a new domicile of choice.

Certain dependent individuals are deemed incapable of choosing a new domicile. They have a *domicile of dependency* which is always fixed by the operation of the law. Dependants for this purpose include minors, women married before 1 January 1974 and mental patients. A child under 16 years of age automatically has the domicile of his father if he is legitimate, and otherwise that of his mother. If, however, a girl of under 16 marries then she takes on her husband's domicile. (Prior to 1 January 1974 the relevant age was 18.) In Scotland a boy has an independent domicile from age 14 and a girl from age 12.

Prior to 1 January 1974, a wife assumed the domicile of her husband while they were married. After the end of the marriage (by death or divorce) the woman kept her former husband's domicile unless she took on a fresh domicile of choice. Since 1 January 1974, however, a wife's domicile is independent of that of her husband. If married before that date, the husband's domicile at 1 January 1974 remains as the wife's deemed domicile of choice until displaced by positive action.

1.7   Residence

Your residence for tax purposes is something which is fixed by your circumstances from year to year and you may sometimes be treated as being resident in more than one country at the same time.

Residence depends on the facts of each case and is determined by the individual's presence in a country, his objects in being there and his future intentions regarding his length of stay. The main criterion is the length of time spent in the country during each tax year. Another point is whether a 'place of abode' is kept in the country (1.7.5).

If you have always lived in this country you are treated as being *ordinarily resident* here. Ordinary residence means that the residence is not casual and uncertain but that the individual who resides in a particular country does so in the ordinary course of his life. It implies residence with some degree of continuity, according to the way a man's life is usually ordered.

If you come to this country with the intention of taking up permanent residence here, it is Revenue practice to regard you as being both resident and ordinarily resident in the UK from your date of arrival. If, however, you originally did not intend to take up permanent residence here, you would not be considered ordinarily resident on arrival. You would normally become ordinarily resident from the time when you have been here for two complete tax years, or earlier, if you keep a place to live in this country.

1.7.1   Individuals
(ICTA 1988 Ss334-336)

If a person visits this country for some temporary purpose only, and not with the intention of establishing his residence here, he is not normally treated as being a UK resident unless he spends at least six months here during the tax year.

An overseas visitor, however, might be treated as acquiring UK residence if he pays habitual substantial visits to this country. This normally means coming here for at least four consecutive years and staying for an average of at least three months each year. If you wish to remain non-resident you must avoid habitual visits.

If you pay only short casual visits abroad you will not lose your UK residence, but if an entire tax year is included in any continuous period spent abroad you will normally be treated as being non-resident for at least that intervening tax year (1.7.6).

1.7.2 **Companies**
(ICTA 1988 Ss749 & 765-767 & FA 1988 Ss66 & 130-132)

The rules for determining the residence of a company were radically altered from 15 March 1988. Subject to transitional provisions (see below), a company which is incorporated in the UK is treated for tax purposes as being resident here. Prior to 15 March 1988, a company was deemed to be resident where its central control and management were carried out. This was not necessarily where the company was registered although normally the central control and management would be exercised in the country in which the company was registered.

If, however, a company simply had its registered office here but carried on all its business from offices abroad and held its board meetings abroad, it was non-resident. Such companies will not come within the new rules for determining residence until 15 March 1993, provided they were already non-resident on 14 March 1988 or became non-resident later with Treasury consent, applied for by that date. (Such companies must, in general continue to carry on business.)

If a company registered abroad transacts some of its business in this country, it will not normally be treated as being UK resident provided its management and control are exercised abroad, which includes all board meetings being held abroad.

Taxes Act 1988 S765 contains penal provisions which prevented a UK company from becoming non-resident without Treasury consent being obtained. Such consent was also required to transfer part or all of its business to a non-resident and for certain share transactions. These sections remained in force despite the abolition of exchange control.

From 15 March 1988, such consent is no longer needed (except for certain share and debenture transactions) and it is replaced by a tax charge on unrealised gains. Companies intending to emigrate must notify the Inland Revenue in advance providing an estimate of their UK tax commitments including tax on unrealised gains, and details of arrangements to settle such tax. If the tax is not paid, penalties may be charged. Furthermore, directors and group companies can be held responsible for tax and interest.

1.7.3 Partnerships
(ICTA 1988 S112)

Where any trade or business is carried on by a partnership and the control and management of the trade are situated abroad, the partnership is deemed to be resident abroad. This applies even if some of the partners are resident in this country and some of the trade is carried on here.

1.7.4 Trusts
(FA 1989 Ss 110 & 111)

A trust is generally treated for capital gains tax purposes as being resident and ordinarily resident in the UK unless its general administration is ordinarily carried on outside this country and a majority of the trustees are neither resident nor ordinarily resident here. (Stricter rules apply for income tax. If there is a UK settlor, all the trustees must be non-resident for the trust to be so treated.)

In general, there are stricter rules for income tax. For these purposes, broadly from 1989–90 (with some exceptions), special rules apply where at least one trustee is UK resident and one is not, depending on the settlor's status when he created the settlement or introduced further funds. If the settlor was then resident, ordinarily resident or domiciled in the UK, for determining the residence of the trust, all of the trustees are treated as being UK resident. Otherwise, they are all treated as being resident outside the UK. (A similar rule concerns the residence of executors, etc.) An important exception is where none of the trustees was UK resident from 1 October 1989 to 5 April 1990.

1.7.5 Place of abode in the UK
(ICTA 1988 S335)

If you maintain a house or flat in this country *available* for your occupation this will usually be a factor towards deciding that you are resident here. You will normally be treated as resident here for any tax year during which you set foot in the UK. Your residence position will, however, be decided without regard to any place of abode maintained for your use in the UK in the following circumstances:

(1)   You work full-time in a trade, profession or vocation no part of which is carried on in this country.
(2)   You work full-time in an office or employment, all the duties of

which (ignoring merely incidental duties) are performed outside the UK.

1.7.6 Visits abroad
(ICTA 1988 S334)

If you are a citizen of the Commonwealth or the Republic of Ireland and your ordinary residence has been in the UK you are still charged to income tax if you have left this country if it is for the purpose of only occasional residence abroad.

In order to obtain non-residence for UK tax purposes your overseas residence must be more than merely occasional — it must have a strong element of permanency. The normal Revenue requirements are as follows:

(1) A definite intention to establish a permanent residence abroad.
(2) The actual fulfilment of such an intention.
(3) Normally a full tax year should be spent outside this country before you are considered non-resident (although short periods in the UK may be allowed by the Revenue). Thus if you leave the country permanently on 30 September 1990 and have some evidence of this (eg, having sold your house and set up house abroad), you will be provisionally treated as being non-resident; but this will only be confirmed after 5 April 1992. If you leave the UK and are treated on departure as being no longer resident nor ordinarily resident, by Revenue concession you will not be charged to capital gains tax on any disposals after your departure.

1.8 Changing your domicile and residence

As has been indicated already, domicile and residence normally run together but domicile is much more difficult to change.

The way in which to change your residence is summarised above. You simply establish a permanent residence abroad and remain out of this country for a complete tax year. (In certain circumstances short visits to the UK are allowed.) After that you must avoid returning to this country for as much as six months in any one tax year, averaging less than three months here every year. If, however, you have a place of abode available for you in the UK you are regarded as being resident here for any tax year during which you pay a visit (no matter how short), unless your residence abroad is for the purpose of an overseas trade or employment.

In order to change your domicile to a new domicile of choice, you should take as many steps as possible to show that you regard your new country as your permanent home.

The following points are relevant to establishing a particular country as your new domicile:

(1) Develop a long period of residence in the new country.
(2) Purchase or lease a home.
(3) Marry a native of that country.
(4) Develop business interests there.
(5) Make arrangements to be buried there.
(6) Draw up your will according to the law of the country.
(7) Exercise political rights in your new country of domicile.
(8) Arrange to be naturalised (not vital).
(9) Have your children educated in the new country.
(10) Resign from all clubs and associations in your former country of domicile and join clubs, etc in your new country.
(11) Any religious affiliations that you have with your old domicile should be terminated and new ones established in your new domicile.
(12) Arrange for your family to be with you in your new country.

The above are some of the factors to be considered and the more of these circumstances that can be shown to prevail, the sooner you will be accepted as having changed your domicile.

● *Reference to the table earlier in this chapter (1.5.1) will illustrate the importance of residence and domicile in ascertaining whether or not an individual is liable to inheritance tax and capital gains tax. If you are able to become non-resident for tax purposes you will avoid liability to UK income tax on many classes of income and if you are also not ordinarily resident here you will not be liable for any UK capital gains tax on sales of assets here or abroad.*

● *If you become neither domiciled nor deemed domiciled (7.5) in this country you will only be liable for UK inheritance tax on assets situated here.*

● *A very effective way of avoiding liability to UK taxes is to emigrate and take all of your assets out of this country. Once you have ceased to be resident and are no longer domiciled nor deemed domiciled here you*

will be outside the UK tax net regarding all income and assets arising
and situated abroad. (You should note that if you have shares in a UK
company with its registered office here, the shares are treated for
inheritance tax purposes as located in this country unless they are
bearer securities—7.26.)

- *If you have a large potential capital gain you should defer taking this
until you cease to be resident and ordinarily resident here; in this way
you will avoid capital gains tax. (If you wish you may then return to this
country in the following tax year.)*

- *As a pure tax-saving exercise, you should only consider emigrating if
you are a very wealthy person; and even then you should only go to a
country where you feel that you will be happy. If, however, you wish to
spend your retirement abroad, then in choosing the country, you should
take into account the tax which you would have to pay there. Once you
have established your foreign residence and domicile, in order to
preserve this situation, you must avoid paying regular visits to the UK
(1.7.1).*

2 Capital gains tax — general

2.1 Introduction

Subject to the specific rules that are summarised in the following pages, you will be charged to capital gains tax in respect of any chargeable gains that accrue to you on the disposal of assets during a given tax year. You deduct from your capital gains any allowable capital losses (2.14).

Individuals are charged to capital gains tax at the same rates as income tax (25% and 40%). However, prior to 6 April 1988, the capital gains tax rate was 30%. An annual exemption of £5,000 applies from 6 April 1988 for individuals and broadly £2,500 for trusts (5.2.1). Companies (6.1) pay corporation tax on their capital gains, subject to special rules for authorised investment trusts and unit trusts (3.3.1).

Most references throughout this chapter are to the Capital Gains Tax Act 1979 which consolidates the relevant legislation from Finance Act 1965 onwards. (Although a short term capital tax had briefly existed earlier, capital gains tax as we now know it was introduced by FA 1965.)

2.2 Chargeable gains
(CGTA S28)

A chargeable gain is a gain which accrues after 6 April 1965 to a tax-payer (including a company, trust, partnership, individual, etc), such gain being computed in accordance with the provisions of the relevant legislation. There must, however, be a disposal of assets in order that there should be a chargeable gain. Disposals include sales, gifts, etc (2.8).

2.3   Liability
(CGTA Ss2, 12 & 14)

Any company, trust, partnership, individual or other taxpayer is chargeable to capital gains tax on any chargeable gains accruing to him in a year of assessment during any part of which he is either resident or ordinarily resident (1.7) in this country.

Also, a non-resident taxpayer who carries on a trade in the UK through a branch or agency is generally liable to capital gains tax accruing on the disposal of: (*a*) assets in this country used in his trade, or (*b*) assets held here and used for the branch or agency.

If you are resident or ordinarily resident here during a tax year your world-wide realisations of assets will normally be liable to capital gains tax. However, if you are not domiciled in this country (1.6) you are only charged to capital gains tax on your overseas realisations of assets to the extent that such gains are remitted here (2.21.1).

2.4   Capital gains tax rates
(FA 1988 Ss98-103)

Prior to 6 April 1988 (apart from the alternative basis before 6 April 1980) capital gains tax was applied at a single rate of 30%, for individuals (and trusts and partnerships). However, from 6 April 1988, the rules have been changed as follows:

(1)   Individuals now suffer capital gains tax at 25% and 40%.
(2)   The rate for accumulation and maintenance trusts and discretionary settlements is generally 35% (5.2).
(3)   Other trusts will in general pay 25%.
(4)   If the settlor or his or her spouse has any interest in or rights relating to a UK settlement, any capital gains will be subjected to his or her rates (5.2).
(5)   The capital gains of companies continue to bear corporation tax at the appropriate rate (6.1).
(6)   To find the rate or rates payable by an individual, you take the total gains less losses for the tax year, deduct losses brought forward and the annual exemption. This is then considered together with the taxable *income* after reliefs and allowances. (Note, however, that income tax losses cannot be set against capital gains.) The first £20,700 attracts 25% and the remainder 40%.
(7)   Thus, if your taxable income after allowances for 1990-91 is

£15,700, you have £20,700-£15,700 = £5,000 of your 25% rate band unused. This means that if your net capital gains for 1990-91 are £15,000, this is reduced to £10,000 by your annual exemption (£5,000). Your capital gains tax is thus:

£5,000 at 25%	1,250
£5,000 at 40%	2,000
	£3,250

(8) Husband and wife were considered together for the above rules for 1988–89 and 1989–90 but not subseqently. Thus they are treated separately for 1990–91 and each has a full basic rate (25%) tax band (2.8.1). This represents a substantial improvement for 1990-91 and future years.

2.5 Annual reliefs

The first £5,000 of your net gains for 1990–91 is exempted from capital gains tax (2.5.3). For 1990–91, but not previously, the £5,000 exemption is available in full for both husband and wife. Exemptions for previous years are shown in the following table. (Prior to 6 April 1980 different rules applied as below.)

2.5.1 Table: Annual exemptions

	Individuals etc £	Certain Trusts £
1980-81 & 1981-82	3,000	1,500
1982-83	5,000	2,500
1983-84	5,300	2,650
1984-85	5,600	2,800
1985-86	5,900	2,950
1986-87	6,300	3,150
1987-88	6,600	3,300
1988-89, 1989-90 & 1990-91	5,000	2,500

Note The full rate applies to individuals, personal representatives (2.5.3), trustees for the mentally handicapped and those receiving attendance allowance. The lower rate broadly applies to other trusts.

2.5.2 Alternative basis of charge before 6 April 1980
(FA 1965 S21; FA 1976 S52 & CGTA S5 & Sch 1))

In calculating your capital gains tax liability prior to 6 April 1980, instead of paying the basic 30% rate you paid a lower amount in certain circumstances. For 1977–78, 1978–79 and 1979–80 your net capital gains (including those of your wife unless you were separated) were taxed at less than 30% broadly, as follows:

(1)   If your chargeable gains were no more than £1,000, no tax was charged.
(2)   The excess over £1,000 was taxed at 15%, provided your total net gains were no more than £5,000.
(3)   If your total net gains were in the band from £5,000 to £9,500, your tax was £600 (£4,000 at 15%) plus half of the excess over £5,000. Thus on total gains of £8,000 you paid £600 + (8,000–5,000)/2 = £2,100.
(4)   Fuller details appear in previous editions of this book.

2.5.3 Annual exemptions from 6 April 1980
(CGTA S5 & Sch 1; FA 1980 Ss77 & 78; FA 1982 S80 & FA 1988 S108)

The annual exemption system was changed from 6 April 1980. The following rules apply (the rates shown are for 1990–91):

(1)   The first £5,000 of your net gains is exempted from capital gains tax. This applies no matter how high are your total gains for the year.
(2)   Any set-off for losses from previous years (2.14) is restricted to leave £5,000 of gains to be exempted. In this way your exemption is protected and you have more losses to carry forward. All losses for the same year must be deducted, however, in arriving at the net gains.
(3)   These rules apply to personal representatives for the tax year of death and the next two years.
(4)   The rules also apply to trusts for the mentally disabled and for those receiving attendance allowance.
(5)   For other trusts set up before 7 June 1978 the first £2,500 of net capital gains each year is exempt (5.2.1).
(6)   Trusts set up after 6 June 1978 by the same settlor each have an exemption of £2,500 divided by the number of such trusts. Thus if you have set up three trusts since that date, they each have an exemption of £834. In any event each trust obtains an exemption of at least £500.

(7)   Trusts where the settlor or the spouse retains an interest do not benefit from any separate exemption. CGT is payable at the settlor's rates.

(8)   Any set off for trust losses from previous years is restricted so that the appropriate exemption (£2,500 etc) is not wasted.

(9)   The above figures apply for future years subject to indexation. Unless Parliament otherwise directs, the exemptions will be increased in line with the increase in the Retail Price Index for the December before the year of assessment compared with the previous one.

(10) Only one annual exemption applied for husband and wife together for 1989—90 and earlier years. However, from 6 April 1990, they have one each.

(11) The annual exemptions from 1980–81 to 1990–91 are detailed in (2.5.1).

2.5.4   £5,000 net gains exemption

● *Make the best use of this relief. If your sales of chargeable assets produce net gains which are not normally far in excess of £5,000 in any tax year, try to spread your realisations so that your net gains are no more than £5,000 each year – you will then pay no capital gains tax.*

● *Remember that each of your minor children (and also your spouse) can realise up to £5,000 of net gains each year and pay no capital gains tax. It is thus a good idea to spread your share dealings, etc throughout your family.*

● *If your net gains are less than £5,000 in any tax year, realise further profits. In this way, you will be able to make better use of the exempt band.*

● *Should your net gains be rather more than £5,000 for a tax year, sell assets to create capital losses to bring the net total for the year below £5,000. If you wish to buy back quoted shares which you have sold in this way, you may do so in the same stock exchange account (bed and breakfast). However, your sale and repurchase must not be on the same day, otherwise they will be matched against each other and the required capital gain or loss will not be created.*

2.5.5   Example: Capital gains tax — £5,000 exemption

Mr A has losses carried forward from 1989–90 of £4,000. He has made no realisation previously in 1990–91 and now wishes to realise £30,000 from share sales in a tax-effective manner. His holdings are as follows and he intends to follow his broker's advice to keep his shares in B Ltd. Ignoring the effects of indexation allowance (2.11) and assuming all shares were purchased after 31 March 1982 (2.10), how should he proceed?

Details	Cost	Value
	£	£
Shares in A Ltd	4,000	7,000
Shares in B Ltd	10,000	6,000
Shares in C Ltd	3,000	9,000
Shares in D Ltd	5,000	15,000
Shares in E Ltd	7,000	6,000
Government Stock	5,000	8,000

It is suggested that Mr A sells all his shares in A Ltd and D Ltd realising 22,000, at the same time selling his shares in B Ltd and buying them back next day (2.14.1).

Sales of Government Stock are free from capital gains tax. Thus the holding worth £8,000 can be sold tax free. As a result of those transactions Mr A will realise £30,000 without any capital gains tax liability as follows:

Details	Cost	Proceeds	Gain (Loss)	
	£	£	£	
Shares in A Ltd	4,000	7,000	3,000	
Shares in B Ltd	10,000	6,000	(4,000)	Repurchased next
Shares in D Ltd	5,000	15,000	10,000	day
Government Stock	5,000	8,000	—	(Exempt)
			9,000	
	Losses B/fwd		(4,000)	
	Annual exemption —			
	1990-91		(5,000)	
	Taxable		Nil	

2.6   Liable assets
(CGTA Ss19–21)

Subject to various exemptions (see below) all forms of property are treated as 'assets' for capital gains tax purposes including:

(1) Investments, land and buildings, jewellery, antiques, etc.
(2) Options and 'debts on a security' (2.7.1)
(3) Any currency other than sterling.
(4) Any form of property created by the person disposing of it or otherwise coming to be owned without being acquired. (This would cover any article which you made or work of art created by you.)
(5) Foreign currency including that held in bank accounts unless for the personal expenditure of you and your dependants (including a residence) outside the UK.

2.7 Exempted assets
(CGTA — see 2.13)

The classes of assets listed in 2.7.1 are exempted from charge to capital gains tax, subject to the relevant rules.

2.7.1 Table: Assets exempted from capital gains tax

(1) Private motor vehicles (S130).
(2) Your main private residence (4.1).
(3) National Savings Certificates, Defence Bonds, Development Bonds, Save-as-you earn investments, etc (S71).
(4) Any foreign currency which you obtained for personal expenditure abroad (S133).
(5) Decorations for gallantry (unless purchased) (S131).
(6) Betting winnings including pools, lotteries and premium bonds (S19(4)).
(7) Compensation or damages for any wrong or injury suffered to your person or in connection with your profession or vocation (S19(5)).
(8) British Government securities FA 1985 s67.
(9) Certain corporate bonds (3.2) issued after 13 March 1984.
(10) Certain 'deep discount' and from 14 March 1989 'deep gain' securities (FA 1989 S139).
(11) Life assurance policies and deferred annuities provided that you are the original owner or they were given to you. If you bought the rights to a policy from its original owner you may be liable to capital gains tax on the surrender, maturity or sale of the policy, or death of the life assured (S143).
(12) Chattels sold for £6,000 or less (4.2).
(13) Assets gifted to charity (4.10).
(14) The gift to the nation of any assets (eg paintings) deemed to be of national, scientific or historic interest; also land, etc, given to the National Trust (S147).
(15) The gift of historic houses and certain other property of interest to the

public, provided they are given access — also funds settled between 2 May 1976 and 6 April 1984 for its upkeep (Ss147–148).

(16) Tangible movable property which is a wasting asset (ie, with a predictable life of 50 years or less). This includes boats, animals, etc, but not land and buildings nor assets qualifying for capital allowances (S127).

(17) Disposals by a close company of assets on trust for the benefit of its employees (S149).

(18) The disposal of a debt is exempt provided you are the original creditor and the debt is not a 'debt on a security' (a debenture, etc). Otherwise capital gains tax applies. Similarly, loss relief is usually restricted to debts on security. However, loss relief may also be available on certain business loans (excluding those from associated companies) made after 11 April 1978, and also on certain business guarantees made after that date (S134 & 136).

(19) Land transferred after 5 April 1983 from one local constituency to another as a result of the Parliamentary boundaries being redrawn (F2A 1983 S7).

(20) Shares issued to you after 18 March 1986 under the business expansion scheme (3.8) provided you are the first holder of those shares.

(21) Transactions in futures and options in gilts and qualifying bonds after 1 July 1986.

(22) Personal equity plans (PEPs) (3.9).

2.8 Disposals
(CGTA Ss19–26)

The following are examples of circumstances in which you will be treated as making a disposal or a part disposal of an asset:

(1) The outright sale of the whole asset or part of it.

(2) The gift of the asset or a part of it — the asset must be valued at the date of gift and this valuation is treated as the proceeds. An election for holding-over the gain is sometimes possible (4.7).

(3) The destruction of an asset eg, by fire.

(4) The sale of any right in an asset, eg, by granting a lease, is a part disposal although if you obtain a fair rent there is normally no capital gains tax liability.

(5) If any capital sum is received in return for the surrender or forfeiture of any rights, this is a disposal. For example, you may receive a sum of money for not renewing a lease in accordance with a renewal option which you possessed.

(6) If you die, you are deemed to dispose of all of your assets at your date of death but no capital gains tax is payable. Whoever inherits your assets does so at their market value at your death.

The following are not treated as disposals of assets for capital gains tax purposes:

(1) The sale or gift of an asset to your husband or wife (see below).
(2) If you transfer an asset merely as security for a debt but retain the ownership this is not a capital gains tax disposal. This would apply, for example, if you mortgaged your house.
(3) If you transfer an asset to somebody else to hold it as your nominee, this is not a disposal provided that you remain the beneficial owner.
(4) Gifts of assets to charities are not treated as disposals (4.10).

2.8.1 Husband and wife

If you give or sell an asset to your spouse this is not treated as a capital gains tax disposal, provided he or she is living with you during the relevant tax year. In that case your spouse is charged to capital gains tax on any subsequent disposal that he or she makes of the asset as if it had been bought when you originally acquired it at the actual cost to yourself.

Capital gains realised by the wife after 5 April 1990 are assessed on her. She has her own annual exemption and rate bands separate from her husband but transactions between them are exempt from CGT. For 1989–90 and earlier years, the capital gains of both spouses were assessed on the husband so that only one set of rate bands and one annual exemption applied.

● *As mentioned above, sales and gifts of assets between yourself and your spouse are not normally liable to capital gains tax. This enables you to redistribute your assets for inheritance tax purposes without paying any capital gains tax. (Some stamp duty – (15.1) may be payable on sales, however.) Your spouse and yourself will then both be able to use your full inheritance tax annual exemptions and nil-rate band if you have sufficient spare assets. If a wealth tax is introduced at some future time, it may help to have your assets split between you if husband and wife are separately taxed.*

● *Dividing assets between yourself and your spouse paves the way to worthwhile capital gains tax savings. If you each realise capital gains, you will each have your own annual exemption and rate bands. (Valuable income tax savings may also result.)*

2.9   Computation of chargeable gains
(CGTA Ss28–36; & FA 1982 Ss 86–89 & Sch 13)

The following general rules should be followed:

(1)   If the asset sold was originally acquired before 7 April 1965, special rules apply (2.17).

(2)   Special rules also apply in the case of leases and other wasting assets (2.18).

(3)   Ascertain the consideration for each of your disposals during the tax year — this will normally be the sale proceeds but in the following cases it will be the *open market value* of the assets (2.16):

   (*a*)   Gifts of assets during the tax year.

   (*b*)   Transfers of assets (by gift or sale) to persons 'connected' with you including close relations other than your spouse and also business partners ('connected persons' is defined in CGTA S63). This also applies to other disposals of assets not at arm's length. (After 9 March 1981, anti-avoidance rules operate to prevent losses being manufactured artificially in this way.)

   (*c*)   Transactions in which the sale proceeds cannot be valued, or where an asset is given as compensation for loss of office, etc to an employee. (For example, if you give your friend a valuable picture on condition that he paints your house regularly for the next ten years, then since this service cannot be accurately valued you are treated as disposing of your picture for its market value.)

(4)   Deduct from the disposal consideration in respect of each asset its original cost (or value at acquisition) together with any incidental expenses in connection with your original acquisition and your disposal of each asset. Regarding post — 5 April 1988 disposals, you generally must deduct the value at 31 March 1982, instead of the cost, if this gives you a better result (2.10). Also deduct any 'enhancement' expenditure, ie, the cost of any capital improvements to the assets not including any expenses of a 'revenue nature'.

(5)   Your incidental costs of acquisition and disposal (see (4) above) include surveyors', valuers' and solicitors' fees, stamp duty and commission in connection with the purchase and sale; also the cost of advertising to find a buyer and accountants'

charges in connection with the acquisition or disposal. No expenses are deductible, however, if they have already been allowed in computing your taxable revenue profits.

(6) If applicable, deduct indexation allowance (see below), based on the original cost (or other base value) of the asset (2.11.1).

2.10 Re-basing to 31 March 1982 values
(FA 1988 S96 & Sch 8)

The following rule applies where you dispose of assets after 5 April 1988, which you owned on 31 March 1982. The base value of each asset is automatically taken as its value at that date, provided this exceeds the cost. Thus, if you bought some shares for £1,000 in 1970 and they are worth £4,000 on 31 March 1982, you use £4,000 as their base value for capital gains tax purposes. Assuming you sell the shares for £10,000 in August 1990, your capital gain is £10,000 — £4,000 = £6,000 (ignoring indexation).

Re-basing to 31 March 1982 does not increase a gain or loss compared with what it would have been under the old rules. Furthermore, where there is a gain under the old system and a loss through re-basing, or vice versa, the transaction is treated as giving rise to neither gain nor loss. For example, if you sell as asset for £1,000 which had cost £500 and was worth £1,500 at 31 March 1982, ignoring indexation you had a gain of £500 under the old rules and a loss of £500 through re-basing; you are therefore treated as having no gain and no loss.

The existing rules for assets held at 6 April 1965 can themselves give rise to disposals being treated as producing no gain and no loss. This is not affected by re-basing.

Even if you did not hold an asset at 31 March 1982, it may still qualify for re-basing if you received it from someone else in circumstances that there was neither a gain nor loss under the rules and their acquisition was before that date. A particular example is where one spouse acquires an asset from another.

You have the right to elect that all of your assets are re-based as at 31 March 1982. There is a time limit for this irrevocable election (ie before 6 April 1990). However, this is extended to two years after the end of the tax year in which you make your first sale after 5 April 1988.

Re-basing does not apply to assets owned at 31 March 1982, but sold before 6 April 1988 in such circumstances that the gain is deferred. An example is where rollover relief applies on the replacement of business assets (4.3). However, special relief is available regarding disposals of the replacement assets, etc after 5 April 1988 (excluding no gain/no loss disposals). A claim is needed to the Inland Revenue within two years of the end of the year of assessment in which the disposal is made.

Your original rolled-over, held-over or deferred gain is then halved (FA 1988 S97 & Sch 9). Thus if you sold a factory, making a capital gain of £20,000 which you were able to roll-over into a new factory costing £100,000 which you now sell for £150,000, your taxable gain would have been £150,000 — (£100,000 - £20,000) = £70,000. However, the special relief reduces the gain by £10,000 (half the rolled-over gain) and so you are taxed on £60,000.

2.11   Indexation allowance
(FA 1982 Ss86–89 & Sch 13 & FA 1985 s68 & Sch 19 & FA 1988 S96 & Sch 8)

If your disposal is after 5 April 1982 (31 March 1982 for companies) the original cost and enhancement expenditure may be increased by *indexation*. For disposals between 5 April 1985 (31 March for companies) and 6 April 1988, you have the option of basing indexation on the value of the asset sold at 31 March 1982. After 5 April 1988, disposals are automatically re-based to their 31 March 1982 values if this is beneficial and so indexation is taken on the base value (2.10).

The expenditure is scaled up in proportion to the increase in the Retail Price Index between March 1982 and the month of disposal for assets held before April 1981. Otherwise, for disposals before 6 April 1985 (1 April 1985 for companies), the Index increase is taken between a year after acquisition and the month of disposal. For subsequent disposals, there is no one-year waiting period. Thus indexation runs from the month of acquisition (or March 1982, if later) until the month of disposal. Recent values for the *Retail Prices Index* have been as follows:

2.11.1 Table: Retail Price Index

	1982	1983	1984	1985	1986	1987	1988	1989	1990
January		325.9	342.6	359.8	379.7	394.5/			
						100.0*	103.3	111.0	119.5
February		327.3	344.0	362.9	381.1	100.4	103.7	111.8	120.2
March	313.4	327.9	345.1	366.1	381.6	100.6	104.1	112.3	121.4
April	319.7	332.5	349.7	373.9	385.3	101.8	105.8	114.3	125.1
May	322.0	333.9	351.0	375.6	386.0	101.9	106.2	115.0	126.2
June	320.9	334.7	351.9	376.4	385.8	101.9	106.6	115.4	126.7
July	323.0	336.5	351.5	375.5	384.7	101.8	106.7	115.5	126.8
August	323.1	338.0	354.8	376.7	385.9	102.1	107.9	115.8	128.1
September	322.9	339.5	355.5	376.5	387.8	102.4	108.4	115.6	
October	324.5	340.7	357.7	377.1	388.4	102.9	109.5	117.5	
November	326.1	341.9	358.8	378.4	391.7	103.4	110.0	118.5	
December	325.5	342.8	358.5	378.9	393.0	103.3	110.3	118.8	

Note: At January 1987 the index base was changed to 100.0. Thus assets acquired before January 1987 and sold after that time must be indexed using both scales. For example, the index figure for March 1987 is taken as 394.5 × 100.6/100 = 396.9.

Every month, the Inland Revenue publish a table of indexation fractions for disposals in the previous month. The table covers fractions to be used for acquisitions in each month from March 1982. For example, an asset held at 31 March 1982 and sold in April 1990 has indexation of 0.575. Because the fractions only go to three decimal places, slightly more favourable results may be obtained by using the Inland Revenue figures compared with making exact calculations based on the Retail Prices Index.

You obtain the full benefit of indexation relief, even to the extent that it creates a loss. However, prior to 6 April 1985 (1 April 1985 for companies), indexation did not operate to create or increase a capital loss (2.14). Special rules apply regarding assets held on 6 April 1965 (2.17) and shares (3.1). The provisions regarding shares should particularly be noted since they give rise to useful planning opportunities.

Transactions between husband and wife do not normally give rise to capital gains tax (2.8.1). Thus if you acquire an asset from your spouse, your deemed acquisition cost is taken to be hers, augmented by any indexation allowance attaching to it at the transfer date. When you sell the asset, you obtain full indexation allowance on your deemed acquisition cost, from the date you took over the asset from your spouse. Similar treatment applies to company intra-group transfers and certain reconstructions. Also, legatees are deemed to acquire assets at the death of the deceased and so obtain indexation allowance as if that was their actual date of acquisition.

Regarding disposals after 5 April 1985 (31 March 1985 for companies) and before 6 April 1988 you had the option of electing for your indexation relief to be based on the market values at 31 March 1982 of the relevant assets, rather than the cost. Each election had to be made within two years of the end of the tax year in which your disposal was made. (For companies, the time limit was two years from the end of the accounting period of disposal.) The election could be revoked within the original two-year time limit (FA 1985 S68 & Sch 19).

2.11.2   Example: Computation of chargeable gain

Mr A sells a block of flats on 10 April 1990 for £400,000. The flats were bought during 1970–71 for £100,000 and subsequent capital expenditure in 1975 amounted to £20,000. Also £10,000 had been spent on decorations and maintenance. The legal costs on purchase were £2,500 and stamp duty was £1,000. Surveyors' fees prior to purchase amounted to £500. £500 was spent in advertising the sale and agents' commission amounted to £12,000. Legal costs on sale were £3,500. At 31 March 1982 the market value was £200,000. Assuming that Mr A's profit will be taxed as a capital gain, his £5,000 annual exemption has already been used and that his income assessable for 1990-91 takes him into the 40% tax bracket, what tax will he pay on it?

Cost of block of flats		£100,000
Add:		
Enhancement expenditure		20,000
(decorations and maintenance not relevant)		
Legal costs on purchase		2,500
Stamp duty on purchase		1,000
Surveyors' fees on purchase		500
Total cost		£124,000
Re-based to value at 31 March 1982		£200,000
Proceeds		£400,000
Less:		
Value 31 March 1982	£200,000	
Advertising	500	
Agents' commission	12,000	

Legal fees on sale	3,500

	216,000
	£184,000

Less: indexation allowance

£200,000 × (394.5 × 125.1 - 313.4)/313.4 = £114,945*   115,000
                          100

Chargeable gain	£69,000

Capital gains tax at 40%	
(25% rate band already used)	£27,600

* The Inland Revenue figure is 0.575 and so the indexation allowance is £115,000
(£200,000 × 0.575)

2.12   Part disposals
(CGTA S35 & 107; FA 1982 Sch 13; FA 1984 S61; FA 1986 S60 & FA 1988 Sch 8)

Where part of an asset is disposed of (including part of a 'pool' holding of shares in a particular company — 3.5) it is necessary to compute the cost applicable to the part sold. This is done in general by multiplying the original cost by the fraction A/(A + B) where A is the consideration for the part disposed of and B is the market value of the remaining property at the date of the part disposal. This calculation is made before working out the indexation allowance, if relevant (2.10). Indexation is only taken on the cost applicable to the part sold. When the remainder is sold, a different indexation factor will probably apply.

Where you held an asset at 31 March 1982 and make a part disposal after 5 April 1988, the fraction A/(A+B) is applied to the value at 31 March 1982 if this exceeds the cost. If a part disposal had taken place between 31 March 1982 and 6 April 1988, the gain on a further part disposal after 5 April 1988 is computed on the basis that 1982 re-basing applied to the earlier disposal.

A special rule applies to small part disposals of land (only a small part of the whole being sold, etc). Provided that your proceeds from such disposals during the tax year do not exceed £20,000 (£10,000 before 6 April 1983), you may deduct the proceeds from your base cost rather than pay tax now. For disposals after 5 April 1986, the proceeds must not exceed one-fifth of the total market value of the land.

2.13   A series of disposals
(CGTA S151 & FA 1985 S71 & Sch 21)

Before 20 March 1985, if you acquired a series of assets (shares etc) from one or more people connected with you, all of the assets were valued together to find the relevant proportionate proceeds and your acquisition figure. After 19 March 1985, however, the rule operates only from the viewpoint of a person splitting up an asset or a collection of assets by two or more transactions to connected persons. The transactions must be within a total period of six years.

2.14   Capital losses
(CGTA S29 & FA 1988 Ss104 & 113)

If your capital gains tax computation in respect of any disposal during the tax year produces a loss, such a loss is deductible from chargeable gains arising during the year. Any remaining surplus of losses is then available to be carried forward and set off against your future capital gains. Any capital loss which you make on an asset transferred to a connected person (2.9) can only be relieved against gains made on transfers to the same person.

In computing your capital losses note the special rules for assets owned at 6 April 1965 (2.11) and that indexation allowance can both create and add to a loss. Also note that losses may be reduced by 1982 re-basing (2.10), but not increased nor created. The losses of one spouse could be deducted from the gains of the other. However, this rule ceased to have effect from 6 April 1990 on the introduction of independent taxation.

A result of indexation allowance creating capital losses was that *building society* share accounts could give rise to capital losses when closed down or reduced. This constitutes a capital gains tax disposal. No real loss is likely but for capital gains tax purposes, prior to 4 July 1987 indexation relief could produce a capital loss. However, from that date, countermanding legislation operates.

Your net capital gains are reduced by losses brought forward down to the tax free amount of £5,000 (£6,600 for 1987–88, etc) and any balance of the losses is carried forward (S5(4)).

2.14.1 'Bed and breakfast' transactions

● *Remember that, if necessary, you may be able to create capital losses by 'bed and breakfast' transactions. These involve selling shares on the stock exchange at a loss and buying them back no earlier than the next day. The costs of such a transaction must be taken into account, however, and will include commission and jobber's turn. The repurchase should be within the same account otherwise $\frac{1}{2}$% stamp duty normally applies. (From 6 April 1982 to 5 April 1985 bed and breakfast transactions were effective only if the shares were repurchased in the following account or later.)*

● *When bed and breakfasting, take account of the different base values you will be establishing for indexation relief.*

● *Note that gilt-edged securities and qualifying corporate bonds (3.1.2, 3.2) cannot be used for 'bed and breakfast' transactions. They do not carry any capital gains or losses.*

2.15 Assessment and payment of capital gains tax
(TMA S29; CGTA S7; FA 1980 S61 & FA 1988 S104)

Your capital gains tax assessments will be raised on you in respect of each tax year as soon thereafter as the Revenue obtain the necessary information. In the case of a company, however, its gains are included in its corporation tax assessment which is due for payment according to the special company rules (6.1).

From 6 April 1990, both husband and wife are assessed to tax on their capital gains separately. Prior to that date, the wife's gains were assessed on her husband.

Your capital gains tax assessment is due for payment on 1 December following the tax year in which the respective gains are made, or 30 days after the assessment is issued, if later. Thus the tax on gains made in 1990–91 would be payable on 1 December 1991 (provided assessed by 1 November 1991).

Interest is normally payable on overdue tax from the earlier of

1 June following the end of the year after the year of assessment or the date when the tax becomes due and payable. However, in no event does interest run from a date earlier than 30 days after the issue of the assessment, unless the information is returned late or you are otherwise at fault. The interest is not deductible for tax purposes and the rates since 1 January 1980 have been as follows:

From	Rate %
6 November 1989	13
6 July 1989	$12\frac{1}{4}$
6 January 1989	$11\frac{1}{2}$
6 October 1988	$10\frac{3}{4}$
6 August 1988	$9\frac{3}{4}$
6 May 1988	$7\frac{3}{4}$
6 December 1987	$8\frac{1}{4}$
6 September 1987	9
6 June 1987	$8\frac{1}{4}$
6 April 1987	9
6 November 1986	$9\frac{1}{2}$
6 August 1986	$8\frac{1}{2}$
1 May 1985	11
1 December 1982	8
1 January 1980	12

Capital gains are treated as arising on the actual date of sale or gift, etc. In the case of a transaction in which a sales contract is used, such as the sale of shares or property, it is the date of the contract which applies. It is not the completion date if this is different. Similar considerations apply to fixing the date of acquisition for capital gains tax purposes.

2.15.1   Payment by instalments
(CGTA Ss8 & 9, & FA 1984 S63)

Regarding certain disposals by gift, etc, from 11 April 1972 to 5 April 1984 of land and buildings, non-quoted shares, or assets used exclusively in your business, you had the option of paying capital gains tax in eight yearly or 16 half-yearly instalments. If you are paying by instalments you must pay interest at the appropriate rate on the overdue tax (see above). For *disposals* after 5 April 1984, the instalment basis no longer applies, although relief may be available if the *consideration* is paid in instalments (see below).

Controlling interests in companies were also included (even if quoted). If you disposed of any of the specified assets (except for land

and investment companies, etc) you obtained relief from interest on the instalments unless they are overdue or the total market value of the assets exceeded £250,000.

Normally, even if the sales consideration is paid to you by instalments over a number of years the gain is assessed for the tax year of the disposal. If, however, you can satisfy the Revenue that you would otherwise suffer undue hardship, payment of the tax can be spread over the period of the instalments (maximum eight years).

2.15.2 Timing

● *Timing your sales of shares or other chargeable assets can have an important bearing on your capital gains tax liability. If you postpone a sale until after 5 April it means that you delay the payment of your tax for one year. Also, if you know that you will be incurring a capital loss during the next tax year you should defer making any potential capital profits until that year because, although capital losses can be carried forward, they cannot be set off against capital profits in earlier tax years. A further point to bear in mind is that the longer you hold an asset, the higher your indexation allowance (2.11) is likely to be on its disposal.*

● *Similarly, if you have already made a lot of capital profits during the current tax year you should consider incurring capital losses during the same year which can then be offset. You should not normally sell investments unless it is sound to do so from a commercial point of view. A loss may be established on a shareholding, however, even if you buy it back later (2.14.1). Such transactions may be taxable, however, if done by companies.*

● *If you have a substantial capital gain on a shareholding which you wish to realise, split it between two tax years by selling part before and part after 5 April. In this way you will be able to offset your annual exemptions (2.5.1) for two years.*

2.16 Valuations
(CGTA S150 and Sch 6)

The values of assets must be found for capital gains tax purposes in various circumstances. These include gifts, transactions between connected persons, acquisitions and on death. Also valuations at 6 April 1965 and particularly 31 March 1982 are required. The general rule is that you must take the 'market value' of the assets at the relevant time. 'Market value' means the price which the assets might reasonably be expected to fetch on a sale in the open market.

You need value only the assets actually being disposed of even though they form part of a larger whole. This is particularly important regarding the shares in a non-quoted company. Suppose you hold 90% of the shares in such a company which are together worth £90,000. If you gift 10% of the company's shares to your son you might assume that their value is £10,000. This would, however, probably not be true since your 90% holding carried with it full control of the company whereas 10% of the company's shares is a minority holding which would be worth considerably less than £10,000 in the circumstances mentioned. The 90% holding would be worth nearly 90% of the total value of the company, but the true market valuation of the gifted 10% holding might only be £1,000 depending on the profits of the company and dividends paid. Note that different valuation rules apply for inheritance tax purposes (7.18).

Unquoted share valuations must take account of all information which a prudent arm's-length purchaser would obtain (CGTA S152). As mentioned above, the size of the holding will be relevant, as will the profits, dividends, net assets and record of the company.

Particular rules relate to the valuation of quoted securities such as shares and debenture stocks. In this case you must normally take:

(*a*)   the lower of the two prices shown in the Stock Exchange Official Daily List plus one quarter of the difference between them, *or*

(*b*)   halfway between the highest and lowest prices at which bargains (other than at special prices) were recorded in the shares or securities for the relevant day.

In valuing quoted shares at 6 April 1965 (3.12) however, you must take the *higher* of:

(*a*)   midway between the two prices shown in the Stock Exchange Official Daily List (ie the middle market price), and

(*b*)   halfway between the highest and lowest prices at which bargains (other than at special prices) were recorded in the shares or securities for 6 April 1965.

Apart from quoted shares other valuations will normally need to be agreed with the Revenue valuation officers such as the district valuers who are concerned with valuing land and buildings.

The valuation of gifted agricultural property is effectively subject to the same reduction as applies for inheritance tax (7.44).

2.17 Relief on sales of assets owned on 6 April 1965
(CGTA Sch 5)

The present system of capital gains tax only operates regarding sales after 6 April 1965. Rules were, therefore, introduced with the purpose of relieving so much of your capital gains as can be related to the period before 7 April 1965. The general rule is that you assume that your asset increased in value at a uniform rate and you are relieved from capital gains tax on such proportion of the gain as arose on a time basis prior to 7 April 1965. This is known as the 'time apportionment' method.

For example, if your total gain is G and you held an asset for A months prior to 6 April 1965 and B months after that date until the date of sale your taxable chargeable gain is $G{\times}B/(A{+}B)$. Note that time apportionment is now calculated on gains net of any available indexation allowance (2.10). Your time apportionment benefit is limited to 20 years prior to 6 April 1965. Thus if you acquired an asset before 6 April 1945 you are treated as having acquired it on that date.

Suppose you bought a property for £50,000 in 1940; time apportionment runs from April 1945, so that if you sell the property on 6 April 1990 for £230,000 your gain is £180,000 and your taxable chargeable gain is £180,000 × 25/45 (6 April 1965 to 6 April 1990) = £100,000. (This ignores indexation relief and re-basing.)

Instead of using 'time apportionment' you have the option of substituting for the cost of the asset its market value at 6 April 1965 (Sch 5 (11)). In order to do this you must make an election to this effect to the Revenue within two years of the end of the tax year in which you make the disposal. (In the case of a company the election must be made within two years of the end of the accounting period in which the disposal is made.) Once you make an election it is irrevocable, even if it results in your paying more tax than on a 'time apportionment' basis.

It is very rare that the market value of an asset at 6 April 1965 is more than at 31 March 1982. Thus, because of the new re-basing rules

(2.10), 6 April 1965 valuations are normally only relevant for asset disposals before 6 April 1988.

The 'time apportionment' basis *does not* apply to quoted shares and securities (3.1). Nor does it apply to land with development value when sold (or which has been materially developed after 17 December 1973). Such land is normally automatically dealt with on the 6 April 1965 valuation basis.

In the same way that your gain is reduced by 'time apportionment' so any loss that you make on a disposal of an asset that you owned at 6 April 1965 is also reduced in this way. Thus if you bought an asset for £5,000 on 6 April 1950 and sold it for £1,000 on 6 April 1990 your total loss is £4,000 of which only £2,500 (£4,000 × 25/40) is an allowable capital loss. An election for 6 April 1965 valuation is not effective to increase a capital loss and if it converts a gain into a loss, you are treated as having no gain and no loss on the transaction.

2.18　Leases and other wasting assets
(CGTA Ss127, 129 & Sch 3)

A 'wasting asset' is defined as an asset with a predictable life not exceeding 50 years, excluding freehold land and buildings, etc. Leases with no more than 50 years still to run are a special kind of wasting asset and have separate rules for capital gains tax (see below).

'Wasting assets' which are also movable property (chattels) are normally exempted from capital gains tax. (This exemption does not generally apply to plant and machinery qualifying for capital allowances.) In the case of other wasting assets apart from leases, you must reduce their original costs on a straight line time basis over the respective lives of the assets. Thus suppose you buy a wasting asset for £10,000 with an unexpired life of 40 years. If you sell it after 20 years for £20,000, assuming the residual value after 40 years would have been nil, your allowable cost is £10,000 × 20/40 = £5,000; thus your chargeable gain is £20,000–5,000 = £15,000. This assumes no indexation allowance (2.10). Any such allowance available would be calculated on the adjusted cost of £5,000 or 31 March 1982 valuation if applicable.

In the case of a lease of land with no more than 50 years of its original term to run (including leases for shorter terms) the original cost must be written off according to a special table under which the rate of wastage accelerates as the end of the term of the lease is reached. If you sell such an interest in a property and lease back the premises at a lower rent for less than 15 years, you may be taxed on all or part of the proceeds either as a trading receipt or under Schedule D Case VI.

The exact computaton of the reduced value of the cost of a lease involves using the following table of percentages according to the number of years still to run. The table below gives an appropriate percentage for each year up to 50 (which is 100%).

2.18.1   Table: Leases of land — restriction of allowable expenditure

Years	%	Years	%	Years	%
50 (or more)	100	33	90·280	16	64·116
49	99·657	32	89·354	15	61·617
48	99·289	31	88·.371	14	58·971
47	98·902	30	87·330	13	56·167
46	98·490	29	86·226	12	53·191
45	98.059	28	85·053	11	50·038
44	97·595	27	83·816	10	46·695
43	97·107	26	82·496	9	43·154
42	96·593	25	81·100	8	39.399
41	96·041	24	79·622	7	35·414
40	95·457	23	78·055	6	31·195
39	94·842	22	76·399	5	26·722
38	94·189	21	74·635	4	21·983
37	93·497	20	72·770	3	16·959
36	92·761	19	70·791	2	11·629
35	91·981	18	68·697	1	5·983
34	91·156	17	66·470	0	0

If the duration of the lease is not an exact number of years the percentage is that for the whole number of years plus one twelfth of the difference between that and the percentage for the next higher number of years for each odd month, counting an odd 14 days or more as one month.

Thus suppose you bought a 20 year lease for £40,000 in 1980 and sell it in 1990, when it has exactly ten years to run, for £50,000. Your base cost of £40,000 must be reduced in the ratio of the relevant percentages at ten and twenty years (ie, 46·695 : 72·770). The capital gain (ignoring indexation allowance and re-basing at 31 March 1982) is:

Proceeds	£50,000
Remainder of cost	
£40,000 = 46·695/72·770	£25,667
Chargeable gain	£24,333

● *When buying a lease in a company, it can prove beneficial to do so through a newly formed subsidiary. Thus if you are buying the lease of premises for £100,000, create a new subsidiary with share capital of £100,000 and buy the lease. Then when your company wishes to dispose of the premises, by selling the subsidiary the base value remains at £100,000. However, if the lease had been sold out of the subsidiary, only a reduced base cost would have been available, in line with the table (2.18.1).*

2.19　Partnership capital gains
(CGTA S60)

When a partnership asset is sold in such circumstances that, if owned by an individual, capital gains tax would have been payable, this tax is assessed on the partners according to their shares in the partnership asset. Thus if a capital gain of £4,000 is made from the sale of a partnership asset on 1 January 1991 and A, B, C and D share equally in the partnership assets, a capital gain of £1,000 each must be added to the capital gains tax assessments for 1990–91 of A, B, C and D respectively (2.21.1).

Where a share in a partnership changes hands, a share in all of the partnership assets is treated for capital gains tax purposes as changing ownership and this might give rise to capital gains or capital losses regarding the partner who is disposing of his share. Thus if A, B, and C are equal partners and A sells his share to D, A is treated for capital gains tax purposes as disposing of a one-third share in each of the partnership assets to D. The Revenue operate concessional treatment which relieves certain capital gains which arise in normal commercial partnership operations, including, in some cases, changes in profit shares.

2.20　Anti-avoidance
(CGTA Ss25, 26, 87 & 88; FA 1986 S58 & FA 1988 Ss114 & Sch 11)

With a tax as complicated as capital gains tax, it is not surprising that various loopholes have been exploited. To counter this a number of anti-avoidance provisions have been introduced. Those concerning non-resident companies are dealt with elsewhere (6.1.8), as are the capital gains tax avoidance rules concerning overseas trusts. In addition, various decisions of the Courts have rendered contrived artificial capital gains tax saving schemes virtually obsolete (eg, *Ramsay* v *IRC* and *Furniss* v *Dawson*).

Rules exist to counter any advantage which you may derive from 'value shifting' schemes. These involve the artificial creation of an allowable capital loss by moving value out of one asset and possibly into another. There are also anti-avoidance rules concerning capital gains tax relief resulting from company reconstructions, takeovers and amalgamations. The rules do not apply if you can show that the arrangements were all carried out for commercial and not tax-saving purposes. A clearance procedure exists under which you may supply full details to the Inland Revenue. They will then, within 30 days, let you know whether or not clearance is granted. Alternatively the Revenue may request further information.

There are provisions in the 1981 Finance Act to prevent the artificial inflation of the capital gains tax acquisition values of your assets. Otherwise, if you sold for true market value, a capital loss would be created. The artificial effect sometimes resulted from the rule that transactions between connected persons are treated as being at market value (2.9); sometimes it arose through reorganisations of share capital (3.3). After 9 March 1981 your capital gains tax cost is only increased to the extent that the capital gains tax position of the person who transferred the asset to you is affected.

Gifts relief (5.2.3) is not available for gifts to non-residents. This was being circumvented by using certain dual-resident trusts, but from 18 March 1986, these are regarded as non-resident for this purpose. Also, gifts relief may be lost where a UK-resident trust becomes dual-resident.

The 1988 Finance Act has introduced, from 15 March 1988, provisions to prevent groups of companies or associated companies from creating artificial capital losses by applying indexation to certain inter-company loans and shareholdings.

Capital gains tax rollover relief (4.3) is not available where a non-resident replaces a business asset within the UK charge with one which is outside it. In general, this rule applies where the old asset is disposed of, or the new one purchased after 13 March 1989.

2.21   Overseas aspects

*(CGTA Ss10–18; FA 1981 Ss79–85 & S88; FA
1984 S66; FA 1989 Ss 126 & 140)*

As already mentioned (2.3), provided you are resident and/or
ordinarily resident in this country you are liable on capital gains anywhere in the world.

Even if neither resident nor ordinarily resident in the UK, a trader
(whether an individual, partnership or company) who carries on a
trade here through a branch or agency is generally liable to capital
gains tax on the disposal of assets (*a*) used in this country in his trade,
or (*b*) held here and used by the branch or agency. From 14 March
1989, this also covers professions and vocations, however, assets are
re-based to their values at that date. Furthermore from that date
deemed disposals may take place for capital gains tax purposes. This
happens if the assets are moved out of the UK or the trade, etc ceases.
The term 'branch or agency' includes any factorship, agency,
receivership, branch or management. Note that it does not include
general commission agents and brokers. Also note that double tax
relief (2.22) may be available.

- *If you know you will be realising a substantial capital gain in the future
and your personal circumstances will allow it, go abroad so that you are
neither resident nor ordinarily resident in the UK (1.7) at the time you
make the gain. This will normally involve establishing your non-
residence to run from the beginning of the year in which you realise the
gain. However, the Revenue concessionally treat you as non-resident
from the time you leave the UK if you are leaving to work abroad. Of
course, you must make sure not to go to a country which will itself tax
you on the gain.*

The *market value* rule (2.9) applies in general to gifts and other
dispositions for less than full consideration involving non-resident
and non-ordinarily resident persons after 5 April 1983 (FA 1984
S66.) From 10 March 1981 until 5 April 1983, however, if you
obtained an asset from such a person, your base cost was restricted to
the actual consideration, if any (CGTA S29A).

Should you be a UK resident investor in an offshore 'umbrella fund'
you will be subjected to a capital gains tax charge when you switch
holdings. This applies to switches made after 13 March 1989.

If you are non-domiciled in the UK, you are only liable to capital
gains tax on *overseas gains* to the extent that they are *remitted* here.

Thus it is important to determine the location of your assets. For these purposes, from 6 April 1984 if you are non-domiciled and have a non-sterling bank account, this is treated as located outside the UK unless both the account is held at a UK branch and you are UK–resident (FA 1984 S69).

If you are UK domiciled, the Revenue have powers to apportion to you the capital gains of certain overseas trusts (5.2.5) and companies. From 10 March 1981 this extends to overseas companies owned by foreign trusts. Overseas aspects relating to companies are included in Chapter 6; for example the tax charge where a company is exported.

2.21.1 The remittance basis

Under the remittance basis you are only liable to capital gains tax on the amount of gain you actually bring into this country in the tax year. Remember, however, that this only applies if you are not domiciled in the UK. Remittances can be made in cash or kind (2.21.2).

If you make no remittances you will have no liability to UK tax on your overseas capital gains taxable on the remittance basis, no matter how high they are in any year, although you might well suffer foreign tax.

2.21.2 Classes of remittance
(S122)

As well as cash and cheques, any property imported or value arising here from property not imported will be classed as remittances. Thus if you buy a car abroad out of your overseas gains and bring it into this country this is a remittance (although strictly speaking the second-hand value of the car at the time of importation should be used instead of the cost of the car). Similarly, if you hire an asset abroad out of unremitted overseas gains, any use that you get from the asset in this country should be valued and treated as a remittance.

If you borrow money against sums owing to you for overseas gains and bring the former into this country, this is a remittance. Similarly, if you borrow money here and repay it abroad out of overseas gains, this is known as a 'constructive remittance' and is taxable. Other forms of 'constructive remittances' include the payment out of overseas capital gains of interest owing in this country, and the repayment out of such gains of money borrowed overseas which was made available to you in this country.

If you use non-remitted capital gains to buy shares in UK companies this is normally treated as a remittance unless you do so through a third party abroad who actually acts as the principal in the transaction.

You are able to use non-remitted overseas gains to cover the cost of overseas visits (including holidays) and provided you bring none of the money back to this country there is no taxable remittance. For this purpose the Revenue allow you to receive traveller's cheques in this country provided they are not cashed here.

● *If you are taxable on a remittance basis in respect of overseas capital gains then isolate the proceeds in a separate bank account, reinvesting the money abroad as required. Any money which you remit back to the UK should be from a clearly defined separate bank account so that you can prove you have not in fact remitted any of your proceeds, including overseas capital gains and it comes from a completely different source.*

2.22 Double tax relief
(CGTA Ss10 & 11)

Your chargeable gains may be liable to tax both in the UK and another country. In that case, relief will be available in the following ways:

(1)   Under a bilateral double tax agreement with the other country, which covers capital gains, if you are UK resident you may be exempted from overseas tax on gains from non-business assets apart from land and buildings. A list of the countries having comprehensive agreements with the UK appears below. Rules vary from country to country and the actual agreements should be examined as necessary; for example, the other country may not operate capital gains tax. In some cases you are only given unilateral relief (see below).

(2)   If there is no bilateral agreement or the agreement does not give you exemption, unilateral relief enables you to set off overseas tax on your gain against the UK capital gains tax on it.

(3)   Should neither of the above apply, then the overseas tax on your gain can be deducted in the UK computation as if it was an expense.

2.22.1 Table: Double taxation relief — List of countries which have General Agreements with the UK

Antigua	India	St Christopher &
Australia	Indonesia	Nevis
Austria	Irish Republic	St Lucia
Bangladesh	Israel	St Vincent
Barbados	Italy	Seychelles
Belgium	Ivory Coast	(terminated)
Belize	Jamaica	Sierra Leone
Botswana	Japan	Singapore
Brunei	Jersey	Solomon Islands
Bulgaria	Kenya	South Africa
Burma	Korea	South West Africa
Canada	Lesotho	(Namibia)
China	Luxembourg	Spain
Cyprus	Malawi	Sri Lanka
Denmark	Malaysia	Sudan
Dominica	Malta	Swaziland
Egypt	Isle of Man	Sweden
Falkland Islands	Mauritius	Switzerland
Faroe Islands	Montserrat	Tanzania
Fiji	Netherlands	(terminated)
Finland	Netherlands	Thailand
France	Antilles (ceased	Trinidad & Tobago
Gambia	31.3.89)	Tunisia
German Federal	New Zealand	Turkey
Republic	Nigeria	Tuvalu
Ghana	Norway	Uganda
Gilbert Islands	Pakistan	USA
(Kiribati)	Philippines	USSR
Greece	Poland	Yugoslavia
Grenada	Portugal	Zambia
Guernsey	Romania	Zimbabwe
Hungary		

Note: In addition to the above general agreements, arrangements of a more restricted kind have been entered into with Argentina, Brazil, Jordan, Lebanon, Venezuela and Zaire covering the double taxation of profits from shipping and air transport. There is an agreement with Iceland covering shipping profits only and agreements with Algeria, Cameroon, Ethiopia, Iran and Kuwait cover only air transport.

3 Capital gains tax — shares and securities

3.1 Quoted shares and securities
(CGTA Ss64–76 & FA 1985 S67)

3.1.2 Government securities

The general rules (3.2.3) do not apply to UK government securities which are exempt from capital gains tax. Before 2 July 1986, if you sold any such 'gilt edged' securities within a year of purchase you were liable to capital gains tax on your chargeable gain. Any compensation stock received on a nationalisation after 6 April 1976 will give rise to a gain or loss when sold. This consists of the gain or loss on your original shares up to the date of issue of the compensation stock.

For sales before 2 July 1986, you must also include the gain or loss on this stock if it had been held for less than 12 months before sale (CGTA S84). Any disposals of 'gilts' after 1 July 1986 are completely free of capital gains tax and similarly cannot create allowable losses. This exemption extends to options, etc in gilts and corporate bonds (3.5).

3.2 Exemption for corporate bonds
(FA 1984 S64 & Sch 13, FA 1985 S67 & FA 1990 Ss84 & 85)

The exemption for capital gains tax for gilt edge securities extends to *qualifying corporate bonds* satisfying the following conditions:
(1)   The bonds are issued after 13 March 1984 or if issued before that date, are acquired after it otherwise than through an excluded disposal (broadly, one deemed to give rise to neither

gain nor loss, or involving a held-over gain, if before the disposal the bond is not yet a qualifying one).

(2)   They are debentures, loan stocks or similar securities, not necessarily secured but 'debts on security'.

(3)   They are normal commercial loans, expressed in and redeemable in sterling.

(4)   At least some of the shares or debentures of the issuing company are quoted.

(5)   The bonds are capable of being marketed but are not issued by a company to another company in the same group.

(6)   Sales from 2 July 1986 are totally exempt and before that date a 12 month holding period was required for exemption to apply.

(7)   Where you sustain a loss on a qualifying corporate bond held on, or issued after, 14 March 1989, you will obtain relief where part or all of the loan is irrecoverable.

In a takeover or reorganisation; etc, the 'paper for paper' holdover reliefs (3.3) are modified unless both your old and new bonds are qualifying bonds.

3.2.1   Bond Washing
(FA 1985 Ss73–77 & Schs 22–23 & FA 1986 Sch 17)

Although government securities and corporate bonds are now generally free of capital gains tax (apart from held-over gains) if you sell with accrued income, you may be liable to income tax under Schedule D Case VI. You will be liable if your *securities* have a nominal value exceeding £5,000 at any time in the tax year. (The £5,000 exempt level does not apply to companies.) In that case you are taxed on the accrued income on your sales 'cum dividend' but as purchaser, you obtain a corresponding credit. You also have a credit if you sell 'ex dividend'. The scheme covers transactions after 27 February 1986, with transitional rules for the previous year.

3.2.2   'Pooling'

All shares of the same company and class that you held prior to 6 April 1982 (1 April for companies) were put into a 'pool'. With the introduction of indexation allowance (2.10) pooling no longer applied to new purchases. However, pooling was reintroduced concerning share *disposals* after 5 April 1985 for individuals and trusts, etc. (For companies the date is 31 March 1985.) You are now treated as having one pool of shares acquired after 5 April 1982 and another before that time.

The 'pool' is considered indistinguishable regarding the various numbers of shares that it comprises. Thus if you bought 100 ordinary shares in A Limited on 1 May 1966 for £200 and another 200 ordinary shares in A Limited on 30 September 1970 for £1,000 your total pool cost is £1,200 (ie £4 per share). If you then sell 100 shares they are not treated as being the original ones which you bought for £200; they are treated as coming from your 'pool' at the average pool cost of £4 per share giving a cost of £400.

'Pooling' does not apply to shares purchased on or before 6 April 1965 unless you elect for all your shares to be valued at that date (3.3.2). In the absence of this election, you allocated any sales prior to 6 April 1982 first against your holdings at 6 April 1965 on a 'first in first out' basis. After these shares were eliminated you then went to the 'pool'.

Each separate purchase or sale of shares of the same company and class results in adjustments to the 'pool' except that if you buy and sell shares on the same day the respective sale and purchase are first matched against each other. Any surplus or deficit is then added to or deducted from your 'pool'. This rule ceased to apply for transactions from 6 April 1982 (1 April for companies subject to parallel pooling – 6.1.3), but was re-introduced from 6 April 1985.

3.2.3 Identification — Sales from 6 April 1982 to 5 April 1985
(FA 1982 Ss88 & 89 & Sch 13 & FA 1983 S34 & Sch 6)

For disposals of quoted shares and securities between 5 April 1982 and 6 April 1985 special identification rules applied. Similarly, shares purchased between those dates were no longer pooled. (For companies, the dates are from 1 April 1982 to 31 March 1985.) Each of your existing share pools was treated as a separate asset with its own pool cost at 6 April 1982, and treated for indexation purposes as if acquired one year earlier.

Disposals after 5 April 1982 but before 6 April 1985 were taken in order and identified first against purchases in the previous 12 months taking the earliest first. Note, however, that purchases and sales in the same Stock Exchange account (or for settlement on the same day) were matched against each other.

As mentioned above, your 'pool' holdings are to be treated as separate entities, so if you purchased 1,000 shares in company A from, say, 1970 to 1978 at an average cost of £5, the sale now of 500 would be taken to cost $500 \times £5 = £2,500$. However, an exception applied where certain dealings in the shares took place in 1981–82 (year to 31 March 1982 for companies). If a holding increased in cost during that year, you effectively treated part as being acquired for indexation purposes in 1981–82, by matching the 1981–82 sales against the purchases in that year. The earliest sales in 1981–82 were matched against the latest purchases (even if later than respective sales). Any unmatched purchases in 1981–82 only qualified for indexation after holding for one year.

3.2.4 Indexation and identification — sales from 6 April 1985
(FA 1985 S68 & Sch 19)

Revised rules apply to share disposals by individuals after 5 April 1985 and by companies after 31 March 1985. However, securities (apart from 'gilts' and corporate bonds) covered by the accrued income provisions to combat bond-washing only came within the new indexation and identification rules after 27 February 1986.

As previously mentioned indexation now runs immediately. An exception is where you buy and then sell the same shares within ten days. Your transactions are then matched and you obtain no indexation relief.

Under the latest rules, you must keep separate pools of shares acquired after 5 April 1982 and those obtained from 6 April 1965 to 5 April 1982. Furthermore, acquisitions prior to 6 April 1965 must be kept separately, unless there is a pooling election, in which case they are included in the 31 March 1982 pool.

If you sell shares after 5 April 1985, they must be identified with your acquisitions of the same shares on a 'last in first out' basis. They are thus first identified with your post 5 April 1982 pool, then with your pre-6 April 1982 holdings and finally with your unpooled pre-6 April 1965 holdings. (For companies the pools run to 31 March 1982 and from 1 April 1982.)

Indexation must be calculated separately on the different parts. Holdings acquired before 1 April 1982 will be valued at 31 March 1982 for indexation purposes if you make the required election. However, re-basing to the value at 31 March 1982 (2.10) will normally apply if more favourable, regarding disposals after 5 April 1988.

Subsequent acquisitions cannot be treated like that. However, every additional purchase will carry indexation relief from the acquisition date until sale and so a careful record is needed to calculate relief from the respective acquisition dates. This is done on a pooled basis by adding indexation relief to the pool prior to each purchase or sale. The total indexation relief in the pool is then found by deducting the total cost and the relief on the sale is simply the proportion appropriate to the number of shares sold.

3.2.5 Example: share identification and indexation—sales after 5 April 1985

Mr A carried out the following share transactions in the ordinary shares of quoted company B Ltd:

	Date	Number	Cost or Proceeds
Purchases	20.6.78	2,000	£3,000
	10.5.80	1,000	2,000
	10.7.83	2,000	4,000
	10.9.84	4,000	11,000
Sale	20.9.90	9,000	30,000

The value of B Ltd shares at 31 March 1982 was £1.80. Calculate Mr A's capital gain assuming the following indexation figures:

March 1982 to September 1990	50%
July 1983 to September 1984	5%
September 1984 to September 1990	20%

(1)   The shares sold are taken first out of the post 5 April 1982 pool:

Cost of 2,000 shares 10.7.83		£4,000
Indexation July 1983 to		
September 1984 5%		200
		4,200
Cost of 4,000 shares 10.9.84		11,000
		15,200
Indexation September 1984 to		
September 1990 20%		3,040
Cost and indexation for 6,000		
shares		£18,240
Proceeds of 6,000 shares		20,000
Capital gain on 6,000 shares from		
post 5 April 1982 pool		£1,760

(2)   The remaining shares sold are then identified against the pre-6 April 1982 pool:

Cost of 3,000 shares (£1.67 each)	£5,000
Re-based to £1.80 per share	5,400
Add indexation relief from March 1982 to September 1990 50%	2,700
	8,100
Proceeds of 3,000 shares	10,000
Capital Gain on 3,000 shares	£1,900

TOTAL CAPITAL GAIN 1990–91	£1,760 + £1,900	£3,660

3.3 Bonus issues, take-overs and company reorganisations
(CGTA Ss77–91; FA 1981 S91; & FA 1982 Sch 13)

If you receive a free scr:y (or bonus) issue of shares of the same class as those that you already hold, you must treat the additional shares as having been bought when your original shares were bought. Thus if you bought 1,000 shares in A Ltd for £2 each in 1975 and you now receive a bonus issue of 1,000 shares you will have 2,000 shares at a cost of £1 each which are all treated as having been bought in 1975. Note, however, that scrip dividend options are normally taxed as income, whether taken in cash or shares.

A company in which you own shares may have a capital re-organisation, in the course of which you receive shares of a different class either instead of or in addition to your original shares. You are not normally charged to capital gains tax on any old shares in the company which you exchange for new ones. Any capital gains tax is only payable when you sell your new holding. The rules for re-organisations including bonus issues hold good under the new 'indexation' system unless new consideration is given.

Previously, if you took up 'rights' to subscribe for additional shares in a company of which you are a shareholder, your rights shares were treated as having been acquired when your original shares were purchased and the cost of the rights shares was added to the original cost of your holding. If you sold your 'rights' on the market without taking up the shares this was considered to be a 'part disposal' of your holding which accordingly was charged to capital gains tax (2.12). (If the proceeds are small in relation to your holding, however, you may elect not to pay tax now but set off the proceeds against the original cost of your holding.) Under the indexation rules which now apply (3.2.3) any new consideration (for rights shares, etc) is treated effectively as a new acquisition so that indexation runs accordingly.

Anti-avoidance rules act to prevent you from obtaining capital loss relief artificially from reorganisations taking place after 9 March 1981. Any increase in the capital gains tax acquisition value of the shares which you obtain through the reorganisation is limited to the actual increase in value.

In the case of a take-over you may receive cash for your shares in which case this is taxed as an ordinary disposal. If, however, you receive shares or loan stock, etc in the acquiring company, you will not normally be liable to pay capital gains tax until you actually sell your new shares or loan stock, subject to certain conditions and anti-avoidance laws (2.20). One of the conditions is that the acquiring company already held, or obtains as a result of the take-over, over 25% of the ordinary share capital of the other company.

• *As a general rule, reorganisations should only be carried out with commercial rather than tax-saving motives. Where possible, it is advisable for the directors to obtain for the company Inland Revenue clearance both in respect of the capital gains tax anti-avoidance provisions and ICTA 1988 Section 703 (1.4).*

In general, when you finally sell all or part of your holding, you use your original cost in computing the gain. However, this will be subject to possible re-basing (2.10) if the sale is after 5 April 1988.

All of the above rules concerning bonus issues, take-overs and company reorganisations apply equally to unquoted shares (3.6).

3.3.1 Investment trusts and unit trusts
(CGTA Ss92–98; & FA 1980 S81)

Special rules apply regarding disposals both of shares owned *by* the trusts and of shares and units *in* the trusts by their shareholders and unit holders.

After 31 March 1980 authorised unit and investment trusts are exempt from tax on their capital gains. However, from 6 April 1980 any disposals which you make of units and investment trust shares carry full capital gains tax (25% or 40%) with no credit.

3.3.2   Holdings at 6 April 1965
(CGTA Sch 5, FA 1982 Sch 13 & FA 1985 Sch 19)

'Time apportionment' (2.17) does not apply to quoted shares. Instead you must consider the mid-market price at 6 April 1965 (2.17). Subject to the election described below, your gain on any sales after 6 April 1965 of shares held at that date is the difference between the proceeds and the higher of the cost of the shares and their value at 6 April 1965. Similarly, any allowable capital loss on such share sales is the difference between the proceeds and the lower of the cost of the shares and their value at 6 April 1965. If the price at which you sell shares held at 6 April 1965 is between their value at that date and their cost then you are treated as having no gain and no loss for capital gains tax purposes (subject to the election described below).

Disposals after 5 April 1982 may entitle you to indexation allowance (2.11). If you have elected for a 6 April 1965 valuation your indexaton allowance will be based on that amount. However, for disposals after 5 April 1982 you have the option of electing for indexation relief to be based on the respective values at 31 March 1982 (2.11.1). Furthermore, disposals after 5 April 1988 are subject to re-basing to 31 March 1982 values (2.10). Otherwise, for quoted shares and securities, indexation relief will be based on the cost, subject to the rules (2.11).

As regards disposals of quoted shares and securities which you held at 6 April 1965, you had the right to elect that any capital gains or losses on such disposals should be calculated by substituting the 6 April 1965 values for the original costs in all cases. (Fuller details are given in previous editions of this book.)

The election for each category was to have been made within two years of the end of the tax year (or accounting year for a company) in which the first sale after 19 March 1968 was made. However this has been extended and is now two years after the end of the tax year in which your first disposal occurs after 5 April 1985 (31 March 1985 for companies). *Thus in many cases elections will have been made* and will now be out of time in most cases.

Making the election was particularly beneficial regarding shares whose cost was lower than their value at 6 April 1965 but which had dropped below the latter value. An election would increase the available capital loss on sale. A further advantage arose if the original costs could not be ascertained in which case, on election, the 6 April 1965 values are used. Otherwise the Revenue would not normally allow any capital losses on the disposal of such shares. The election was originally a most important tax planning tool and is still available in some limited cases (see above).

Regarding sales after 5 April 1988, re-basing (2.10) is likely to occur. This results in the value at 31 March 1982 being used rather than the 6 April 1965 value in most cases.

3.4 Planning

● *Basic capital gains tax planning regarding quoted shares, etc, should include the following*

    (1) *Use your annual exemption (£5,000) to enhance the base cost of your shares. This will also increase your indexation allowance for future sales.*

    (2) *If you have realised gains in the current tax year in excess of £5,000, realise losses to cover such excess, possibly by means of 'bed and breakfast' transactions (2.14.1).*

    (3) *In order to maximise the annual exemptions available, split share purchases between yourself and your adult children.*

    (4) *So that you and your spouse are able to use your respective annual exemptions (£5,000 each) available from 1990-91 onwards, split share purchases between you.*

    (5) *Always weigh carefully any potential tax savings against investment criteria.*

3.5 Traded options
(FA 1980 S84; FA 1984 S65; FA 1986 S59 & F2A 1987 S81)

Options to buy or sell quoted shares are dealt with on the Stock Exchange. Prior to 6 April 1980 they were treated as wasting assets (2.18), but from that date they are no longer so regarded which means that the entire cost is deductible on a sale. Also from 6 April 1980 the abandonment of a traded option is treated as a disposal so that its cost is an allowable loss. From 6 April 1984, this treatment also applies to all traded options quoted on recognised stock exchanges or the London International Financial Futures Exchange.

However, after 1 July 1986 transactions in futures and options in gilts and qualifying bonds are exempt from capital gains tax.

3.5.1 Commodity and financial futures
(FA 1985 S72 & F2A 1987 S81)

Prior to 6 April 1985, profits from futures which were not part of a trade were taxed under Schedule D Case VI. However, from that date, any profits less losses which you realise are normally covered by capital gains tax and not income tax This applies to commodity futures or financial futures dealt in on a recognised futures exchange.

The 1987 Finance Act brought into effect broadly similar capital gains tax treatment for commodity and financial futures which are dealt in over the counter. This same applies to traded options which are handled in this way.

3.6 Unquoted shares
(CGTA S152 & Sch 5; FA 1981 S64; & FA 1982 S51)

Many of the above points regarding quoted shares and securities apply also to unquoted shares but the following special rules should be noted:

(1) Regarding holdings of shares at 6 April 1965 the 'time apportionment' rule normally applies to sales after that date subject to the right of election for valuation at 6 April 1965 (2.17). This is not a 'blanket' election for all your non-quoted shares as is the case for quoted shares. If you have elected for a 6 April 1965 valuation, your indexation allowance will be based on that amount unless you elect for a 31 March 1982 valuation. Otherwise, time apportionment applies to the gain *net* of indexation allowance. Thus indexation may affect the desirability of an election. (For disposals after 5 April 1988, re-basing to 31 March 1982 values is likely — 2.10.)

(2) If after 6 April 1965 there is a capital reorganisation or takeover regarding a non-quoted company in which you have shares, 'time apportionment' normally stops at that time and on any future sales you have a time apportioned gain or loss to the date of reorganisation or takeover and the full gain or loss after that time.

(3) If a reorganisation or take-over as in (2) above occurred before 6 April 1965 any shares still held at that date must automatically be valued at 6 April 1965 and time apportionment

does not apply. You still consider, however, the cost of your original holding when computing any capital gain or loss on a future sale.

(4)   Prior to 6 April 1982 (1 April for companies) the 'pooling' rules (3.2.2) applied to shares acquired after 6 April 1965 but not to acquisitions before that time which must be separately considered on a 'first in first out' basis.

(5)   The indexing rules (2.10) apply to non-quoted shares as for quoted ones.

(6)   The rule in (4) above regarding shares held at 6 April 1965 was modified, so that the 'last in first out' basis applied for disposals between 5 April 1982 and 6 April 1985.

(7)   Any relief which you obtain against your income, from the business expansion scheme (below) is not also available to create a capital loss. Thus if you eventually sell the shares at a profit, you will obtain full relief for the cost in calculating your capital gain, but not in a loss situation.

3.7   Losses on unquoted shares in trading companies
(ICTA 1988 Ss573-576)

Special rules apply to disposals after 5 April 1980 of shares in 'qualifying trading companies'. Provided you or your wife was the original subscriber, you can elect to obtain income tax relief for any loss on a full priced arm's-length sale, liquidation, etc. The election is required within two years after the tax year in which the relief is applied.

A 'qualifying trading company' is, broadly, one which has always been UK resident but never quoted and has traded for at least six years, or from within a year of incorporation if less. The company is permitted to have stopped trading within the previous three years provided it has not become an investment company in the meantime. 'Trading' excludes dealing mainly in shares, land or commodity futures. The relief originally applied only to individuals, but was extended to certain investment companies regarding disposals of shares held in 'qualifying trading companies' after 31 March 1981.

● *This relief is interesting because it allows you income tax relief for what otherwise would be a capital loss. If you are able to realise the loss in a year when your income tax top rate is particularly high, so much the better. An even more direct way of obtaining income tax relief from a capital transaction is through the business expansion scheme (see below).*

3.8   Business Expansion Scheme
(ICTA 1988 Ss289-312, FA 1988 Ss50-53 & Sch 4, FA 1989 S47 & FA 1990 S73)

Since 1981–82, first the Business Start-Up Scheme and then the Business Expansion scheme have operated to give you the opportunity of obtaining income tax relief on subscriptions for shares in certain companies.

The Business Start-Up Scheme operated for 1981–82 and 1982–83. During that period you obtained relief from income tax including investment income surcharge in respect of amounts subscribed in a year of assessment for shares in a qualifying company. A *qualifying company* exists to carry on one or more *qualifying trades* — broadly, manufacturing, wholesale and retail business but not leasing and financial activities, etc. Also, your subscription in the company needed to be during the first five years of its trade. A 51% subsidiary company does not qualify.

The scope of the Business Start-Up Scheme was considerably widened regarding shares issued from 6 April 1983 and it is now known as the *Business Expansion Scheme.* Particular features include the following:

(1) The life of the scheme was first extended to 5 April 1987 and then indefinitely.
(2) As well as covering investment in new companies, shares issued by established unquoted trading companies satisfying certain conditions are now included.
(3) As before, the scheme excludes employees. paid directors and 30% + shareholders.
(4) The annual total investment limit was doubled to £40,000 but the minimum remains at £500 unless made through approved investment funds. The previous 50% restriction was removed so that any quantity of shares may be included.
(5) Shares on which relief is claimed must in general be held for at least five years.
(6) Claims for relief can now be made once the company has carried on its qualifying trade for four months; and normally must be made within two years after the end of the year of assessment to which the claim relates.

(7) The relief does not normally reduce the cost for capital gains tax purposes. Also, shares issued after 18 March 1986 are exempt from that tax when first disposed of.

(8) The *qualifying trade* rules are similar to those for the Business Start Up Scheme (see above) with some modifications. For example, in respect of shares issued between 13 March 1984 and 19 March 1986, farming was not a qualifying trade.

(9) In general, a trade whose income is mainly from royalties and licence fees does not qualify, but an exception now applies for film producing companies.

(10) From 6 April 1985, companies whose business consists of research and development will, in general, qualify.

(11) After 19 March 1985 and before 19 March 1986 property development was not a qualifying trade where the company doing the development had an interest in the land being developed.

(12) Ship chartering is a qualifying trade for shares issued after 18 March 1986. Charters must not exceed one year and the ships must be UK registered and owned, managed and navigated by the company. (Pleasure craft are excluded.)

(13) After 18 March 1986, wholesaling or retailing goods normally collected or held as investments is not a qualifying trade, unless the company actively tries to sell them. Examples are fine wines and antiques.

(14) Certain parent companies have already been qualifying companies if all their subsidiaries have been wholly owned. After 18 March 1986, this extends to tiers of companies provided they are each at least 90% owned. Subsidiaries can even be resident abroad if the group's trade is mainly within the UK.

(15) Share capital issued in excess of £50,000 in total in any year does not qualify for relief if the company broadly has more than half its assets consisting of land and buildings. This applies regarding shares issued after 18 March 1986 only. The land content test applies at any time within three years after either the issue of the shares, or the commencement of trade if later. In calculating the land and buildings fraction, you deduct from the land liabilities secured on it and certain unsecured long-term liabilities and preference shares.

(16) If you buy qualifying shares after 5 April 1987, half of your investment can be carried back to 1986-87, provided it is made before 6 October 1987. The relief carried back in this way is limited to £5,000. You must elect for this treatment and your total relief for any tax year must not exceed £40,000. Similar relief applies for 1987-88 and future years.

(17) If you invest in an approved BES fund which closes after 15 March 1988, you obtain relief when it becomes closed for investment, rather than when it invests in BES shares. The fund must invest 90% of your investment within six months of the closing date.

(18) Regarding BES shares issued after 1 May 1990, a maximum amount of £750,000 capital raised by a company qualifies for relief in any period of 12 months. After 15 March 1988 and before 1 May 1990, this limit was £500,000. However, a £5,000,000 limit applies for certain ship chartering and private rented housing (below).

(19) From August 1988, BES relief extends to investment in companies enabling them to buy properties for letting under new-styled *assured tenancies* when the new system starts (towards the end of 1988). The company must provide tenancies over at least a four-year period from when the BES shares are issued. Properties valued at over £125,000 in Greater London and otherwise £85,000 are excluded. (Improvements in the locality are ignored for the purposes of valuations after 19 March 1990).

(20) Tax relief for interest on a loan to buy BES shares issued after 13 March 1989 in a close company is not available where BES relief can be obtained.

3.9   Personal Equity Plan
(ICTA 1988 S333)

A special scheme to encourage the purchase of shares operates from 1 January 1987. It is called the Personal Equity Plan (PEP) and broadly speaking the rules are as follows:

(1) Provided you are resident and ordinarily resident in the UK you will be eligible.

(2) A maximum of £6,000 can be invested each year from 6 April 1990 (£500 each month if preferred). Previous limits were £4,800 for 1989–90, £3,000 for the calendar year 1988 and £2,400 for 1987.

(3) For tax relief to apply, investments needed to be held for at least one complete calendar year from 1 January to 31 December. However, from 6 April 1989, there is no minimum holding period.

(4) Generally, your contributions must be invested in the ordinary shares of public companies quoted on a UK stock exchange or dealt in the Unlisted Securities Market. However, there can be

an investment trust or unit trust element if desired. From 6 April 1990, the limit is £3,000 (£2,400 for 1989–90); thus you can have a unit trust-only PEP. From 6 April 1990, the unit or investment trusts themselves must invest at least 50 per cent in UK equities, subject to certain relaxations. Previously this figure was 75%. Also, for schemes existing before 14 March 1989 there is an option to use a limit of £750 for 1989–90 and £900 from 6 April without the 50% rule.

(5) A manager must look after your PEP investments but they will belong to you and you are able to choose which you buy if your own scheme permits this.

(6) Re-investment of dividends and proceeds is allowed in excess of the limits.

(7) Subject to the above, re-invested dividends are free of income tax. Similarly re-invested capital profits are not subjected to capital gains tax.

(8) Also, subject to the above, share sales and withdrawals will be free of capital gains tax.

(9) Prior to 6 April 1989, for the year that a plan is started, up to the entire investment limit could be left in cash. After the first year, broadly 10% could be held in cash. After 5 April 1989, there is no limit on the amount of cash that can be held. However all interest on the cash is subject to composite rate tax.

(10) From 6 April 1989, you are allowed to buy shares through new issue offers and transfer all or part of your allocation into a PEP. This includes privatisation issues and also issues of shares in building societies converting to plc status. This must be done within 30 days from the day the share allocation is announced and the value at the offer price goes towards your total PEP entitlement for the year.

(11) The PEP rules are amplified by Regulations.

● *The advantages from investing in a PEP will grow each year as the accumulated fund and thus income and capital gains increase. If you do not use much of your annual capital gains tax exemption of £5,000, however, it is unlikely that the PEP capital gains tax relief will provide any additional benefit. From this point of view, a PEP will be of more interest if you have already used your annual capital gains tax exemption.*

4 Capital gains tax — special reliefs

4.1 Main private residence exemption
(CGTA Ss101–105; FA 1980 S80; FA 1984 S63 & FA 1988 S111 & Sch 8)

The house or flat where you live is normally exempt from capital gains tax when you sell it, subject to the following rules:

(1) The house must have been your only or main residence during the time that you owned it subject to various allowable absence periods (see below). You ignore all periods before 6 April 1965 for these purposes.

(2) The following periods of absence will not entail the loss of your exemption:

   (a) The last 24 months of ownership.

   (b) Periods of absence totalling three years.

   (c) Any period throughout which you work abroad.

   (d) Any periods up to four years in aggregate when you are prevented from living in your house due to your employment being elsewhere.

   (e) Any period during which you live in job-related accommodation from 31 July 1978, but intend to return to your main residence.

   (f) For disposals after 5 April 1988, any period before 1 April 1982.

   Provided you have no other residence which you claim to be exempt during the above periods they are taken cumulatively and so you could have a long period of absence and still not lose your exemption. You must, however, return to your main residence at the end of periods (b), (c) and (d) above or else you may lose part of your relief.

(3) Any periods of absence subsequent to 6 April 1982 in excess of those allowed (see above) result in the relevant proportion of

your sale profit being charged to capital gains tax. For example, if you bought your house in June 1983 and sold it in June 1990 at a profit of £7,000 having lived elsewhere for reasons unconnected with your employment for the middle five years, your chargeable gain is £7,000 × 1/7 = £1,000. (You are only allowed three years of absence and the last two in any event, leaving one year taxable.) For disposals before 6 April 1988, all periods of absence after 6 April 1965 needed to be considered.

(4)   If a specific part of your house is set aside for business purposes then that proportion of your profits on sale of the house will be taxable. Thus if you have eight rooms of which two are wholly used for business purposes you would normally claim 25% of your house expenses against your business profits and when you sell your house you will pay capital gains tax on 25% of your total gain (arising after 6 April 1965). If, however, you use no rooms exclusively for business purposes you will not normally be liable for any capital gains tax if you sell your house even though you claim part of your house expenses against your business profits.

(5)   Regarding disposals before 6 April 1980 if part of your main residence was let, your capital gain on that part was not covered by the exemption. (This restriction does not apply to periods of absence covered in 2(1)–(4) above.) However, if your disposal is on or after that date and part has been let for residential purposes, you may obtain further exemption, which is related to the gain on that part. However, the extra amount is not to exceed the exemption on the part occupied by you, or £20,000 if smaller. (Before 6 April 1983, this figure was £10,000.)

(6)   If you have two residences you can give written notice to the Revenue within two years of acquiring your second residence to elect which of the two should be treated as your main private residence and thereby be exempted from capital gains tax. If you do not elect then the Revenue will decide in the light of the time that you spend at each of your residences which of these is your main private residence.

(7)   For the purposes of the exemption your main residence is taken to include land of up to one acre (including the site of the house). If the house is large and its character requires a larger garden than one acre, this will normally be allowed.

(8)   Subject to the above rules, full relief is available for disposals after 5 April 1988, provided the house or flat has been your only or main residence since 31 March 1982. This ties in with the re-basing legislation (2.10).

Previously, you also obtained capital gains tax exemption on no more than one residence owned by you and occupied by a dependent relative (not able to keep him or herself — also the widowed or separated mother of either your spouse or yourself). However, this relief was withdrawn for disposals after 5 April 1988 unless the dependent relative had remained in occupation from an earlier date.

● *Ensure that you gain the maximum benefit from the private residence exemption. If you have two residences, claim within two years of the date of purchase of your second abode which should be treated as your main private residence to be free of capital gains tax. You have a free choice in this matter and so should select the house or flat likely to increase in value the most. The new re-basing rules may well affect your decision.*

● *Remember that the election could apply to a residence which you rent, as well as one which you own. Thus, if you have one of each, you should elect that the freehold (or long-leasehold) home is your main residence.*

● *Also, if you use part of your house for business, if possible do not claim specific rooms for income tax but merely make a general claim for expenses (see (4) above).*

4.2 Chattels
(CGTA S128; , FA 1982 S81 & FA 1989 S123)

A chattel is an asset which is tangible movable property such as a chair, a picture, or a pair of candlesticks. For these purposes a set is treated as one chattel. If you dispose of a chattel for no more than £6,000 you pay no capital gains tax and if your proceeds exceed £6,000 your capital gain is restricted to five-thirds of the excess. Thus if you sell a set of antique chairs for £6,300 (original cost £500) your capital gain is restricted to $5/3 \times (£6,300–£6,000) = £500$.

If you buy a chattel for more than £6,000, and sell it for less than £6,000, your allowable loss is restricted to the excess of the cost over £6,000.

For the years 1982–83 to 1988–89 inclusive, the limit was £3,000. A £2,000 exemption limit applied from 1978–79 to 1981–82. Before 1978–79, the limit was £1,000 and the capital gains tax was limited to half the excess over £1,000.

● *Planning your sales of chattels to take full advantage of the relief can save considerable tax. For example, you may have a valuable brooch whose real worth lies in four diamonds. By selling the stones separately for less than £6,000 the chattels exemption would apply. However, the brooch as a whole would raise, say, £20,000 so that no relief would be obtained. Similarly if you have a set of valuable objects whose value as a set is not much enhanced then sell them separately to different buyers so as to secure relief which you would not otherwise obtain.*

● *The chattels exemption should be borne in mind when you build up a collection of, say, antiques or pictures. By choosing items in a moderate price bracket, you stand a good chance of being able to sell them within the £6,000 exemption, or whatever it is at the time.*

4.3   Replacement of business assets
(CGTA Ss115–121, FA 1988 S112 & Sch 8 & 9, FA 1989 Ss129 & 133 & Sch 15 & FA 1990 S65)

You are liable for capital gains tax in respect of gains realised on sales of assets used in your business. Similarly a company is liable regarding its sales of business assets. If further business assets are purchased within one year preceding and three years after the sale, 'roll-over' relief can be obtained as a result of which the gain on the disposal is deducted from the cost of the new business assets. Thus, the gain is 'rolled over' and no tax is paid until the new business assets are sold, unless the latter are in turn replaced. (Furnished holiday lettings are treated as a trade for the purposes of 'roll-over' relief— FA 1984 Sch 11.)

To obtain full relief, the old asset needs to have been used in the business during the period of ownership. However, where the disposal takes place after 5 April 1988, the old asset only needs to have been used for business since 31 March 1982 for full relief to apply (if otherwise due). A special situation which might apply is where you obtain roll-over relief in the period from 1 April 1982 to 5 April 1988 and the original asset was acquired before the earlier date. If you now sell the replacement asset after 5 April 1988, no re-basing relief is available. However, you are given special relief equal to half of the rolled-over gain from the original disposal (2.10).

In order for the relief to be obtained the old and new assets must be 'qualifying'. This means that they must be within the following categories:

(*a*)   Land and buildings (but not trading stock).

(*b*) Fixed plant and machinery not forming part of a building.
(*c*) Ships, aircraft and hovercraft.
(*d*) Goodwill.
(*e*) Milk and potato quotas after 29 October 1987.
(*f*) Satellites, space stations and spacecraft, etc after 27 July 1987.

Since plant and machinery only qualifies if it is fixed, items such as motor vans, fork lift trucks and movable machines are excluded.

To get the relief you must use the old and new assets in the same business. However, if you carry on several trades, they are treated as one for this purpose. (This applies if there is a gap of no more than three years between one trade ceasing and the other starting). Also, roll-over relief applies regarding purchases and sales by you of personally owned assets used in your 'family company' (4.9). Note that to obtain total relief, the entire proceeds must be invested, otherwise you pay tax on your capital gain up to the extent of the shortfall.

If you are non-resident and replace a business asset chargeable to UK tax with one which is not, roll-over relief is generally no longer available. This covers the situation where you sell an asset used in your business in the UK and buy one overseas. This new rule normally applies where you dispose of the old asset or acquire the new one after 13 March 1989; but not if the new asset was acquired before that date and the old asset disposed of within one year.

If the new business asset is a wasting asset (2.18), unless it is replaced by a non-wasting asset within ten years, the rolled-over gain becomes chargeable. This also applies to assets which will become 'wasting' within ten years, such as a lease with 59 years to run. However, this clawback does not apply to a held-over gain arising before 31 March 1982 and becoming chargeable after 5 April 1988 (FA 1989 Sch 15).

For disposals or acquisitions after 13 March 1989, subject to transitional rules, dual-resident companies obtain no roll-over relief where they replace a UK business asset with one overseas. From 20 March 1990 roll-over relief is denied where the replacement asset is outside the UK tax charge and is acquired by a dual resident group member.

'Roll-over' relief is applicable to companies (6.1). Also a special extension of the rules covers 'gilts' obtained by companies in exchange for group companies in the aircraft and shipping industries on compulsory acquisition through nationalisation. An election is required within four years of the exchange and then the normal new compensation stock rules do not apply.

- *Always remember that to obtain full roll-over relief you must reinvest the full proceeds within the next three years (or the previous year). This will be a strong argument in favour of, say, buying the freehold of a new factory rather than leasing one, finances permitting.*

4.4 Roll-over relief on compulsory purchase
(CGTA Ss111A & 111B)

From 6 April 1982 a form of roll-over relief, similar to that available on business assets (above) applies to certain property which is sold to local authorities. The property must either be compulsorily bought from you or the purchasing local authority must have compulsory acquisition powers. The relief is not available if your replacement property qualifies for main residence relief (4.1).

4.5 Transfer of a business to a company
(CGTA S123 & FA 1988 Schs 8 & 9)

You will obtain this form of roll-over relief if you transfer your business as a going concern to a company, wholly or partly in exchange for shares in that company. You must transfer all of the assets of your business except for its cash, which you need not pass over to the company. The relief equally applies to the transfer to a company of a partnership business but not one already carried on by a company.

If you obtain nothing but shares as your consideration, your entire gain is rolled-over and you will pay no tax until you sell some or all of the shares. However, if you receive part of your consideration in other form, such as cash or even a debt owing to you, you will immediately be liable for the capital gains tax attributable to that part of the consideration (subject to your annual exemption of £5,000). Thus if your total gain is £4,000 and your consideration is shares worth £4,000 and cash of £12,000, you will pay tax now on £4,000 × £12,000/16,000 = £3,000; the remaining £1,000 being rolled-over.

When you sell your shares after 5 April 1988, you will obtain relief of half the original deferred gain (2.10), provided the original business existed at 31 March 1982 and was incorporated after that date and before 6 April 1988.

● *The decision of whether to take part of the consideration in cash or other taxable form provides an opportunity for tax planning. If you take all shares, your entire gain will be rolled over. However, if you have not used all your annual exemption (£5,000) it will be beneficial to take enough of the consideration in cash, etc, to cover it.*

4.6   Gifts of business assets
(CGTA S126 & Sch 4 & FA 1988 Sch 9)

A form of 'hold-over' relief applied to certain transfers of assets, other than bargains at arm's length, made after 11 April 1978. The assets covered were any used in your trade or 'family company' (4.9); also shares in such a company. A claim was required from both the recipient and yourself, similar in effect to that for general gifts (4.7). A more general relief applies for individuals after 5 April 1980 and for settlements after 5 April 1981 (4.7). The old relief remains for gifts to companies, however. Gains held-over after 31 March 1982 and before 6 April 1988 on assets held at 31 March 1982 qualify for 50% relief (2.10) on sales after 5 April 1988. From 14 March 1989, the general relief for gifts no longer applies and the old rules for gifts of business assets are expanded.

4.7   General relief for gifts
(FA 1980 S79; FA 1981 Ss78 & 79; FA 1982 S82; FA 1986 Ss58 & 101 & FA 1988 Sch 9)

In general, transfers of assets which you made after 5 April 1980 and before 14 March 1989, other than bargains at arm's length, are covered by 'hold-over' rules. Only UK resident or ordinarily resident *individuals* (1.7) were covered up to 5 April 1981. However after that date gifts *to trusts* were included and from 6 April 1982 gifts *from* trusts were covered. Note that the donee had to be UK resident or ordinarily resident.

A claim was required from you both, whereupon your gain was reduced to nil and the recipient deducted your original capital gain from his acquisition value for the asset. (If your gift was to the trustees of a settlement, you alone needed to elect.) Should you have received some consideration the claim covered only the gift element, if this was less than your total gain. If you were entitled to retirement relief (below) this reduced the held-over gain. The special 50% reduction for certain held-over gains applied (2.10). The assets needed to be held at 31 March 1982, the gains held-over after that date and before 6 April 1988, the sale being after 5 April 1988.

Capital transfer tax may have been paid on the gift based on its market value. Following the introduction of inheritance tax, however, such tax on gifts is now less likely. If any inheritance tax or capital transfer tax (7.1) is payable on the transaction, to the extent that this is no more than the original gain, the acquisition value is increased for the recipient. This even applies to inheritance tax eventually payable on potentially exempt transfers (7.3).

If you have received a gift after 5 April 1981 and made the election, then the held-over gain is assessed on you, subject to certain exceptions, should you become neither resident nor ordinarily resident in the UK before having sold the asset. The exceptions are:

(1)   Working wholly abroad being the reason for you having become non-resident returning within three years and becoming UK resident or ordinarily resident once again.
(2)   Not becoming non-resident until at least six years after the gift.

The exclusion of non-resident donees was being avoided by using certain dual-resident trusts. However, from 18 March 1986 these are regarded as non-resident for this purpose.

4.8   Gifts relief from 14 March 1989
(CGTA S126 & FA 1989 Ss124 & 125 & Sch 14)

With the removal of general gifts relief from 14 March 1989, the business gifts relief (4.6) has been expanded so that it now includes other items. The scope is now:

(1)   Business assets used in a trade profession or vocation carried on by the giver or his family company, etc.
(2)   Certain agricultural property (normally where the giver has vacant possession).
(3)   Shares and securities in family trading companies or non-quoted trading companies. (These categories include the holding companies of trading groups.)
(4)   Gifts of heritage property and to maintenance funds.

(5)   Gifts to political parties which qualify for inheritance tax exemption.

(6)   Gifts which give rise to an immediate charge to inheritance tax, for example, into a discretionary settlement (8.3). Potentially exempt transfers (7.3) do not qualify for this relief. However, if a gift is covered by the nil rate band and exemptions for inheritance tax but would otherwise be taxed, the gifts election is available.

(7)   Distributions of capital from accumulation and maintenance settlements may also qualify for the election. However, the beneficiary must not obtain the capital later than the income entitlement.

(8)   Subject to an election by donor and recipient, gifts to a housing association (FA 1989 S125).

(9)   Certain assets not mentioned above, which are not eligible for gifts relief may qualify for the tax on disposal to be paid by instalments (7.32.1).

(10) The relief is only available if the donee is UK resident and/or ordinarily resident.

(11) A similar rule regarding recoupment of the relief on the emigration of the donee applies as previously (4.7).

● *If you are making gifts subject to a 'hold-over' election, consider having some payment so as to enable you to use up your own £5,000 annual exemption if you have not already done so; also retirement relief (see below) if applicable. Thus if you wish to give your son some shares which cost you, say, £5,000 and are now worth £20,000, sell them to him for £10,000 so that your capital gain of £5,000 is covered by the annual exemption. Effectively, your son obtains a base cost of £10,000 because the gain of £10,000 is 'held over'.) With larger gifts, inheritance tax will need to be considered (7.1).*

● *With the abolition of general gifts relief for capital gains tax purposes, the choice of the subject matter of your gifts is important. Cash is free of the tax as are gilt edge securities. Otherwise, gifts of business assets, including family company shares, are eligible for a gifts relief election, subject to the rules.*

● *The type of settlement which you use may determine whether or not you may elect for gifts relief to apply on its creation. Discretionary settlements qualify in any event. Otherwise, gifts relief will only be available if the assets settled qualify.*

4.9   Business retirement relief

*(CGTA Ss124 & 125, FA 1984 S63; FA 1985 Ss69
& 70 & Sch 20 & FA 1988 S110)*

If you are over 60 and dispose by gift or sale of the whole or part of a business which you have owned for the past ten years, you are exempted from capital gains tax on the first £125,000 of any gain arising in respect of the 'chargeable business assets' of the business. If you have several businesses your total relief is restricted to £125,000.

For disposals after 5 April 1988, not only is the first £125,000 of gains exempted from capital gains tax; the next £375,000 is given 50% relief. thus if you are over 60 and sell your business, giving rise to a chargeable gain of £405,000, £125,000 of this is exempted from capital gains tax, as is 50% × (£405,000 - £125,000) = £140,000. You are taxed on only £405,000 - (£125,000 + £140,000) = £140,000. (This example assumes that you have not used any retirement relief previously.)

For disposals before 6 April 1987 and after 5 April 1985 the maximum relief was £100,000. For disposals before 6 April 1985 £100,000 was available at age 65 with tapering relief between 60 and 65. Prior to 6 April 1983, this figure was £50,000, with £20,000 before 12 April 1978, and £10,000 before 3 July 1974.

Note that you do not actually need to retire to obtain the relief.

After 5 April 1985, you are also able to obtain relief if you retire younger than age 60 for reasons of ill-health. You must show that you are likely to remain incapable of performing your previous work and will require a medical certificate.

'Chargeable business assets' include assets used for the trade, etc, of the business, and also goodwill. Assets held as investments, (including shares in subsidiary companies—see below), are not classified as chargeable business assets, however. Also excluded are assets where there could be no capital gains tax liability if you sold them; for example, trading stock (part of your trading profit) or cash (exempt).

The above relief also covers any disposal of shares in a trading company which has been your 'family company' for at least the last ten years during which time you have been a full-time director of the company. A 'family company' is one in which you have 25% of the voting rights or your immediate family has at least 50% (51% before

6 April 1985) including 5% held by yourself. Only the proportion of the gain on the shares attributable to the 'chargeable business assets' of the company compared with its total chargeable assets qualifies for the relief. Since 6 April 1985, but not before, subsidiary companies in a trading group are regarded as owning chargeable business assets.

The relief also applies if you personally dispose of an asset used rent-free by your 'family company' in its trade. To obtain this relief, you must have been a full-time working director of the company throughout your period of ownership of the asset. Limited relief is available if you receive less than a market rent. Similar rules apply in certain circumstances concerning assets owned by partners and used in the partnership business.

Before 6 April 1985, if your age was between 60 and 65 your relief as above was limited to £20,000 (£10,000 before 6 April 1983, etc for each year by which your age exceeded 60. (Add a corresponding fraction of £20,000 for the odd months.) Thus if you were $63\frac{1}{2}$ your relief was restricted to £20,000 × ($63\frac{1}{2}$ – 60) = £70,000. If your wife complied with the above requirements, she too was eligible for the relief if she sold her business or shares in a 'family company'.

Concerning disposals of the whole or part of a business which you have owned for less than ten years, you obtain 10% of the full relief if you owned the assets for at least one year prior to disposal, 20% relief for at least two years of ownership and so on, adding a further 10% for each year up to ten. From 6 April 1988, the fraction is applied separately to the £125,000 full relief and the 50% relief components.

If your wife complies with the requirements, she too will be eligible for the relief if she sells her business or shares in a 'family company'.

From 6 April 1985, the relief covers disposals by a settlement of assets used by a beneficiary for his own or his family company's business. Also shares in a family trading or holding company are covered. The beneficiary must have an interest in the possession in the settlement and must retire.

- *If you have a family business or company and are at least 60 years of age, use the capital gains tax retirement relief to its best advantage. This may mean continuing to work in it until disposal. Remember that, subject to the rules, your wife can also get the relief if she works in the business and owns part of it.*

- *Note the importance of the proportion of chargeable business assets in your company. In particular, remember that this proportion is only relevant when you dispose of your shares. This leaves scope for improving the 'mix'.*

4.9.1 Example: Business retirement and gifts relief

Mr A is 63 and holds all of the share capital in B Ltd, of which company he is a full-time director. His shares are worth £325,000, on which a capital gain of £175,000 would arise on disposal at that price. Assume that all the value represents chargeable business assets and Mr A has owned the shares for eight years; also that he has used none of his £5,000 exemption for 1990–91. How should Mr A gift or sell his shares to his son, C, in the most tax-efficient way? Ignore re-basing to the value at 31 March 1982, capital gains indexation allowance and inheritance tax and assume that Mr A is a 40% rate taxpayer.

Disposal proceeds of shares in B Ltd		£325,000
Chargeable gain before reliefs		175,000
Retirement relief available for period of ownership:		
8/10ths × £125,000	100,000	
50% × (£175,000 - 8/10ths × £125,000)	37,500	
	137,500	
Annual exemption	5,000	142,500
		£32,500
Capital gains tax on gift without election at 40%		£13,000

If both A and C make a gift hold-over election, then A will not be assessed to the capital gains tax but the base value of the shares for C will be reduced by the gain *before* the annual exemption, becoming £325,000 – £37,500 = £287,500. C's base cost could be increased to £292,500 without A paying any capital gains tax if C buys the shares for £292,500. This will leave A with a gain of £5,000, covered by his annual exemption. (C could borrow the money from A to purchase the shares.) The transaction would also involve a gift element of £32,500 for which a gift election should be made. Also, the inheritance tax position (7.1) should be watched.

4.10 Charities
(CGTA Ss145 & 146)

Charities are exempted from capital gains tax in respect of any gains on the disposal of assets provided that such gains are applied to charitable purposes.

If you make a gift of an asset to a charity you pay no capital gains tax on this disposal.

- *Thus if you wish to make a generous gift to a charity of a capital amount (rather than recurring annual amounts under deed of covenant) you will save yourself future capital gains tax if you gift a chargeable asset on which you have a large potential profit. For example, if you wish to give £20,000 to a charity and own shares in A Ltd which cost £4,000 in 1984 and are now worth £20,000 you should gift those shares. (If you sold the shares and donated cash they would only produce £12,000 net of say 40% capital gains tax, assuming your £5,000 exemption has already been used and ignoring indexation.)*

- *From 1 October 1990, an even better combination is likely to be to sell the shares first and then donate the cash. Provided the amount is at least £600, 'gift aid' relief will be available, subject to the rules. Thus, if you pay higher rate tax, a gross gift of £1,000 to the charity will only cost you £600 after tax relief. You pay the charity £750 (£1,000 – £250) and obtain £150 higher rate tax relief). Your capital gains tax in realising the money for your gift would certainly be less than £400 (your total income tax relief).*

5 Capital gains tax — trusts and estates

5.1 Introduction

This chapter deals with capital gains tax (CGT) as it applies to trusts and estates. Other taxation matters relating to trusts and estates are covered in Chapter 9 The legal aspects of trusts are dealt with in Chapter 12 and the administration period of estates is considered from a legal point of view in Chapter 11.

5.2 Trusts

(CGTA Ss51–58 & 126 & Sch 4; FA 1980 S78; FA 1981 S78, Ss86–87 & 89; FA 1982 Ss80, 82 & 84; FA 1985 S70 & Sch 20 & FA 1988 Ss100 & 109 & Schs 8 & 10)

Regarding realisations by trusts after 5 April 1988, a 25% capital gains tax rate applies, except for discretionary and accumulation trusts. Regarding the latter, a rate of 35% applies. This is equivalent to the basic and additional rates. Where the settlor (or spouse) has an interest in or rights relating to a UK settlement, the 25% rate may be increased. Any gains are taxed at the settlor's top rate. Also, the trust's annual exemption is lost, but the settlor's annual exemption will be available to the trust to the extent it has not already been used (FA 1988 S100). Prior to 6 April 1988, trusts were charged to capital gains tax at 30% on all gains from the sales of chargeable assets (less capital losses) during each tax year.

5.2.1 Annual exemptions

For 1988–89 the £5,000 annual exemption (2.5.3) applies to trusts for the mentally disabled and those receiving attendance allowance. Other trusts formed before 7 June 1978 obtain a straight annual exemption of £2,500 no matter how high their gains. Regarding trusts formed from that date, the exemption of £2,500 must be split between all those with the same settlor. Thus if you have settled two such trusts they each have an annual exemption of £1,250. If there are more than five, however, they each still have an exemption of £500. For future years, these figures will be increased with the retail price index (unless the Treasury order otherwise), rounding up to the nearest £100 as necessary.

For 1980–81 and 1981–82 the £3,000 annual exemption (2.5.3) applied to trusts for the mentally disabled and those receiving attendance allowance. (From 6 April 1981 only broadly half the property and income need be applied to the disabled.) Other trusts formed before 7 June 1978 obtained a straight annual exemption of £1,500 no matter how high their gains. Regarding trusts formed from that date the exemption of £1,500 was split between all those with the same settlor. Thus if you have settled four such trusts they each had an annual exemption of £375. If there are more than five, however, they each still had an exemption of £300. For subsequent years the corresponding exemptions are:

	Disability trusts	*Other trusts*	*Minimum*
1982-83	£5,000	£2,500	£500
1983-84	5,300	2,650	530
1984-85	5,600	2,800	560
1985-86	5,900	2,950	590
1986-87	6,300	3,150	630
1987-88	6,600	3,300	660
1988-89	5,000	2,500	500
1989-90	5,000	2,500	500
1990-91	5,000	2,500	500

5.2.2   Assets settled

When any chargeable assets are introduced into the trust by the settlor this is a disposal by him on which he pays capital gains tax if applicable. For example, if A bought 1,000 shares in B Ltd for £1,000 in May 1983 and gifts them in June 1990 to a settlement that he created, the shares must be valued at that time. If the shares are then worth £2,000 (ignoring indexation allowance) he has a chargeable gain of £1,000 for 1990–91. If, however, the shares are worth only £600 at that time, he has an allowable loss of £400 (£1,000–£600), which he can only set off against any capital gains resulting from other transactions between A and his trust. This is because they are treated as being 'connected persons' (2.9).

Any capital loss arising on property transferred to a beneficiary, which cannot be used by the trust in that tax year becomes available for use by the beneficiary in that and subsequent years against general gains.

5.2.3 Gifts relief

The general gifts relief (4.7) applied to all kinds of gifts *to* trusts after 5 April 1981, but gifts *by* trusts were only covered if made after 5 April 1982. Prior to this the business assets gifts relief applied. Between 11 April 1978 and 6 April 1981, where business assets, including shares in 'family companies' were settled, the trustees and settlor could jointly claim for any gain on the assets to be rolled over (4.3). The effect was that the settlor had no CGT to pay on the settled business assets, etc, and the acquisition value for the trustees was correspondingly reduced.

The general gifts relief does not apply after 13 March 1989. However, from 14 March 1989, the old business assets relief applies with some extensions (4.9).

5.2.4 Disposals, etc

The disposal of an interest in a trust by one of the original beneficiaries is normally exempt from CGT. However, after 9 March 1981 this does not apply to non-resident settlements.

Where a capital asset of a trust is distributed to a beneficiary this is a chargeable event which can give rise to a capital gain in the trust. (This even applies for minors, etc, who are not yet able to legally own the property.) Thus if a trust bought 1,000 shares in B Ltd for £2,000 in April 1983 and it distributes them to beneficiary C in July 1988 when their market value is £3,000 the trust will have a capital gain of £1,000 (£3,000–£2,000), which is assessable for 1988–89 subject to the annual exemption and indexation allowance. (An exception to this rule is where a beneficiary under a will receives his entitlement — 5.3.4.)

Prior to 6 April 1982, where a *life interest* ended in a discretionary settlement, CGT could arise on the excess of its value over the base cost. This did not apply on a death, however. From 6 April 1982 this charge is removed, provided the property remains in trust. However, on a subsequent disposal the original base value must be used. (FA 1982 S84.)

- *CGT planning for trusts is similar in many ways to that for individuals. Thus, for example, the £2,500 annual exemption should be used where appropriate and losses created (2.14.1) to cover gains made in the tax year.*

5.2.5   Foreign trusts
(CGTA S17; FA 1981 Ss80–85 & 88; FA 1984 Ss66, 70–71 & Sch 14 & FA 1989 Ss110 & 111)

A trust is generally treated as being resident abroad for capital gains tax purposes if a majority of the trustees are so resident and its administration and management is carried out overseas. Such a trust is exempt from CGT on realisations of assets in the UK and elsewhere. There are, however, rules under which the Revenue can sometimes assess UK resident beneficiaries with their shares of any capital gains (provided that the settlor is UK domiciled and resident or ordinarily resident either when he made the settlement or when the capital gain is made). Prior to 6 April 1981, this applied whether or not the beneficiaries received any part of the gains. However, tax assessed prior to 6 April 1984 in respect of gains arising before 6 April 1981 could be deferred until the benefit passed, provided the tax was unpaid at 29 March 1983. After 5 April 1981, however, UK beneficiaries are only charged to tax to the extent that they receive capital payments attributable to such gains.

A different system applies regarding the gains after 5 April 1981 of overseas settlements (settlor UK domiciled and resident or ordinarily resident). Where the capital gains by the overseas trust and capital payments to UK beneficiaries are in different tax years, the beneficiaries are taxed in the later one. There are rules to prevent CGT being avoided by transfers between settlements and by a trust changing its residence. From 1984–85, for the purposes of the rules, the term 'settlement' is enlarged to include dispositions, arrangements and agreements. Similarly 'settlor' takes in those making reciprocal arrangements or undertaking to provide funds indirectly.

For *income tax* purposes, broadly, for 1989–90 (with some exceptions) and subsequent years if at least one trustee is UK resident and at least one is not, special rules apply, depending on the settlor's status when he introduces funds into the settlement. If the settlor was then resident, ordinarily resident or domiciled in the UK, the non-resident trustees are treated as UK resident for determining the trust's residencce for income tax purposes. Otherwise, all of the trustees are treated as non-UK resident. If the settlement arises on death, the residence, etc of the deceased at the date of death applies for deeming the residence of the trustees and a similar rule applies concerning the personal representatives (5.3).

If you are a beneficiary of a foreign trust and obtain an asset from it after 5 April 1983, as a general rule, your base value is taken to be the market value of the asset. (From 10 March 1981 to 5 April 1984, except in certain cases where the trust was liable for UK capital gains tax, your base value was limited to the amount of any consideration which you actually gave for the asset—normally nothing.)

● *In an overseas discretionary settlement with some resident and some non-resident beneficiaries, UK CGT can be saved by distributing the gains to overseas beneficiaries in one tax year and then making capital distributions to UK beneficiaries in the next. (If all the beneficiaries had received distributions in the same tax year, those resident in the UK would have been assessed on their shares of the capital gain.)*

5.3 Estates of deceased persons

5.3.1 The CGT liability of the deceased
(TMA Ss40, 74 & 77)

When a person dies, CGT must be settled on all his capital gains up to the date of his death. Any of this tax that is not paid during his life-time must be settled by his executors or administrators out of his estate.

If the deceased has not been assessed to tax on all his capital gains prior to his death, the Revenue are allowed to make assessments on such gains within three years after the end of the tax year in which death occurred. In the case of fraud, wilful default or neglect by the deceased, however, the Revenue may make assessments in respect of any tax years ending within six years before the date of death, but no earlier years can be assessed.

5.3.2 The administration period
(Ss426–433)

The administration period of an estate is the period from the date of death of the deceased until the assets are distributed to the beneficiaries according to the will of the deceased or according to the rules of intestacy. Where, however, a trust is set up under a will the administration period normally lasts only until the trust takes over the residue of the estate. (See Chapter 11 for details.)

5.3.3   Capital gains tax during the administration period
(CGTA Ss5 & 49 & Sch 1)

No capital gains tax liability accrues to the estate of the deceased on the passing of his assets at death. The executors or administrators of the estate are regarded as acquiring the assets at their market value at the date of death and if they later sell any of the assets during the administration period the estate is assessed to capital gains tax on any surplus. The rate is 30% up to 5 April 1988 and 25% thereafter. Thus suppose part of the estate of A, deceased, consisted of 1,000 shares in B Ltd whose value at his death on, say, 30 June 1984 was £2,000. If those shares are sold on 1 November 1990 for £3,000 (in order to pay inheritance tax, for example), the estate is assessed to capital gains tax on £1,000 (£3,000–£2,000) for 1990–91. (This ignores indexation allowance.)

In computing the capital gains the executors or administrators are allowed to deduct their costs of establishing title. For gross estates not exceeding £400,000 the Revenue allow the use of a scale now extending from ·75% to 1·5% of the probate value of the asset sold. Also selling costs are, of course, deductible. .

5.3.4   Transfers of assets to beneficiaries

No CGT is charged on the estate on unconditional transfers of its assets to beneficiaries, in settlement of their entitlements under the will of the deceased. Instead, each beneficiary is treated for capital gains tax purposes as if he had acquired the assets at the same time as the personal representatives acquired them and at the same value.

Thus in the example mentioned above, if instead of selling the 1,000 shares in B Ltd for £3,000 on 1 November 1990 the executors gave them to C on that day in satisfaction of a legacy provided by the will of A, deceased, C is treated as having acquired the shares on 30 June 1984 for £2,000 only. (The value of £2,000 was the probate value of the shares at the date of death.) Thus no CGT is payable by the estate in respect of the transfer. If, however, C were to sell the shares on 1 December 1990 for £3,500 his chargeable gain will be £1,500 (£3,500–£2,000), although the shares have only gone up in value by £500 since he received them. This is because his entitlement to the legacy is considered for capital gains tax purposes to extend back to the date of death. Note that any indexation allowance for C would also relate back to that time, subject to the rules (2.10).

5.3.5 Annual exemption

For the year of assessment in which death occurs and the next two years, the first £5,000, etc of net gains is exempted (depending on the annual exemption for that year), as for an individual. (Prior to 1980-81 the special reliefs for aggregate net gains not exceeding £9,500 applied (2.5.2).)

5.3.6 Deeds of family arrangement

If the terms of the will (or intestacy) are varied by means of a deed of family arrangement (7.25) within two years of death, no CGT results at that time. (However, a deed of family arrangement is ineffective for income tax purposes.) Furthermore, new beneficiaries receive their legacies without the estate incurring any chargeable gains, but on future disposals their base value will be the probate value.

- *Make use of the annual exemption (£5,000 etc) where practicable in the year of death and next two years. This will probably save CGT for the beneficiaries. Assets with high capital gains which have arisen since death should be transferred direct to respective beneficiaries to avoid crystallising any capital gain. If it is agreed that certain members of the family should have particular assets, this could be facilitated by a deed of family arrangement (see above).*

6 Capital gains tax — companies

6.1 Companies' capital gains tax
(Ss267–276 & 278–281, TA 1988 Ss345-347, 400 & 435 & Sch 29 & FA 1988 Ss106, 107, 114 & 115)

The capital gains of companies are now charged to corporation tax at the normal rates. This applies for gains realised from 17 March 1987. Thus a gain made by a company with £1m profits bears 35% tax. However, a gain of £20,000 made by a company with £50,000 other taxable profits pays the small companies rate of 25% on the gain. (The rate was 29% if the gain arose in the period from 17 March to 31 March 1987 and 27% for the year to 31 March 1988.)

An exception concerns the capital gains which life assurance companies make for their policyholders. These remain taxed at 30%. This only applies to the policyholders' funds; any shareholders' profits are now taxable under the new arrangements.

Capital losses in accounting periods are offsettable against gains so that the net gains are taxable. Where an accounting period straddled 17 March 1987, it is regarded as being two separate periods, one before and one starting on that date, for capital gains purposes. Any allowable capital losses in the second period could be carried back and set against gains in the first.

For any accounting period ending before 1 April 1983, 15/26ths of the chargeable gains of a company, computed according to the normal CGT rules (2.9), were added to the assessable profits of the company and charged to corporation tax at 52%. Even if the lower rate (38%) applied to the company's profits, 15/26ths of the capital gains were still subjected to the 52% rate. This produced an effective rate of 30%, as for individuals, etc.

As the rates of corporation tax were cut, the taxable fractions of capital gains were adjusted to keep the effective rate at 30% (even if the small companies rate applied). Details are:

Year to 31 March	Tax rate	Taxable fraction of capital gains
1984	50%	3/5
1985	45%	2/3
1986	40%	3/4
1987	35%	6/7

Companies pay tax on their gains at the same time as the rest of their corporation tax liabilities. The due date is normally nine months after the year-end in the case of companies which started trading after March 1965. If the corporation tax assessment is issued later than the date given above, the due date becomes 30 days after the date of issue of the assessment (unless there is an appeal).

6.1.1   Dividends

• *Under the present system of taxing company capital gains, the Advance Corporation Tax (ACT) on dividends paid can be set off against the mainstream corporation tax. Thus if a company is paying the full 35% rate, 25% relief is available for any ACT leaving 10%. If the 25% small companies rate is paid by the company for the year in question, the net charge on the gain would be nil, if the entire gain is distributed. Shareholders may pay an extra 15% income tax if they are 40% top rate tax payers. However, dividends now represent an efficient way of getting capital gains realised by the company into shareholders' hands.*

6.1.2   Asset ownership

• *An important tax planning point to consider when buying a valuable asset for use in your company's business is whether you should own the asset personally or whether your company should be the purchaser. For example, the company which you control could buy a new building or you could buy it and let it to the company. If the company buys the asset and sells it later, making a capital gain, the company will pay tax on it (subject to possible roll-over relief — see 4.3). Should you then liquidate the company you will probably incur CGT on any increase in the value of your shares. The double CGT effect is an argument for holding the asset direct, but this could be over-ridden by commercial considerations. There is, however, the useful route of making dividend payments out of the capital gain (6.1.1). Also, consider the possible loss of retirement relief, particularly where you let the asset to your company (4.9). Note, however, the benefits of a wasting asset, such as a lease, being held by a company (2.18).*

6.1.3 Parallel pooling
(FA 1983 S34 & Sch 6, FA 1984 S67 & FA 1985 Sch 19)

The parallel pooling provisions applied only to companies. A formal and irrevocable election was needed which then covered all disposals, after 31 March 1982, of 'qualifying securities'. Disposals were first matched against acquisitions within the previous twelve months, taking the earliest first. Then, the pooled shares were regarded as being disposed of and finally non-pooled 6 April 1965 holdings. Two pools of costs were required, one indexed and one not. The costs of disposals were calculated in proportion to the shares sold, using the indexed pool. The indexation factor was reduced or eliminated to avoid producing a loss. A parallel pooling election could be revoked by written notice before 1 April 1987 otherwise, it has no effect regarding disposals after 31 March 1985.

6.1.4 Capital losses

Chargeable gains can be relieved by means of capital losses in the same period or those brought forward from previous periods. Trading losses can be set off against gains of the same period or the previous period. Gains can also be off-set by group loss relief claims (below). Note that the chargeable gains are first reduced to the appropriate fraction (6.1) for periods to 16 March 1987 and the trading losses are deducted from the remainder. Trading losses brought forward from previous periods, however, can only be set off against future trading profits and not against future chargeable gains.

Capital losses (2.14) incurred by a company can only be set off against any capital gains of the company in the same accounting period or a future accounting period. They cannot be set against trading profits, as a general rule, for any year. Unused capital losses can be carried forward to future years even if the company has ceased trading whereas a cessation prevents trading losses from being carried forward.

Unlike individuals, rules apply to prevent a company from manufacturing capital losses by sales from large holdings (2% upwards) of another company's shares and buying them back within a month if quoted and six months otherwise (F2A 1975 S58).

6.1.5   Groups of companies
(Ss272–280; FA 1973 S28; FA 1984 Ss46 & 47; ICTA 1988 Ss402–413; FA 1988 Ss114 & 115; FA 1989 Ss97–102 & FA 1990 S66)

Special rules concerning CGT relate to groups of companies (broadly, parent and subsidiaries). A subsidiary company is classified according to the percentage of its ordinary capital owned (directly or indirectly) by its parent. Thus a 51% subsidiary is over 50% owned by its parent; and a 75% subsidiary is not less than 75% owned by its parent.

Some of the main rules affecting chargeable gains in groups of companies are as follows:

(1)   Group loss relief is available in respect of a parent company and its 75% subsidiaries subject to various rules. This enables a capital gain in one group company to be relieved by a trading loss surrendered from another company in the same group.

(2)   Subject to certain rules, group relief also applies to a consortium of companies which own a substantial part of another. Up to 26 July 1984, a consortium was limited to five companies which had to own at least 90% of the ordinary shares. After that date, only 75% need be owned in total, with each consortium company having at least 5% of the ordinary shares.

(3)   Transfers of assets within a group consisting of a parent and its 75% subsidiaries (all resident in the UK) do not normally give rise to CGT. This excludes certain dual resident companies after 19 March 1990. (From 14 March 1989, the parent must be effectively entitled to over 50% of the profits of the subsidiary and of its assets on winding up.) When the asset leaves the group, however, CGT is paid on the entire chargeable gain on the asset whilst it was owned by any of the companies within the group.

(4)   For the purposes of CGT 'roll-over relief' (4.3) in a UK group consisting of a parent company and 75% subsidiaries, the gain on an asset sold by one trading company may be 'rolled over' against the purchase of an asset by another trading company in the group. Property holding companies are also included, where they hold assets used for their trades by trading companies in the group.

(5)   As from 15 March 1988, the exploitation of capital gains tax indexation allowance through inter-group financing has been countered. From the same date, the rules have been amended

to ensure that share exchanges by companies in the same group do not result in capital gains or losses being charged or allowed more than once.

- *In a group situation, you should be alert to the advantages sometimes to be obtained from transferring an asset into another group company before selling it. For example, company A might be carrying forward a capital loss of £500,000 with no immediate prospect of gains to set against it. If company B in the same group as A is planning to sell an asset, making a capital gain of £600,000, it is advisable to transfer the asset into A. Then A will sell the asset, thus realising the capital gain and offsetting the £500,000 loss, leaving a net assessable balance of £100,000.*

- *If a capital loss is carried forward in a company it remains available even if its trade ceases. Thus such a company in a group should not be liquidated until the loss is used. Alternatively it may be possible to sell the company to a group or single company which could transfer its own asset into it before selling the asset at a gain and offsetting the old loss.*

- *Note that the Revenue may try to invoke the* Ramsay, Burmah Oil *or* Furniss v Dawson *decisions to counter partly artificial group CGT schemes. However, commercial arrangements with no artificial tax-saving links should be safe.*

6.1.6 Demergers
(TA 1988 Ss213-218)

Sometimes it is wished, for commercial reasons, to split a group into two or more separate parts. Rules now operate which make it easier for two or more trading businesses to 'demerge' where they are carried on by a single company or a group. In demergers, subject to the detailed provisions:

(1) Where a company distributes shares in a 75% subsidiary (6.1.5) to its shareholders this is not treated as a distribution and no advance corporation tax or income tax arises for the company or its shareholders.

(2) Relief also applies where one company transfers a trade to a second company which in turn distributes its shares to the shareholders of the first.

(3) CGT relief applies to any distribution which you receive in the above circumstances until you sell the actual shares.

(4) There was previously certain relief from development land tax and stamp duty in demergers.

(5)   The new provisions only apply to the genuine splitting off of trades or trading subsidiaries. There are anti-avoidance provisions to counter, for example the extraction of tax-free cash from companies subject to an advance clearance procedure.

(6)   To obtain clearance from the Revenue, full particulars should be sent and the Revenue must then either signify their approval or require further details within 30 days.

6.1.7   Unquoted company purchasing its own shares
(TA 1988 Ss219-229)

The 1981 Companies Act enabled companies to purchase their own shares and issue redeemable equity shares. If the proceeds exceed the original cost, the excess would be treated as a distribution under existing law and taxed in the same way as a dividend. (Thus the company would pay ACT at 25/75ths on the excess and an individual receiving the payment would pay higher rate tax on the grossed up excess less a tax credit.) In order to remove the disincentive of this heavy taxation, relief is provided in certain circumstances so that the company pays no ACT and the shareholder's liability is restricted to CGT (unless he is a share-dealer, in which case the gain is treated as his income).

Thus the relief in general involves reducing taxes on income and normally substituting taxes on capital at often lower rates. (Stamp duty relief applied up to 27 October 1986 but not subsequently.) Because of the importance of unquoted companies repurchasing their own shares as a tax planning tool, the basic conditions for relief are given below:

(1)   The company must not be quoted nor be the subsidiary of a quoted company. (Shares dealt with on the Unlisted Securities Market are not treated as quoted.)

(2)   The company must be a trading company or the holding company of a trading group.

(3)   The purchase or redemption of the shares must be mainly to benefit a trade of the company or its 75% subsidiary.

(4)   The shareholder must be UK resident and ordinarily resident, having normally owned the shares for at least five years.

(5)   If the shares were inherited, the shareholder is required to have normally owned the shares for at least three years, including ownership by the deceased.

(6)   If the payment is used for inheritance tax or capital transfer tax within two years after a death, (4) and (5) above do not apply

and relief is due, provided that to pay the tax out of other funds would have caused undue hardship.

(7) If the shareholder keeps part of his shareholding in the company (or its group) his shareholding must be substantially reduced. Broadly, this means reducing his interest by at least 25% and not being 'connected' (ie, holding 30% of the shares, etc).

(8) The relieving provisions apply to payments after 5 April 1982 and advance clearance application may be made to the Revenue.

(9) As indicated, the above rules do not apply where a company buys back its shares from a dealer. Instead, the company remains liable for ACT on the excess of the proceeds over the original cost and the dealer is taxed under Schedule D Case I or II (1.3), receiving no tax credit.

● *Although tax is generally saved by having the distribution taxed as capital, this is not always true. For example, low taxpayers may pay less if a 'share buy-back' is treated as a distribution liable to income tax. The same would apply for certain trusts. Thus the refusal of clearance should not necessarily rule out a share 'buy-back'. This is particularly so following the reduction of income tax rates and introduction of matching capital gains tax rates.*

6.1.8 Overseas companies
(CGTA S15 & FA 1981 S85)

Any UK resident and domiciled shareholders of an overseas company can have certain of its capital gains apportioned to them if the company would have been close if UK resident. The gain is apportioned between the shareholders according to their entitlement on liquidation and any with less than 5% avoid assessment. The rule also covers overseas trusts with shares in such companies. The effect is that UK beneficiaries of the trusts could then be taxed on capital payments to them.

● *S15 does not apply if the gain is distributed within two years. Thus UK capital gains tax can be saved if the gain is distributed to non-domiciled shareholders, who are neither resident nor ordinarily resident in the UK.*

After 13 March 1989, any gains made on switches of holdings in offshore 'umbrella' funds by UK investors attract CGT.

6.1.9   Dual resident companies
(FA 1989 Ss132 & 133 & FA 1990 S65)

After 13 March 1989, where an asset of a dual resident company ceases to be within the UK CGT charge due to a double tax agreement, the company is deemed to have disposed of the asset.

Regarding replacements of business assets after 13 March 1989 (either the disposal or replacement) rollover relief is not available if a UK asset within the CGT charge is replaced by an asset which is not.

From 20 March 1990, rules operate which are designed to prevent a company transferring assets tax-free to a dual resident company in whose hands any gain would be outside the UK tax charge. Similarly, from that date, rollover relief (4.3) is denied on the replacement of business assets where one member of a group disposes of an asset and a dual resident group member replaces it with an asset outside the UK tax charge.

6.1.10   Company migration
(FA 1988 Ss105-107)

Taxes Act 1988 S765 contains penal provisions to prevent a UK company from becoming non-resident without Treasury consent being obtained. Such consent is also required to transfer part or all of its business to a non-resident and for certain share and debenture transactions. From 15 March 1988, such consent is no longer needed (except for certain share and debenture transactions) and it is replaced by a tax charge on unrealised gains.

Where a company is being 'exported', there is a deemed disposal of all of its assets at market value for capital gains tax purposes. This broadly applies to companies migrating after 14 March 1988, from which time only those incorporated outside the UK will be able to become non-resident. Furthermore, roll-over relief (4.3) does not apply where assets are sold before and replaced after migration. If a company which migrates continues to trade in the UK through a branch or agency, any connected assets will be exempted from the deemed disposal.

There is also deemed to be a disposal of assets for capital gains tax purposes where a company continued to be resident in the UK but becomes resident elsewhere under the terms of a double tax agreement. This applies where assets cease to be liable to capital gains tax under the Agreement. Such assets are valued at that time and capital gains tax charged on that basis.

Companies intending to emigrate must notify the Inland Revenue in advance providing an estimate of their UK tax commitments including tax on unrealised gains, and details of arrangements to settle such tax. If the tax is not paid, penalities may be charged. Furthermore, directors and group companies can be held responsible for tax and interest.

If a foreign registered 75% subsidiary of a UK company migrates, tax on the capital gains attributable to its foreign assets can be deferred. Parent and subsidiary must make a joint election and the tax becomes payable if any of the foreign assets are sold or if the parent-subsidiary relationship ceases.

After 30 June 1990, Treasury consent is no longer needed regarding certain transactions relating to companies within the European Community. This applies to issues and transfers of shares and debentures of overseas subsidiaries within the EC. Where *special* Treasury consent was previously needed, reporting to the Revenue is now required with non-compliance penalties of up to £3,000.

6.2 Capital gains tax — sales of subsidiaries
(FA 1989 Ss135-136)

From 14 March 1989, certain schemes to save tax on capital gains where a group disposes of one or more subsidiaries are curbed. For example, the value of a subsidiary may be reduced before sale by distributing assets to fellow group members at less than market value; such undervalue is added to the sale proceeds in calculating the capital gain on the sale of the subsidiary. However, the new legislation is not intended to catch distributions which could be made out of normal profits and reserves.

Another situation which has been countered, is where the commercial control of a subsidiary is sold, whilst keeping it within the group for capital gains relief on inter-group transfers etc through using special shares. From 14 March 1989, the benefits of group membership only apply if the parent company of the group has, directly or indirectly, an interest of over 50% in the income and assets of the company.

7 Inheritance tax

7.1 Introduction

The following is a brief outline of inheritance tax (IHT) stressing various planning points. This tax is highly complicated, however, and some of its complexities are beyond the scope of this book.

In some ways, inheritance tax is simply a new name for capital transfer tax (CTT). The name change took place as from 25 July 1986 and the new rules relating to IHT are effective for transfers and deaths on and after 18 March 1986. However, the new rules have radically altered the nature of the tax. In most circumstances, the focal point has become death, and the majority of lifetime transfers are only taxed if death comes within seven years. These are known as potentially exempt transfers (PETs) (7.3). In general CTT applied to transfers when made, subject to certain exemptions. However, for IHT, this only covers certain settlements and other 'non-PETs'. Otherwise, IHT is normally payable following death.

The rules for CTT were originally included in the 1975 Finance Act, which received Royal Assent on 13 March 1975. Substantial changes were made in subsequent Finance Acts and the legislation was consolidated into the Capital Transfer Tax Act 1984, now known as the Inheritance Tax Act 1984 (ITA). The tax applied to lifetime gifts made after 26 March 1974, transfers on deaths occurring after 12 March 1975 and settled property (8.1). (As mentioned, IHT on lifetime transfers after 17 March 1986 is much curtailed.)

CTT replaced estate duty which does not apply to deaths occurring after 12 March 1975. (Where property passed on deaths after 12 November 1974 and before 13 March 1975, estate duty applied at CTT rates.) Whereas estate duty only arose on death, CTT also applied to transfers made during your lifetime. However, after 17 March 1986, lifetime transfers between individuals and certain trusts (PETs) are only taxed if death occurs within seven years (7.3).

● *The essence of IHT planning is the conservation of wealth. Remember that in general, provided you survive three years, gifts carry less tax than the property would have borne on your death. Indeed, as mentioned, potentially exempt transfers (PETs) are free of IHT if you survive for seven years (7.3).*

Thus in broad terms you should aim to spread assets amongst your family to minimise the effect of IHT. Do not make gifts which you cannot afford, however, nor give too much money outright to young or irresponsible children.

7.2   Property chargeable
(ITA Ss1-6 & 10)

The property which you leave, when you die, will need to be considered (7.20). Also, subject to various exemptions and reliefs (7.14 *et seq*) you will be charged IHT on the decrease in value of your assets less liabilities which you suffer as a result of any transfer of your assets (chargeable transfer). Since the PET rules (7.3) did not apply for CTT, most lifetime gifts not covered by exemptions were taxable immediately. Now, IHT on PETs is only triggered off, should death occur within seven years. Normally, arm's length transactions are ignored if they are not intended to confer any gratuitous benefit. Any CGT which you pay is ignored in calculating the decrease.

If you are domiciled (1.6) in the UK or deemed domiciled here (7.5), IHT applies to all of your property wherever situated (7.26). Otherwise it only applies to your property in this country.

7.3   Potentially exempt transfers
(ITA S3A, FA 1986 S101 & Sch 19 & F2A 1987 S96 & Sch 7)

If you make gifts (other than gifts covered by an exemption) after 17 March 1986 to other individuals, or to accumulation and maintenance settlements (8.2) or trusts for disabled persons, they are classed as 'potentially exempt transfers' (PETs). This means that no IHT will be payable on these gifts unless you die within seven years. Should that happen, however, the PETs (less exemptions) become *chargeable transfers*. Your tax must then be recalculated as later indicated (7.20) but using the rate scale applying at death (7.8) and subject to possible tapering relief (7.4).

Note that transfers into discretionary and some other settlements are not PETs. However, from 17 March 1987, lifetime transfers concerning interest in possession trusts are classified as PETs. Such trusts are broadly those in which one or more beneficiaries have the income, or use of property, as of right. Transfers into these trusts are PETs, as are transfers out, except on death.

Certain transfers of value arising from transactions concerning close companies are not PETs. For example 'non-PETs' include transfers of value resulting from alterations in the capital and associated rights of such companies (7.32.7).

7.4 Tapering relief
(ITA S7 & FA 1986 Sch 19)

Where an individual dies within seven years of making a potentially exempt transfer (PET) (7.3) a proportion of the full tax is payable as follows:

Interval in years between PET and death	%
0–3	100
3–4	80
4–5	60
5–6	40
6–7	20
7+	0

Regarding those lifetime transfers (non-PETs) which attract IHT immediately at half the full rates (7.8), the tax is increased to full rates if death occurs within three years. Otherwise, the above tapering scale is applied to the rates current at death unless this produces a lower charge than that originally paid. In that case the original basis holds good. (Normally, some increase in the amount of IHT is likely if death occurs within five years.)

7.5 Deemed domicile
(ITA S267)

You are deemed to be domiciled in the UK if:

(1)   you were domiciled here on or after 10 December 1974 and

within the three years preceding the date of the chargeable transfer; or

(2)   you were resident here on or after 10 December 1974 and in not less than 17 of the 20 years of assessment ending with that in which you made the chargeable transfer.

7.6   Change of domicile

● *As already mentioned above, you are only liable to inheritance tax on your assets situated in the UK, provided you are neither domiciled nor deemed domiciled here. Hence to cease to be liable on your overseas assets, you will need to emigrate and lose your UK domicile and deemed domicile.*

Changing your domicile and residence is discussed in Chapter 1 (1.8). The two concepts are related but for IHT mainly domicile and deemed domicile (see above) are significant. Provided that you establish your domicile there, it is now sufficient if you move to the Channel Islands or the Isle of Man. Wherever you go, you will need to be treated as domiciled abroad for at least three years before the exemption applies.

7.7   Associated operations
(ITA S268)

Special rules enable the Revenue to treat two or more transactions related to a certain property as forming one 'chargeable transfer'. Where transactions at different times are treated as associated operations, the chargeable transfer is treated as taking place at the time of the last of these transactions.

● *This is one of the most important anti-avoidance provisions for IHT purposes and can be used to counter many arrangements which otherwise would be successful in avoiding the tax. If you have any plans to save IHT in a complicated way, you should always have regard to the associated operations rules.*

7.8   Rate scale
(ITA 1984 S7; FA 1984 S101, etc)

Capital transfer tax was charged on the cumulative total of all your lifetime transfers after 26 March 1974 together with the property passing on your death. There was a ten year limitation on cumulation (7.10).

The IHT scheme applying from 18 March 1986 only has a seven year limitation on cumulation. Also, as previously mentioned (7.3) lifetime potentially exempt transfers (excluding transfers to discretionary settlements, etc) are not cumulated unless you die within seven years. There are, however, various exemptions from the general rules (7.14 *et seq*).

Prior to 18 March 1986 the tax was charged at progressive rates shown in the appropriate tables. A lower scale applied to lifetime gifts and a higher one to property passing on death. If you died within three years of making a chargeable transfer, additional tax was payable to bring the charge on it up to the scale applicable on death. This rule still applies where death is within three years of a pre-18 March 1986 gift.

In general terms, if you made a chargeable transfer, you had two options. Either you paid the tax yourself, based on the value of the transfer plus the tax; or the recipient paid your tax, calculated on the transfer value excluding the tax. If you give cash, however, you could deduct the tax from the amount given.

For example, suppose that having previously made £130,000 of chargeable transfers, you wished to make an £8,000 cash gift to your son in June 1985. Tax on the £8,000 was payable at 20% and so you could keep £1,600 for the tax and pay £6,400 to your son. If you wanted him to get £8,000 net, however, one of you would have had to pay the capital transfer tax of £2,000; ie 20% × (£8,000 + £2,000).

Inheritance tax is charged according to the following Table 7.8.1 which applies to *chargeable transfers* and property passing on death after 5 April 1990. There is only one scale but lifetime gifts which are not PETs are charged at 50% of those rates. This applies basically to transfers into discretionary settlements, charges on such settlements (8.3.3) and chargeable transfers arising from close company transactions. Tax is paid on such transfers soon after they are made, cumulating them with others within the previous seven years to calculate the amount. If death occurs within three years, however, tax is adjusted using the full rates, with possible tapering relief (7.4) where death is later.

On death within seven years of a PET (7.3) inheritance tax must be calculated by treating it as a *chargeable transfer* and cumulating it with any earlier chargeable transfers within seven years of the PET. Tax is calculated using the value of the gift when made but using the scale current at the date of death. On gifts more than three years before death, some tapering relief will be available (7.4).

In general, the current rate scale applies to chargeable transfers and on deaths after 5 April 1990. Previously the rate scales have been modified on 11 occasions. Each time the burden had been reduced. The full tables appear later (7.34). Even if you have paid IHT or CTT on the old scales, a chargeable transfer after 5 April 1990 is taxed by reference to the new scale.

On death within three years of chargeable transfers at the old pre 18 March 1986 rates, any additional tax is found by taking the difference between the tax already paid and that payable at the new rates applying on death. However, even if the total IHT on the new scale is less than the tax already paid, no refund will be made.

7.8.1 Table: Inheritance tax rates after 5 April 1990

Slice of cumulative chargeable transfers	Cumulative total	% on slice	Cumulative total tax
The first £128,000	£128,000	Nil	£Nil
The remainder		40	

7.9 Indexation of rate bands
(ITA S8)

For the year to 5 April 1992, the IHT rates shown in Table 7.8.1 will apply subject to indexation. The threshold (£128,000) will be increased in proportion to the rise in the retail prices index from December 1989 to December 1990 and each threshold will be rounded up to the nearest £1,000. This applies for 1991–92 and similarly for future years unless Parliament otherwise directs. Thus the threshold for 1992–93 would be increased in line with the index increase from December 1990 to December 1991, and so on.

7.10 The ten year cumulation period
(ITA S7)

For CTT there was a ten year limitation on cumulation. If you made a chargeable transfer it was added to all chargeable transfers which you made in the previous ten years and any made before that time dropped out. Since CTT applied after 26 March 1974, the earliest that any transfers fell out of cumulation was 1984. Thus suppose you gifted £40,000 in May 1974 and then nothing more until June 1984; your CTT on a gift then of £64,000 was calculated completely ignoring the earlier gift. In fact it would have been covered by the nil rate band.

7.11 The seven year cumulation period
(ITA S76 & FA 1986 Sch 19)

Regarding chargeable transfers and deaths occurring after 17 March 1986, the cumulation period is seven years. This means that any transfers which you made in the three years to 17 March 1979 immediately fell out of cumulation regarding transfers after 17 March 1986.

Remember that only a limited category of transfers come into charge immediately (7.1). PETs (7.3) are only cumulated and charged to IHT if you die within seven years. Then the PETs become chargeable transfers and are brought into cumulation with previous chargeable transfers within seven years of each PET (including the PETs within seven years of death). The estate left at death (7.20) is then added to the chargeable transfers in the last seven years in order to compute the IHT on those assets.

7.12 Gifts within the nil rate band

- *Gifts are one of the main ways of saving IHT. The smaller exempt transfers are dealt with later (7.14 et seq), but in considering the seven year cumulation period it is worth remembering that, in addition to the annual £3,000 gift exemption (7.15) and other exempt amounts, £128,000 can be gifted each seven years within the nil rate band. (This ignores future indexation — 7.9) Thus, every seven years a fresh nil rate band will be available. Gifts within your nil rate band are particularly useful regarding discretionary settlements and other 'non-PETs' (7.3). These carry IHT when made, if they exceed your unused nil rate band and exemptions. Regarding PETs (7.3), since IHT is only payable on them if you die within seven years, the nil rate band is less important. However, the recipient would normally be liable for any IHT on the gift and his or her position is better if the PET is out of your nil rate band.*

- *Indexation increases the nil rate band. Thus, suppose you have previously used your entire £128,000 nil rate band, if indexation is at 10% you will have a further 10% × £128,000 = £12,800, rounded up to £13,000 available for gifts, etc in 1991–92, as well as the £3,000 annual exemption, etc.*

- *For elderly people with small estates it is not necessarily advisable, however, to gift merely the £128,000 nil rate band since this is tax free on death and it could be better to retain this sum for contingencies. This assumes that the rate scale is not changed adversely in the meantime.*

- *Remember that the capital gains tax gifts election is only available in certain circumstances. An example is regarding discretionary trusts. Thus care must be taken regarding the assets comprised in your gifts (4.8).*

7.13   Larger gifts

- *If you have a large estate, you should consider making more substantial gifts which may entail the payment of IHT in the case of 'non-PETs'. The rate will be nil for the first £128,000 of such chargeable transfers, however, (7.12) and effectively far more if business property relief (7.29) or agricultural property relief (7.30) applies. After that, half the rate scale will apply unless you die within broadly five years of the gift. (This eventuality can be covered by life assurance to pay the extra tax.)*

- *The effect of making substantial PETs (7.3) is beneficial in two ways. Firstly, no IHT is payable when you make the gifts, etc. Secondly, once you survive for seven years, under present law, the PETs are then ignored for IHT purposes. Furthermore, tapering relief (7.4) should help reduce the tax, should you die more than three years and less than seven years after making the PET. Particularly if you are in reasonable health and of moderate age, the potential IHT liability can be covered at modest expense by life assurance for the seven year period (7.3). The cost is likely to be far less than the contingent IHT. Thus, particularly bearing in mind that cumulation now ceases after seven years, so that you will then have the use of a fresh nil rate band, you should be able to make useful IHT savings by larger gifts. This applies both to PETs and non-PETs.*

7.14 Exempt transfers

(ITA Ss18–27 & Sch 6(2))

Broadly, exempt transfers can be divided between those which apply both on death and during your life and those which are only exempt if the transfers are during your life. The first category includes transfers between your wife and yourself.

7.14.1 Transfers between husband and wife

Transfers between your wife and yourself both during your lives and on death were exempt from CTT. This exemption also applied for estate duty purposes on deaths after 12 November 1974. A similar exemption applies for IHT.

These exemptions do not apply, however, if the recipient of the property is not domiciled (or not deemed domiciled) in this country (1.8) (unless the giver is also non-domiciled at the time). In this case, only the first £55,000 (£50,000 to 9 March 1982 and £25,000 prior to 26 March 1980) transferred to the non-domicilied spouse is exempt.

Under the estate duty rules, if you left property in trust for your wife for life, duty was paid when you died; but none was payable on her subsequent death. Where the first death occurs after 12 November 1974, the present relief applies and so no CTT or IHT is payable on property passing to the surviving spouse. For this reason, when the latter dies, full CTT or IHT is payable on the trust property. However, if the surviving spouse had property left in trust by a husband or wife who died before 13 November 1974, no CTT or IHT arises on that property on the death of the survivor (because estate duty would have been payable on the first death).

7.14.2 Equalisation of assets of husband and wife

- *Provided the recipient is UK domiciled (or deemed domiciled) no IHT is payable on transfers which you make to your wife or she makes to you, either during your lives or on death (above). But do not keep all of your assets until you die and then leave them to your wife because this may ultimately result in high IHT on her death which is more than the combined tax if your estates were equal and you each left your assets to your children.*

- *Thus, suppose you have £328,000 and your wife has nothing. If you die first, leaving it all to her, no tax is then payable. But if she still has £328,000 when she dies and has made no previous chargeable transfers, the IHT at present rates will be £80,000 (Table 7.8.1). If you had given your wife £164,000 before you died, however, and left your remaining £164,000 to your children, on your death £14,400 would be paid in IHT. Similarly, on your wife's death £14,400 would be paid making a total of £28,800, compared with £80,000 IHT paid if your wife inherits all your wealth. However, make sure that your wife has sufficient to live on.*

- *If your wife otherwise has insufficient funds, giving her assets will also enable her to make exempt gifts to your children; thus you both take advantage of the exemptions. Also, she could make larger PETs (7.3). Should there be insufficient funds for your widow if money is left or given to your children, the use of a small discretionary trust (8.3.4) is useful. From this trust, either created in your lifetime or by your will, your widow could draw income or capital as required. The amount settled would normally be within the nil rate band.*

- *A further point in favour of equalising your estate with your wife's is that wealth tax, if it is ever introduced, would be expected to apply separately to husband and wife at progressive annual rates. Thus less tax is payable on two smaller estates than on one larger estate. Of course, these tax planning considerations must be tempered by practical points such as making sure your wife has sufficient to maintain her, should you die first. Also, a certain mutual trust is necessary. Your planning should also take account of your respective ages and states of health by arranging for a larger share to be in the hands of the one likely to live longer.*

- *A most vital reason for equalising the estates of husband and wife is the onset of the new rules for independent taxation (3.4). Savings in both income tax and capital gains tax may result.*

7.14.3 The matrimonial home

- *If you are buying a new home, put it into the joint names of your wife and yourself. Since the matrimonial home often comprises the major part of the assets of a married couple, this would be a very useful step towards equalising your respective estates.*

- *You can own your house jointly with your wife as joint tenants or tenants in common (10.15). Under a joint tenancy the share of the first of you to die passes automatically to the survivor on death. Thus the security of your wife is best served by having the house owned in this way and this is certainly the simplest method, advisable for smaller cases.*

- *For IHT planning purposes, however, it is likely to be better for your wife and yourself to own the house as tenants in common. In this way you will each have a clearly defined share in the house, normally half each, although you could have different fractions. You will then be able to dispose of your share independently, either by lifetime gift or in your will. However, take care not to fall foul of the rules concerning gifts with reservation (7.22). Thus, you should not gift all or part of your home (unless to your spouse) and continue to live there, unless you pay a proper rent.*

The above does not normally appy to bequests in your will. Thus, you could leave your share by your will to your son and express the wish that he allows your widow to live in the house for as long as she wishes. (You will need to trust your son but the executors should be able to exert some influence, if required.) In this way your £128,000 nil rate band will be more or less used at your death, if not already absorbed. Otherwise, in order to use your nil rate band it may have been necessary to gift to your son (or others) liquid assets needed by your wife to live on.

7.15 Exempt transfers — lifetime gifts

The following transfers are only exempt if made by an individual during his life. They do not apply to transfers made by trustees nor to assets passing on death. In any one fiscal year to 5 April, you can make all of these exempt transfers cumulatively and so can your wife. Note, however, the limitation in (2) below regarding small gifts.

(1) *Transfers each year up to a value of £3,000*
     Prior to 6 April 1981 the annual limit was £2,000 and before 6 April 1976 it was £1,000. If you do not use up the full £3,000 allowance in one year, you can carry the unused part forward for one year only. If your transfers taken against this exemption reach £3,000 in one year, you have nothing available to carry forward, even though you may have had £3,000 carried forward from the previous year.

     For example, if you made no chargeable transfers in the year to 5 April 1990, you have £6,000 (£3,000 + £3,000) available for exempt transfers under this category in the year to 5 April 1991. If, however, you transferred £1,000 in the year to 5 April 1990 you have £2,000 carried forward and so can transfer £5,000 in the year to 5 April 1991.

     A special allocation rule (FA 1986 Sch 19) applies from 18 March 1986. In any year to 5 April, your annual exemption first reduces those lifetime transfers which are not PETs; and then your PETs. (Deaths within seven years may cause the re-allocation of your annual exemptions, regarding amounts originally set against your 'non-PETs' for the following year.)

(2) *Small gifts*
Outright gifts to any one person not exceeding £250 for each year to 5 April are exempt. Up to 5 April 1980 the annual amount was £100. This applied in addition to the £2,000 exemption. However, from 6 April 1981 the £250 exemption cannot be used against gifts larger than that amount. Thus you can make an unlimited number of exempt gifts of £250 to different people but any gifts of £251 or more must be set against the £3,000 and other exemptions with the excess being taxable (if the nil rate band has been exhausted).

(3) *Normal expenditure out of income*
To qualify under this exemption, a transfer must be part of your normal expenditure. This means that there must be an element of regularity. Life assurance premiums (7.33) are particularly suited for this. Further conditions are that the transfer is out of your after-tax income and you are left with enough income to maintain your usual standard of living.

Life policy premium payments will not qualify for this exemption, however, if they are made out of an annuity purchased on your life, unless you can show that the policy and the annuity were effected completely independently of each other. This rule even applies if you make gifts out of your annuity receipts and the donee pays the premiums on the policy on your life.

If you buy an annuity, and make transfers from it, only the income proportion of the annuity (14.5) is treated as your income for the purposes of the normal expenditure rule; the capital element is not.

- *It may be beneficial for you and your spouse to split your income between you. Not only will the benefits of independent taxation be enhanced (2.8.1), but also you will both be able to use the IHT exemption for normal expenditure out of income.*

(4) *Gifts in consideration of marriage* made to one of the partners of the marriage or settled on the partners and their children, etc. The limits are £5,000 if the donor is a parent of one of the

marriage partners, £2,500 if a grandparent or great-grandparent or one of the parties themselves, or otherwise £1,000. (From 6 April 1981, the relief extends to marriage gifts from settlements where an interest in possession ends.)

- *Note that if your son gets married, your spouse and yourself can each give £5,000 to him and his bride making £10,000 in all, and the bride's parents could do likewise. If you would like to make more substantial gifts to the couple, these could be found from your annual exemption and nil rate band and those of your spouse. Such larger gifts would normally be PETs (7.3) and perhaps partly taxable if you die within seven years.*

(5) *Family maintenance*
     If you make any of the following gifts during your life, they are not treated as transfers of value (ITA S11):
     (a) For the maintenance, education, etc of your child, former spouse or illegitimate child.
     (b) For the maintenance or education of a child not in his parent's care, who has been in your care during substantial periods of his minority.
     (c) For the care or maintenance of a dependent relative.

7.15.1 Reducing your assets by exempt gifts

- *Take advantage of the various exempt transfers (above). By this means you can gift to your children, and others you may wish to benefit, considerable amounts over a period of years free of actual or potential tax. As seen, gifts to your spouse are normally free of IHT (7.14.1).*

- *If you have funds surplus to your requirements, you can make gifts totalling £3,000 in any year (7.15). In addition, you can make outright gifts of up to £250 each year to any number of other individuals apart from the recipients of the gifts totalling £3,000. Furthermore, if you have surplus after-tax income you can make normal expenditure gifts out of income (7.15). Do not overlook the reliefs applied to marriage gifts for your children and grandchildren, etc (7.15). By means of all the above transfers you can reduce your estate without incurring any IHT liability, even if you die within seven years. Furthermore, by making the required election (4.7) any CGT will be held over until the recipient's disposal.*

- *Remember that the above exemptions apply to both your spouse and yourself. Also, do not forget that unused portions of the £3,000 limit can be carried forward for one year only. Thus if, say, your spouse wishes to give a £12,000 necklace to your daughter, it can be done free of IHT if you each give her £6,000 in cash (covering two years, assuming no gifts last year) and she then buys the necklace from your spouse for £12,000. (This could involve a CGT liability, however: see 2.2).*

7.16   Exempt transfers — during life and on death

The following transfers are in general exempt, whether made during your life or on death. Similar rules also apply to trusts (8.1).

(1)   *Transfers in the course of trade, etc* are exempt if allowed as deductions in computing the profits for income tax purposes. This applies equally to professions and vocations, as well as allowable deductions from other forms of profits or gains for the purposes of income tax and corporation tax.

(2)   *Gifts for national purposes, etc* made to certain bodies. These include the National Trust, National Heritage Memorial Fund, National Gallery, British Museum and similar organisations including universities and their libraries; also museums and art galleries maintained by local authorities or universities.

(3)   *Gifts for public benefit* of property deemed by the Treasury to be of outstanding scenic, historic, scientific or artistic merit including land, buildings, pictures, books, manuscripts, works of art, etc.

(4)   *PETs (7.3) of property held for national purposes etc.* This exemption applies where, prior to the death of the recipient, the property is sold by private treaty (or gifted to an organisation as mentioned above (2).

(5)   *Gifts of shares* to an employee trust provided it will then hold at least half of the ordinary shares of the company.

(6)   *Gifts to charities* are exempt without limit if made after 14 March 1983. If made before 15 March 1983 and on or within a year of death, however, the first £250,000 was exempt. The exemption was £200,000 before 9 March 1982 and £100,000 before 26 March 1980. Gifts to settlements for charitable purposes are covered by the exemption, as are gifts to charities from other trusts.

(7)   *Gifts to political parties* after 14 March 1988 (FA 1988 S 137) are wholly exempt. Prior to 15 March 1988, the exemption was limited to £100,000 for gifts made within one year of death. For these purposes a 'political party' is one with at least two

members sitting in Parliament or one member and not less than 150,000 votes for its candidates at the last General Election.

(8) *Gifts to housing associations* or sales of land to them at under-value after 13 March 1989 (FA 1989 S171).

7.16.1 Gifts to charities, etc

- *As noted above, gifts to charities and political parties are exempt. Thus you should consider making such gifts during your lifetime and bequests in your will. Both will reduce the value of your estate for IHT purposes, and CGT relief applies concerning charitable dispositions (4.10).*

- *If you have a really large estate and are charitably disposed, then you should consider making large donations to charity during your lifetime, so that no IHT is paid, even if you die within seven years. (A charitable settlement may be appropriate in this connection.) Also, you should not overlook the advantages of making regular payments by deed of covenant (9.3), which will attract useful income tax benefits.*

7.17 Excluded property
(ITA S6)

As well as the various transfers mentioned above being exempt from IHT and previously CTT, certain categories of property must be 'excluded' from your estate for these purposes. The following 'excluded property' must be left out of the value of your estate, regarding both lifetime transfers and property passing on death:

(1) Property outside the UK (7.26), if you are neither domiciled nor deemed domiciled in this country. As already noted (7.5), this has important planning consequences.

(2) A reversionary interest, unless either you bought it or it relates to the falling in of a lease which was treated as a settlement (8.1). However, certain anti-avoidance rules apply to prevent misuse.

(3) Cash options under approved retirement pension schemes, provided an annuity becomes payable to your dependants instead of the cash option itself.

(4) Certain property in this country belonging to visiting forces and NATO headquarters staff.

(5) Certain overseas pensions from former colonies, etc, including death payments and returns of contributions.

(6) Savings such as national savings certificates and premium

bonds, if you are domiciled in the Channel Islands or the Isle of Man.

(7)　Those UK government securities on which interest may be paid gross to non-residents, provided you are neither domiciled nor ordinarily resident here (see Table 7.17.1).

7.17.1　Table: United Kingdom securities exempt for certain non-residents

$2\frac{1}{2}\%$	Treasury Loan, 2024	$9\frac{1}{2}\%$	Convertible Loan, 2011
$3\frac{1}{2}\%$	War Stock 1952 or after	$9\frac{1}{2}\%$	Treasury Loan, 1999
$5\frac{1}{2}\%$	Treasury Stock, 2008-12	10%	Treasury Loan, 1994
$5\frac{3}{4}\%$	Funding Loan, 1987-91	10%	Treasury Convertible, 1991
6%	Funding Loan, 1993	10%	Treasury Loan, 1993
$6\frac{3}{4}\%$	Treasury Loan, 1995-98	$10\frac{1}{2}\%$	Treasury Convertible, 1992
$7\frac{3}{4}\%$	Treasury Loan, 2012-15	11%	Exchequer Loan, 1990
8%	Treasury Loan, 1992	$12\frac{1}{2}\%$	Treasury Loan, 1993
8%	Treasury Loan, 2002-06	$12\frac{3}{4}\%$	Treasury Loan, 1995
$8\frac{1}{4}\%$	Treasury Loan, 1987-90	$12\frac{3}{4}\%$	Treasury Stock, 1992
$8\frac{1}{2}\%$	Treasury Loan, 2000	13%	Treasury Stock, 1990
$8\frac{1}{2}\%$	Treasury Loan, 2007	$13\frac{1}{4}\%$	Treasury Loan, 1997
$8\frac{3}{4}\%$	Treasury Loan, 1997	$13\frac{1}{4}\%$	Exchequer Loan, 1996
9%	Treasury Loan, 1994	$13\frac{3}{4}\%$	Treasury Loan, 1993
9%	Treasury Loan, 1992-96	$14\frac{1}{2}\%$	Treasury Loan, 1994
9%	Conversion Stock, 2000	$15\frac{1}{4}\%$	Treasury Loan, 1996
9%	Treasury Loan, 2008	$15\frac{1}{2}\%$	Treasury Loan, 1998

● *If you are neither domiciled nor ordinarily resident in the UK but have substantial assets here, sell some of them and reinvest the proceeds in exempt gilts (see above). In this way your UK estate for IHT purposes will be reduced. Also, the income will be exempt from UK income tax.*

7.17.2　Example: Calculation of capital transfer tax — lifetime gifts

Mr A made the following gifts in excess of his normal expenditure:

(1)　3 April 1974 to his son D £21,100 cash*

(2)　10 April 1976 to his son B £3,000 cash

(3)　15 April 1976 to his wife W £20,000 cash

(4)　31 May 1976 to B £10,100 cash on his marriage

(5)　30 September 1976 to C shares worth £4,600

(6)　1 December 1979 to B £14,100 cash

(7)　30 June 1981 to D £5,000 cash

(8)　15 August 1981 to B £250 cash

(9) 20 August 1982 to charity £100,000
(10) 30 June 1984 to B £16,000
  *Less CTT Paid by Mr A.

What CTT was payable on the above by Mr A during his lifetime?

Capital transfer tax payable during Mr A's life.

(Gift 3 was exempt, being to his wife, and gifts 2, 7 and 8 were covered by the respective small gifts and annual exemptions including carry forwards. Gift 9 was covered by the exemption for charitable gifts.)

			Amount Chargeable	Rate	Tax Payable
(1)	3 April 1974 to D		£21,100		
	Less:				
	Small gift exemption	£100			
	Annual exemption	£1,000			
		——	£1,100		
			——	£20,000	£15,000 at Nil	—
				£5,000 at 5%	£250
(4)	31 May 1976 to B on his marriage		£10,100		
	Less:				
	Small gift exemption	£100			
	Marriage exemption	£5,000			
		——	£5,100	£5,000	£5,000 at 7½%	£375
(5)	30 September 1976 to C shares worth		£4,600		
	Less:				
	Small gift exemption		100		
			£4,500	£5,000 (grossed)	£5,000 at 10%	£500
(6)	1 December 1979 to B		£14,100		
	Less:				
	Annual exemption	£2,000			
	Annual exemption bought forward	£2,000		£5,000 at 7½	
	Small gift exemption	100			
		——	£4,100	£10,000	£5,000 at 10%	£875
	Gift (1) falls out of cumulation on 3 April 1984			(20,000)		

(10) 30 June 1984 to B		£16,000			
Less:					
Annual exemption	£3,000				
Annual exemption brought forward	£3,000	6,000	£10,000	Nil	—
Cumulative totals of chargeable gifts and tax			£30,000		£2,000

7.17.3   Example: Inheritance tax on PET

Mr A made the gifts shown in the previous example and then no others until 10 November 1986, when he gave cash of £124,000 to his son, C. This is a PET (7.3) and thus no IHT is then payable. However, if Mr A dies on 31 January 1991, IHT will be payable as follows:

		Amount Charge-able	Rate	Tax Payable
PET — gift to C 10 November 1986		£124,000		
Less: Annual exemption	£3,000			
Annual exemption brought forward	3,000	6,000		
		£118,000		
Prior chargeable tranfers net of exemptions within seven years (6)	£10,000			
(10)	10,000	20,000		
		£138,000	£128,000 at nil	—
			£10,000 at 40%	£4,000
				£4,000
Less IHT on prior transfers within seven years			£20,000 at nil	—
				£4,000

IHT payable on PET allowing for tapering relief (death in fifth year) $£4,000 \times 60\% = £2,400$

Notes: (1) This example does not cover IHT on any subsequent transfers nor on the estate left by Mr A at death.

(2) If Mr A had delayed his gift to C until December 1986, it would have escaped cumulation with gift (6), saving eventual IHT of £2,400 in this example.

7.18 Valuation
(ITA Ss 160-170)

For IHT (and CTT) purposes your assets are normally valued at their open market value at the transfer date. If the value of an asset which you keep is affected by the transfer, you will need to value your 'estate' both before and after the transfer in order to calculate the resultant fall on which you are taxed. Your liabilities must be taken into account in valuing your total 'estate'. Any 'excluded property' (7.17) must be left out of the totals, both before and after the transfer.

For further comments on valuation, please refer to Chapter 2.

7.19 Valuation of related property
(ITA S161)

Certain property (such as shares in a private company) is worth more valued collectively than if considered as the sum of the individual items. Where the value of any of your property is less than the appropriate proportion of the value of the aggregate of that and any 'related property' you must value your own property as the appropriate portion of the value of that aggregate.

'Related property' is property belonging to your spouse, or property in a settlement in which you or your spouse has an interest in possession. Also included is any property transferred by you or your spouse after 15 April 1976 to a charity or charitable trust (unless leaving again more than five years ago.

This rule is particularly significant regarding the valuation of unquoted shares. For example if you and your spouse each have 40% of the shares of an unquoted company, then the value of 80% of the shares is normally much higher than twice the value of 40% of the shares. This is because an 80% holding carries with it full control of the company. Thus splitting a shareholding in a non-quoted company between your spouse and yourself, so that neither of you has control, is not effective (so far as the first transfer is concerned) in producing a lower aggregate value for IHT purposes. Similarly, if you gift to your child, say, 2% out of a combined 51% holding, IHT falls on the difference between the controlling 51% and 49% minority holdings — far more than the value of 2% in isolation.

Special relief applies where you sell the related property which you inherited within three years of the death for less than the value on which tax was originally paid. Subject to various conditions including the requirement that the sale is at arm's length for a freely negotiated price, you can claim for the related property in question to be revalued at death on the basis that it was not related to any other property.

● *Concerning gifts of cash, quoted shares or other securities there is normally no valuation problem. However, regarding substantial gifts of other items like land, businesses, antiques, shares in unquoted companies or paintings you would be well advised to obtain professional advice before you make the gift, from an estate agent, surveyor, valuer or accountant. In this way you can form an idea of your likely IHT liability. This will be payable if the gift is not a PET. In the case of a PET, IHT is only payable if you die within seven years, but you may well require a valuation to take out life assurance to cover the potential IHT liability. Also, professional valuers will be able to assist you, your lawyers and accountants in negotiating with the Capital Taxes Office an agreed value on which IHT is paid. In the case of PETs, should you die within seven years it will be helpful to have valuations made at the time of the gifts since IHT is payable on that basis. Remember that the Revenue will bring in their own valuation experts and so you will need valuation expertise on your side to negotiate as low a value as possible.*

7.20 Inheritance tax on death
(ITA S4)

IHT on your death is charged as if immediately before your death you made a chargeable transfer equal to the *net value* of your estate, subject to certain adjustments and exemptions (7.16) if appropriate. The same applied for CTT on deaths before 18 March 1986.

The *net value* of your estate is determined by making certain deductions (7.21.1) from the *gross value* of all the property passing on your death.

The general rule is that if you are domiciled (or deemed domiciled — 7.5) in the UK at the time of your death, all of your assets, wherever they may be situated, form part of the *gross value* of your estate (7.21).

If you are not domiciled in the UK at your death then the tax is only chargeable on those assets which are situated in the UK (7.26)

CTT payable was calculated from the special rate scale which applied at death (7.8) taking account of cumulative lifetime gifts after 26 March 1974 (and within ten years of death) to ascertain the starting level on the scale.

If any chargeable transfers had been made within three years before death, then additional CTT was payable to bring the charge up to what it would have been on death. The property transferred was aggregated with the estate at death, CTT calculated and any tax already paid on those transfers deducted (7.8.1). This rule still applies to chargeable transfers made before 18 March 1986 where death is after that time.

For deaths after 17 March 1986, the IHT rules apply and the tax is calculated from the single scale taking account of your cumulative lifetime gifts within *seven* years of death. These gifts include PETs (7.3) on which no tax was previously paid. As previously explained, death may lead not only to tax on the estate but also on lifetime gifts. Tax is first calculated on the PETs within seven years of death, taken in succession. Each PET must be cumulated with chargeable transfers made in the previous seven years, including earlier PETs within seven years of death. Finally IHT on the estate left at death is calculated.

As mentioned previously (7.4), if death occurs within three years of a post-17 March 1986 chargeable transfer (which is not a PET) the IHT is increased to the full rates at the time of death. Thus additional IHT will, in general, be payable compared with the half-rates already paid. However, if death is between three and seven years from such a transfer, tapering relief will apply which could involve extra tax if death is in year four. (This is less likely now, as a result of the IHT rate drop to 40%.)

7.20.1 Wills
(See also Chapter 10)

- *You should think carefully about the preparation of your will and, of course, obtain legal advice. Substantial IHT savings can result from a well drawn will. For example, you should ensure that both your wife and yourself by your separate wills leave at least £128,000 to other people so that you each get the benefit of the £128,000 nil rate band. (This presupposes that the free band has not been exhausted by lifetime gifts and also that you each have adequate funds for your old age. You must consider not only lifetime transfers which have borne tax, but also PETs within the last seven years. As each of these becomes more than seven years old, the IHT on your death changes. In substantial cases, you may even wish to change your will — perhaps leaving more to your children or grandchildren).*

- *Avoid leaving too much directly to your children if they are already wealthy; it is more beneficial for tax planning purposes to leave money in trust for your grandchildren. Such will trusts, might be discretionary, but more usefully of the accumulation and maintenance variety (8.2).*

- *If you wish to ensure that your widow has sufficient funds to live on, and at the same time utilise your nil rate band of £128,000, you should consider creating a trust by your will. This could give the trustees discretionary powers to advance funds to your widow if she needs them. Unless your estate is large, the amount comprised in the trust should be no more than your nil rate band which should ensure that there is no IHT in the trust unless its funds appreciate (8.3.4).*

7.21   Gross value of estate
(ITA S5)

This includes all your property situated anywhere in the world, such as land, shares, the goodwill of a business, debts owing to you, etc. Certain other amounts must also be included in your gross estate, even though they do not belong to you or only arise after your death, such as the proceeds of a life policy held by you on your own life, or any death benefit under a pension scheme which is payable to your estate (rather than under the more usual discretionary disposal clause contained in most pension schemes).

Also to be included in your gross estate are various interests in trusts (8.1). In these cases the trustees may pay the tax appropriate to the trusts but the rate is calculated by reference to the value of the estate including the trust interests. A further important category to be included is gifts with reservation made after 17 March 1986 (7.22).

7.21.1   Deductions from gross estate

The more common deductions which are made from the gross value of your estate in order to arrive at its *net value* are as follows:

(1)   Excluded property (7.17) and certain exempt transfers (7.16).
(2)   Funeral expenses.
(3)   Debts owing by you at the date of death which are payable in the UK. For IHT purposes, there are important limitations (7.21.2).

(4) Debts due to persons outside the UK (normally only deductible from the value of assets situated outside this country).

(5) Whilst legal and other professional fees owing at the death may be deducted as debts, no deduction is given for probate and executors' expenses.

(6) Liabilities for income tax and CGT up to the time of death, whether or not assessments were made before that time. (No deduction can be made for IHT or CTT payable on your death, nor tax liabilities regarding income and capital gains arising for periods subsequent to your death).

7.21.2 Debts — Special IHT rules
(FA 1986 S103)

In calculating the net value of your estate immediately before your death (7.21.1) certain debts may be disallowed in whole or part, if you had made connected gifts to the creditors. This may also apply if the liability had not been incurred for full consideration for your benefit. The rules cover post-17 March 1986 debts.

These rules prevent any IHT advantage being obtained, for example, where you give property worth £40,000 to your son and borrow this amount back. The £40,000 debt will not be deductible from your estate, when you die. However, if he lends you £50,000, only £10,000 would be so deductible.

7.21.3 Example: Calculation of IHT payable on death

Mr A (see Examples 7.17.2 and 1.17.3) made no further lifetime gifts and died on 31 January 1991 leaving a net estate of £300,000. Of this he left £100,000 to his wife and £50,000 to charity. IHT on the death will be paid as follows:

	£	£	
Net estate		300,000	
Less:			
Bequest to wife	100,000		
Charitable bequests	50,000		
	———	150,000	
Chargeable to IHT		150,000	
Cumulative transfers (net of exemptions)			
to date of death (7.17.3)	30.6.84	10,000	
	10.11.86	124,000	£134,000

The nil rate band of £128,000 is fully used by gifts within seven years of death. Thus the entire estate passing at death which is chargeable to IHT bears tax at 40%, ie IHT payable is £150,000 at 40% = £60,000

Notes:
(1)   The bequests to the wife and to charity are exempt.
(2)   The IHT on the PET of £124,000 is first calculated—amounting to £2,400 (7.17.3). The IHT on the estate at death is then found, cumulating with chargeable transfers (including the PET) in the seven previous years.

7.22   Gifts with reservation
(FA 1986 S102 & Sch 20)

If you make a gift after 17 March 1986 but reserve some benefit, this will normally result in the property remaining yours for IHT purposes on your death. (This could also apply if you later enjoy the benefit of the gifted property or if the donee does not take possession of it.) However, if you subsequently release the reservation, you will be treated as making a PET (7.3) at that time. Thus IHT could be due if you die within seven years.

A particular example is where you gift a house other than to your spouse but remain living there. The rule does not apply if your benefit is minimal (eg you do not live in the house but only pay occasional visits). If you give full value for any benefit (eg pay a full rent for the house), the rule is also set aside. There is a further exception where the reservation represents reasonable provision by a relative for the care and maintenance of an elderly or infirm donor whose circumstances have changed since he made the gift.

The rules do not normally catch regular premium insurance policies made before 18 March 1986 and not altered since then (14.4.12). Also outside the rules are certain exempt transfers including small gifts, inter-spouse gifts and marriage gifts (7.15), and gifts for charity, national purposes, public benefit, employee trusts and political parties (7.16)

• *Considerable care should be taken not to be caught by the provisions regarding gifts with reservation. The position of the matrimonial home has been considered earlier (7.14.3). Problems may also be encountered with investments, family companies, and some life assurance arrangements (14.4.12). Also, a settlor who is a beneficiary of a discretionary settlement would be vulnerable.*

7.23 Land sold within three years of death
(ITA Ss190-198)

If land or buildings are sold within three years of a death for less than probate value, the person paying the IHT (or, previously, CTT) can claim that the sale proceeds are substituted, and the tax adjusted. There are a number of conditions including the requirement that the shortfall is at least the lower of £1,000 and 5% of the probate value of the land. Relief is extended beyond the three years regarding a compulsory purchase notified before the end of the three years.

- *Only rarely should this rule be allowed to persuade the executors to sell land which otherwise would have been kept. Possible circumstances might be where an unfairly high probate value was fixed, or the market drastically falls but funds are needed. However, if a sale is intended and the price is below probate value then you should ensure that contracts are exchanged within the three year period.*

7.24 Quoted securities passing on death
(ITA Ss178-189)

Where quoted shares or securities or holdings in authorised unit trusts are realised within one year of death, the persons liable to pay IHT can claim that the total of the sale prices should be substituted for the original probate values of the investments. (Note that the executors are normally liable to pay the IHT and so, if they do pay it, they must sell the shares for the relief to be due.) Where, however, the proceeds are re-invested by those persons in quoted shares or unit trusts after the death and within two months after the last sale, the above relief may be reduced or lost.

- *This rule should be borne in mind by the executors in dealing with the quoted securities during the administration period (11.11.1). If the stock market is falling and seems likely to do so for some months, then the executors (in consultation with their stockbrokers) could do well to sell within 12 months of the death. They could then distribute cash to beneficiaries under the will who could reinvest in shares if they wished, without disturbing the IHT relief.*

7.25   Deeds of family arrangement
(ITA S17)

Neither IHT (nor CGT) is charged on certain variations in the destination of property passing on death. Nor is it charged on the disclaimer of title to property passing on death. The variation or disclaimer must be within two years of the death. An election to the Revenue is required within six months of the variation or disclaimer (5.3.6, 10.24). Note that the variation normally has no effect for income tax purposes.

This exemption operates similarly, but without time limit, where a surviving spouse's life interest under an intestacy is redeemed. It also applies if an interest in settled property is disclaimed unless there is some consideration in money or money's worth.

- *Deeds of family arrangement are a valuable IHT planning tool. Transfers free of the tax can be effected in this way so that, for example, if you are one of the legatees, you might arrange for money to go direct to your children (this could result in your bearing income tax on the income if the children are minors). If all the estate has gone to the widow under the will then up to £128,000 of this could be diverted to other members of the family without any IHT arising.*

In large estates, deeds of family arrangement could include substantial amounts for charities. This would normally substantially reduce the IHT liability at a relatively modest cost to the beneficiaries.

7.26   Overseas property

If you are neither domiciled nor deemed domiciled in the UK (7.5) it is important to ascertain the situation of your particular property for tax purposes. This is because you will normally only pay IHT on your assets situated here. It is also important with reference to double taxation relief (7.28). The situation of property for IHT purposes is generally deemed to be as follows:

(1)   Cash — its physical location.
(2)   Bank accounts — the location of the bank or branch (see also below).
(3)   Registered securities — the location of the share register.
(4)   Bearer securities — the location of the title documents.
(5)   Land and buildings — their actual location.
(6)   Business assets — the place where the business is conducted.
(7)   Debts — the residence of the debtor.

7.27 Foreign currency bank accounts
(FA 1982 S96)

Regarding deaths after 8 March 1982 foreign currency accounts with
UK banks are exempted from IHT (or CTT) if the deceased is not UK
domiciled (or deemed domiciled). This also applies if the deceased
had an interest in possession (8.1) in a settlement with such an
account, unless the settlor was UK domiciled when he made the
settlement or the trustees were so domiciled.

- *Should you now be, or later become, neither domiciled nor deemed
domiciled in the UK, you will be able to minimise your liability to IHT
by careful planning. This need not only consist of taking cash and other
assets abroad. If you have land and buildings here, which you wish to
keep, you could form an overseas company to acquire the property.
Your company and all its assets will be regarded as property outside the
UK and thus outside the IHT net, to the extent that you own the shares.*

  *An overseas-based holding company could also be used for holding UK
quoted securities and other assets but the effect of other taxes should
always be carefully investigated.*

- *You may be neither domiciled nor deemed domiciled in the UK but
know that this status will soon change. Before you become UK
domiciled, consider gifting assets situated overseas (see above) which
you will be able to do free of IHT in this country. Also consider settling
overseas assets. This could provide continuing IHT savings. Highly
specialised advice from a solicitor and/or accountant should be taken,
beforehand, since there are both capital and income tax pitfalls.*

7.28 Double taxation relief
(ITA Ss158–159)

Various other countries also operate systems of IHT or CTT. The
government of the UK is empowered to enter into agreements with
them for the avoidance of the double payment of such tax both here
and in the other country.

Concerning IHT and CTT payable on death, relief is continued for
estate duty payable on the same property in other countries if there
was a 'double estate duty' agreement with the countries in question
as at 12 March 1975. The following countries have agreements with
the UK covering estate duty and/or CTT or IHT.

France	Pakistan
India	South Africa
Ireland	Sweden
Italy	Switzerland
Netherlands	United States of America

Unilateral double taxation relief is available for overseas tax paid on death or a lifetime transfer. The tax must be of a similar nature to IHT or CTT and if the property is situated in the overseas country, a credit is given against the UK tax of the amount of the overseas tax. If the property is either situated *both* in the UK and the overseas country, or in *neither* of those places, the credit against the UK tax is $C \times A/(A+B)$. A is the amount of IHT or CTT, B is the overseas tax and C is the smaller of A and B.

7.29   Relief for business property
(ITA Ss103–114, FA 1986 Ss105–106 & Sch 19 & FA 1987 S58 & Sch 8)

A reduction is allowed in the values for IHT (and CTT) purposes of 'relevant business property'. This applies both during life and on death.

'Relevant business property' includes a business or part of a business; shares owned by the controller of a company; unquoted minority shareholdings; and land, buildings, plant and machinery used in your partnership or a company which you control. Control of a company for these purposes includes shareholdings which are 'related property' (7.19) in relation to your own shares.

In general, investment company and land or share-dealing company shareholdings do not qualify for the relief. However, UK stockjobbing qualifies for relief, as does 'market making' from October 1986. You must normally own the business property, or business property which has directly replaced it for at least two years prior to the transfer or else it is not 'relevant business property' and so no relief is due.

Relief is available at the following rates:
(1)   The whole or part of a business — 50%.
(2)   Qualifying company shares to be valued on a control basis — 50%.
(3)   Property transferred by you which is used in a trade by a

company controlled by you or partnership in which you are a partner — 30%.

(4) Shares in an unquoted trading company to be valued on a minority basis — 30% (20% prior to 15 March 1983). After 16 March 1987, holdings over 25% attract 50% relief. Shares dealt in on the USM qualified for relief up to that date, but not subsequently.

Relief applies to certain business assets owned by trusts. After 9 March 1981, the 30% relief category is extended to cover the transfer by a beneficiary with an interest in possession of trust assets (land, buildings, plant or machinery) used in his business.

Business property relief is available against PETs which fall into charge following the donor's death within seven years. However, the relief is lost if the recipient disposes of the property before the donor's death (or his own). But relief is not lost if the gifted business property is disposed of, but replaced by other qualifying assets within one year. Also, the property must remain 'relevant business property' during that period. If these conditions are satisfied for only part of the property, the relief is proportionately reduced. These rules also apply to other lifetime transfers within seven years of death.

Where part of an estate is left to the surviving spouse and thus attracts no tax, and part to others, the allocation of business property relief and relief for agricultural property (7.30) has been unclear. However, from 18 March 1986 specific gifts of such property must be reduced by the relief. Otherwise, the relief is spread proportionately over the estate.

7.29.1 Protecting family companies

- *The 'related property' valuation rules (7.19) may make it potentially costly for you to transfer valuable holdings in your family company to your children, etc. This is because IHT would be payable if you died within seven years of making such PETs and the valuations could be on a controlling basis (7.19). The charge on the shares on your death is far more certain, however, and so you should plan to transfer shares to your children before they become too valuable, and your spouse should do the same. The best time would be on the formation of a new company or early in its development.*

- *Watch out for CGT complications – for example higher valuations resulting from several transfers to connected persons (2.9). However, gifts elections will be effective to 'hold over' the gain (4.6) and should be considered carefully as a means of deferring CGT.*

● *Business property relief is very beneficial if you wish to pass part of your business or shares in your family company to your children. This is effective immediately for 'non-PETs', such as transfers into discretionary and certain other trusts. The relief is also effective regarding PETs, subject to the rules; and on death.*

● *Watch carefully the point when your holding in your unquoted family company drops to 25% (taking your wife's shares into account). The relief rate will go down from 50% to 30% regarding your next transfer of the shares. Therefore try to make the transfer which takes you below 25% a large one, since it attracts 50% relief. (Similar considerations apply regarding controlling holdings in quoted companies.)*

● *If you are planning a new business venture, then do not put it into your main family company. Form a new company whose shares are owned by your children (or others whom you wish to succeed to your business). The new company should be allowed to handle as much business as possible and you may even let your old company run down. In this way the next generation of your family eventually will be left controlling the major company.*

● *In the case of a partnership, the interest of each partner is valued on the appropriate share of the underlying assets. If, however, the partnership is incorporated into a company, the value of each partner's interest is normally reduced appreciably, if it is a minority holding.*

7.30   Relief for agricultural property
(ITA Ss115–124 & FA 1986 S105 & Sch 19)

The system of agricultural relief was changed as from 10 March 1981. Before that date the relief applied to transfers on death and lifetime transfers by 'working farmers'. To qualify you needed to have been mainly or wholly engaged in agriculture as a farmer, farm worker or student in five of the seven preceding years. The relief applied to land including farmhouses and buildings occupied for farming by you for at least two years before the transfer.

Under the new scheme you must have either occupied the property for the purposes of agriculture for at least two years before transferring it, or owned it for seven years up to that time, with others farming. The rules are relaxed where you inherit the property or where you have replaced one agricultural property by another. Both the present and previous systems extend relief to controlling shareholders in farming companies. For the purposes of the relief, 'agriculture' includes stud farming (FA 1984 S107). The grant of a tenancy of agricultural property is not treated as a transfer of value if it is made for full consideration. The relief only applies to agricultural property in the UK, the Channel Islands or the Isle of Man. Effectively the value of the agricultural property is reduced by 50% or 30%.

Relief of 50% is obtained if you enjoy the right to vacant possession or can obtain this within the next 12 months. Otherwise, the relief is normally 30% (20% before 15 March 1983), which applies to tenanted situations, etc. After 9 March 1981, the grant of a tenancy of agricultural property is not to be treated as a transfer of value if it is made for full consideration (FA 1981 S97). If you would have qualified for 50% relief under the old but not the new rules, you still obtain 50% relief regarding property held at 9 March 1981 and transferred after that date, up to the old limit of 250,000 or 1,000 acres if more valuable. The excess is then relieved at 30% only.

From 18 March 1986, similar rules to those for business property relief apply regarding lifetime gifts within seven years of death and the allocation of relief to partially exempt estates (7.29). Thus relief can be lost if the recipient disposes of the property before the death of the donor or himself.

- *Agricultural property relief is generally as beneficial as business property relief and takes priority. Regarding deducting the annual and small gifts exemptions, the same order is followed as for business property relief so that the exemptions are applied afterwards. In this way, the agricultural relief is maximised.*

Although you only obtain 30% relief if your farmland is tenanted instead of 50%, its value is normally accepted to be much less – possibly less than 50% of its unencumbered worth. Hence the established practice of granting a tenancy to members of your family is still worth considering as a means of saving IHT. However, you should take careful advice since the authorities might argue that a tenancy to people connected with you should be disregarded for valuation purposes.

7.31   Woodlands

(ITA Ss125-30)

The old estate duty relief for growing timber applied in general before 13 March 1975. After that a corresponding but more restricted relief applied to the CTT charge on your death provided you either owned the woodlands for at least five years, or acquired them by gift or inheritance.

Under the current system, provided that within two years of your death the inheritor elects, IHT is not charged in respect of the timber on your death. If, however, before the recipient dies, the timber is sold or given away, tax is charged on the proceeds or value of the gift. The tax rate is found by adding such proceeds to the estate at your death. Remember that the relief applies only to the timber and not the land on which it grows.

Where timber is disposed of after 26 October 1977, the rates prevailing at the date of disposal are applied, even if the death was before they take effect. Furthermore, the disposal value is halved in charging the tax, if the death was after 12 March 1975 and the new business property relief would have been obtained, except that the death was too early.

7.32   Administration and collection

(ITA Ss215-261, etc & FA 1986 Sch 19.)

IHT (and CTT) are under the care and management of the Board of the Inland Revenue. Generally speaking, the rules for administration, appeals and penalties resemble those for income tax.

Chargeable transfers must be reported to the Inland Revenue within 12 months from the end of the month of transfer or death.

As for estate duty, tax chargeable on death must be paid on at least an estimated figure before probate is granted. IHT (and CTT) on death are now payable out of the residuary estate unless there is a contrary direction in the will. However, property situated outside the UK continues to bear its own tax. Recipients of PETs are primarily responsible for the relevant tax.

Returns of lifetime gifts were not required for CTT purposes if these were covered by your exemptions (£3,000 etc). Also, no account needed to be submitted if the amount of your gift and any other chargeable transfers in the same year to 5 April did not exceed £10,000 and your cumulative total (including the latest gift) was no more than £40,000. Returns are not normally required of PETs unless the donor dies within seven years.

Interest on unpaid tax runs from when the tax is due. The due date is six months after the end of the month in which death occurs. For lifetime transfers it is six months after the end of the month in which the transfer is made. In the case of lifetime transfers between 5 April and 1 October, the due date is 30 April in the following year. From 16 December 1986 there was a single rate of interest on overdue IHT of 8%, reducing to 6% from 6 June 1987 and then increasing to 8% from 6 August 1988. From 6 October 1988, the rate is 9% and from 6 July 1989, it is 11%.

From 1 May 1985 until 16 December 1986, interest ran on overdue CTT and IHT at 9% on death and 11% on other transfers. For IHT purposes, the 9% rate applied to PETs. Between 30 November 1982 and 1 May 1985 the rate of interest was 6% for transfers on death and 8% otherwise. Prior to 1 December 1982 the respective interest rates were 9% and 12%. This interest is not deductible for income tax purposes. If you overpay CTT or IHT you will get non-taxable interest at the same rates, up to the date on which the repayment of the excess tax is made.

7.32.1 Payment of tax by instalments
(ITA Ss227–229 & FA 1986 Sch 19)

CTT or IHT on death on certain assets may be paid by annual instalments over ten years. (For deaths before 15 March 1983, instalments were yearly or half-yearly but limited to an eight-year period.) This applies to land and buildings, controlling holdings of shares in companies and certain other unquoted shares, as well as business assets. (PETs which become chargeable only qualify for the instalments basis if the recipient had kept the property until the death of the donor.)

Instalments paid on time concerning the shares and business assets mentioned above are free of interest. Land and buildings qualify for this relief only if they are held as business assets, otherwise interest is payable, currently at 11% (from 6 July 1989). A limit of £250,000 on assets qualifying for this relief existing before 10 March 1981 but was removed completely. After 9 March 1981, tax in respect of property qualifying for the new agricultural relief may be paid in interest free instalments as above.

The above provisions apply to lifetime transfers if the donee bears the tax and for settled property which is retained in a settlement. If interest is payable it is currently at 11%. The interest free category is extended to include lifetime disposals of timber. In the case of minority holdings of unquoted shares, these must be worth at least £20,000 (£5,000 before 15 March 1983), in order to qualify for the instalments option. Also, they must be at least 10% holdings. Where paying the tax in one sum would cause undue hardship and the recipient keeps the shares, the instalments basis of payment may also be allowed.

- *The interest rates are moderate by current standards and so it is worthwhile considering opting for the instalments basis. When realty comprised in the estate of a deceased person is sold, however, the balance of IHT (or CTT) on that property will become payable.*

7.32.2   Quick succession relief
(ITA S141)

Quick succession relief reduces the tax payable on death where the deceased himself received chargeable transfers within five years of his death on which IHT or CTT was paid. The deduction is, broadly, a proportion of the original tax, being 100%, 80%, 60%, 40% or 20%, depending on whether the period between the transfer and the death is one, two, three, four or five years or less in each case. Similar relief was given where the previous transfer was a death on which estate duty was payable. Where there are two or more transfers of the same property within five years of each other, special rules apply.

7.32.3   Mutual and voidable transfers
(ITA Ss148–150 & FA 1986 Sch 19)

Complicated rules were introduced which refer back to periods before the 1976 Finance Act was passed, as well as after. Broadly, both the giver and receiver were relieved from CTT, where the receiver later returned the property, etc, concerned to the original giver. (A similar rule is found in ITA S150 concerning voidable transfers.)

From 27 March 1980, anti-avoidance rules operate to prevent CTT being saved by *gifts-back,* where the original gift had obtained business property (7.29) or agricultural property relief (7.30). Those reliefs were ignored in the calculations. Also savings from exploiting the rules for valuing life assurance policies in conjunction with gifts-back were blocked.

The above rules concerning exemptions for mutual transfers have been abolished where the donee's transfer (the gift back) is after 17 March 1986.

7.32.4 Avoiding double charges
(FA 1986 S104)

Rules were introduced to prevent double charges to IHT on transfers of value and other events occurring after 17 March 1986. The rules in part take the place of the previous rules (7.32.3) regarding mutual transfers. The situations covered include where a PET (7.3) becomes chargeable and immediately before the death the estate includes property acquired from the person who received the PET for less than full price.

7.32.5 Waivers of dividends and remuneration
(ITA Ss14 & 15)

In relation to dividends and remuneration there are rules which apply from the inception of CTT. No IHT (or previously CTT) accrues on the waiver of any dividend to which you have a right, provided you waive the dividend by deed within the 12 months before it is due.

If you waive any remuneration to which you are entitled, this normally does not produce any IHT (or CTT) liability, provided the amount waived would otherwise have been assessable to income tax under Schedule E and your employer obtains no income tax or corporation tax relief for the waived remuneration.

7.32.6 Conditional exemption for certain objects and buildings, etc
(ITA Ss27, 30–35,78–79, Schs 4 & 5, FA 1985 Ss94–95 & Sch 26 & FA 1987 Sch 9)

Property similar to that mentioned in (2) and (3) in the exempt transfers list (7.16) is exempt from IHT (and CTT) on death provided the recipient undertakes to keep it in the country, preserve it and allow reasonable access to the public. If it is later sold the tax is payable unless the sale is to an institution such as the British Museum, National Gallery or National Trust.

A similar relief applies to lifetime transfers subject to various conditions. The recipient must give the required undertaking. The relief extends to historical and artistic buildings and objects comprised in settlements. It also applies to settlements set up to maintain historic buildings and objects historically associated with them, together with land of outstanding interest. Such settlements must tie up the capital for at least six years for maintenance purposes only, but after that funds may be withdrawn subject to IHT in certain circumstances.

With effect from 9 March 1982 special rules apply regarding maintenance settlements for approved objects and buildings, etc. Provided the Board of the Inland Revenue (previously the Treasury) are satisfied that the trusts and trustees comply with certain requirements, transfers to such a settlement are exempt (7.15) for IHT purposes. In general, the trust funds must be used for the maintenance of approved assets for at least six years; also, certain reasonable improvements. The trustees must be resident in the UK and at least one must be a solicitor, accountant or trust corporation.

From 17 March 1987, the exemption applies where someone with a life interest in a trust dies and within two years the property goes into a heritage maintenance fund. Heritage property can be offered in lieu of IHT and, from that date, there is the option of calculating the value of the property at the date of the offer instead of acceptance.

Land is exempted which is essential to a building of historic or architectural interest. Furthermore, it is no longer necessary for the land to touch the building.

7.32.7   Close companies
(ITA Ss94–102 & FA 1986 Sch 19)

Close companies making transfers of value are brought within the IHT and CTT net. (This even includes deemed transfers resulting from certain capital alterations.) Broadly, tax is charged on the company as if each of the participators had made a proportionate transfer according to his or her interest in the company. The rules are extended to cover close companies being owned by trusts or being their beneficiaries. Following the introduction of changed provisions regarding discretionary trusts (8.3.3), the close company rules were correspondingly modified as from 9 March 1982.

Transfers of value arising from alterations in the capital and associated rights in a close company are not PETs (7.3). Thus, such transactions may give rise to the immediate payment of IHT.

7.32.8 Free loans
(ITA S29)

From 6 April 1976 to 5 April 1981, subject to certain exemptions, if you allowed someone else the use of money or property at no interest or less than the market rate, you were treated as making a chargeable transfer for each year to 5 April that the arrangement continued. The amount of the chargeable transfer was the shortfall of the interest (less tax), or other benefit which you got, compared with the market rate. These taxing provisions ceased to have effect after 5 April 1981 although interest-free loans for a fixed stated period can still be treated as a chargeable transfer under general principles.

● *Free loans now constitute a valuable part of IHT planning. However, care must now be taken that certain anti-avoidance provisions do not apply. These include the special rules for debts (7.21.2) gifts with reservations (7.22) and associated operations (7.7).*

7.33 IHT and life assurance
(See also Chapter 14)

If you effect a policy on your life for your own benefit, the proceeds payable on your death will be taxable as part of your net estate.

● *You may however, effect a policy in trust for some other person or persons absolutely, such as for example your wife and children. In this case the policy proceeds will not be paid into your own estate but will be paid to the trustees for the beneficiaries. Each premium payment, however, will constitute a separate potentially exempt transfer (7.3) by you. Thus they could be taxable if you die within seven years, unless an exemption applies such as the £3,000 or £250 reliefs (7.15), or the normal expenditure rule (7.15), or the policy is for your wife. If premiums are paid to a non-absolute trust and no exemption applies, each premium will be chargeable at the time and may give rise to recalculation of tax if death occurs within seven years.*

Furthermore, for policies effected after 17 March 1986, the gifts with reservation rules (7.22) may apply. Broadly if you have a retained benefit in the policy the proceeds will form part of your estate at death.

● *If someone else effects a policy on your life and pays the premiums, then the proceeds are not taxable on your death. This is known as a 'life of another' policy. If the person who effects the policy predeceases you, however, then the surrender value of the policy at the date of death of that person is normally included in his taxable estate. Please refer to Chapter 14 for further details concerning this subject.*

7.33.1   Providing the funds to pay IHT on death

- *You may not be able, or indeed wish, to avoid leaving a large estate when you die. In this case you should ensure that sufficient funds are available for paying the IHT. This avoids forced realisations of assets and, for example, the sale of shares in a family company which it might be desirable to keep.*

- *Life assurance provides one of the best means of providing money to pay IHT arising on your death, as well as being a very suitable vehicle for exempt gifts. Ensure, however, that the policy proceeds themselves are not subject to the tax, which could happen if the policy were taken out (with no trust provisions) by you on your own life. Consider taking out policies in trust for your children where you leave assets to them; this will put cash into their hands to pay the tax. This should be a 'whole of life' policy, under which a capital sum, with or without profits or one that is unit-linked to combat inflation, is payable when you die.*

- *If both you and your spouse have large estates then you should each insure your respective lives in trust for your children, assuming that you each leave your estates to them. If, however, you each leave assets to the other by your will, then a joint life last survivor policy could be useful, under which a payment is made only on the second death. If the policy is correctly drawn (in trust for the eventual heirs on the second death) and the premiums are within the annual exemptions (7.15), it will not attract IHT. Further, the premium rate for such a policy is usually substantially lower than for two individual policies.*

- *The policy can be written under a suitable trust for your heirs. Take care that there is at least one trustee other than you so that the proceeds may be claimed without delay on your death.*

- *Temporary life assurance may be used to cover the five-year period following a gift or settlement on which you have paid IHT at the lifetime rate. The amount covered should be the additional tax payable on that transfer should you die within five years (7.4). Normally extra IHT would be payable in such circumstances.*

- *Temporary life assurance written in trust is also most useful for covering any inheritance tax payable on a gift (PET) if you die within seven years. The amount to be covered is the full tax for three years and*

*then 80%, 60%, 40%, and 20% of the tax for the remaining years
respectively. The recipient of the gift will be liable for the tax and so
should receive the policy proceeds. Additional life cover is worth
considering in such circumstances. A PET will still require to be
cumulated with the rest of the estate for the full seven years. Thus the
extra IHT due on death within seven years could well be covered by
temporary life assurance for a seven year term.*

7.33.2 Annuities

• *If you need to increase your income, annuities provide a means of doing
this which at the same time immediately reduces the value of your
estate. For example, if you buy an annuity for £10,000 which produces,
say, £1,400 yearly until your death, no part of your original capital
outlay is charged to IHT on your death. You have thus saved potential
tax on your death at your top rate band. Do not overlook the effects of
inflation, however; an annuity which is sufficient for your present needs
soon may be worth too little to maintain you.*

• *If you do not need the income, you may use the annuity to make gifts to
your beneficiaries. For the purposes of the normal expenditure gifts
exemption, however, it is only the income element and not the capital
portion which is taken into account (7.15).*

7.34   Appendix — capital transfer tax rates

Before 27 October 1977

Slice of cumulative chargeable transfers	Total	CTT Payable			
		Lifetime scale		On death	
		% on slice	Cumulative total tax	% on slice	Cumulative total tax
The first £15,000	£15,000	Nil	£Nil	Nil	£Nil
The next 5,000	20,000	5	250	10	500
5,000	25,000	7.5	625	15	1,250
5,000	30,000	10	1,125	20	2,250
10,000	40,000	12.5	2,375	25	4,750
10,000	50,000	15	3,875	30	7,750
10,000	60,000	17.5	5,625	35	11,250
20,000	80,000	20	9,625	40	19,250
20,000	100,000	22.5	14,125	45	28,250
20,000	120,000	27.5	19,625	50	38,250

30,000	150,000	35	30,125	55	54,750
50,000	200,000	42.5	51,375	60	84,750
50,000	250,000	50	76,375	60	114,750
50,000	300,000	55	103,875	60	144,750
200,000	500,000	60	223,875	60	264,750
500,000	1,000,000	65	548,875	65	589,750
1,000,000	2,000,000	70	1,248,875	70	1,289,750
The remainder		75		75	

from 28 October 1977 to 25 March 1980

The first					
£25,000	£25,000	Nil	£Nil	Nil	£Nil
The next					
5,000	30,000	5	250	10	500
5,000	35,000	7.5	625	15	1,250
5,000	40,000	10	1,125	20	2,250
10,000	50,000	12.5	2,375	25	4,750
10,000	60,000	15	3,875	30	7,750
10,000	70,000	17.5	5,625	35	11,250
20,000	90,000	20	9,625	40	19,250
20,000	110,000	22.5	14,125	45	28,250
20,000	130,000	27.5	19,625	50	38,250
30,000	160,000	35	30,125	55	54,750
50,000	210,000	42.5	51,375	60	84,750
50,000	260,000	50	76,375	60	114,750
50,000	310,000	55	103,875	60	144,750
200,000	510,000	60	223,875	60	264,750
500,000	1,010,000	65	548,875	65	589,750
1,000,000	2,010,000	70	1,248,875	70	1,289,750
The remainder		75		75	

from 26 March 1980 to 9 March 1981

The first					
£50,000	£50,000	Nil	£Nil	Nil	£Nil
The next					
10,000	60,000	15	1,500	30	3,000
10,000	70,000	17.5	3,250	35	6,500
20,000	90,000	20	7,250	40	14,500
20,000	110,000	22.5	11,750	45	23,500
20,000	130,000	27.5	17,250	50	33,500
30,000	160,000	35	27,750	55	50,000
50,000	210,000	42.5	49,000	60	80,000
50,000	260,000	50	74,000	60	110,000
50,000	310,000	55	101,500	60	140,000

200,000	510,000	60	221,500	60	260,000
500,000	1,010,000	65	546,500	65	585,000
1,000,000	2,010,000	70	1,246,500	70	1,285,000
The remainder		75		75	

from 10 March 1981 to 8 March 1982

The first					
£50,000	£50,000	Nil	£Nil	Nil	£Nil
The next					
10,000	60,000	15	1,500	30	3,000
10,000	70,000	17.5	3,250	35	6,500
20,000	90,000	20	7,250	40	14,500
20,000	110,000	22.5	11,750	45	23,500
20,000	130,000	25	16,750	50	33,500
30,000	160,000	30	25,750	55	50,000
350,000	510,000	35	148,250	60	260,000
500,000	1,010,000	40	348,250	65	585,000
1,000,000	2,010,000	45	798,250	70	1,285,000
The remainder		50		75	

from 9 March 1982 to 14 March 1983

The first					
£55,000	£55,000	Nil	£Nil	Nil	£Nil
The next					
20,000	75,000	15	3,000	30	6,000
25,000	100,000	17.5	7,375	35	14,750
30,000	130,000	20	13,375	40	26,750
35,000	165,000	22.5	21,250	45	42,500
35,000	200,000	25	30,000	50	60,000
50,000	250,000	30	45,000	55	87,500
400,000	650,000	35	185,000	60	327,500
600,000	1,250,000	40	425,000	65	717,500
1,250,000	2,500,000	45	987,500	70	1,592,500
The remainder		50		75	

from 15 March 1983 to 12 March 1984

The first					
£60,000	£60,000	Nil	£Nil	Nil	£Nil
The next					
20,000	80,000	15	3,000	30	6,000
30,000	110,000	17.5	8,250	35	16,500
30,000	140,000	20	14,250	40	28,500
35,000	175,000	22.5	22,125	45	44,250

45,000	220,000	25	33,375	50	66,750
50,000	270,000	30	48,375	55	94,250
430,000	700,000	35	198,875	60	352,250
625,000	1,325,000	40	448,875	65	758,500
1,325,000	2,650,000	45	1,045,125	70	1,686,000
The remainder		50		75	

from 13 March 1984 to 5 April 1985

The first					
£64,000	£64,000	Nil	£Nil	Nil	£Nil
The next					
21,000	85,000	15	3,150	30	6,300
31,000	116,000	17.5	8,575	35	17,150
32,000	148,000	20	14,975	40	29,950
37,000	185,000	22.5	23,300	45	46,600
47,000	232,000	25	35,050	50	70,100
53,000	285,000	27.5	49,625	55	99,250
The remainder		30		60	

from 6 April 1985 to 17 March 1986

The first					
£67,000	£67,000	Nil	£Nil	Nil	£Nil
The next					
22,000	89,000	15	3,300	30	6,600
33,000	122,000	17.5	9,075	35	18,150
33,000	155,000	20	15,675	40	31,350
39,000	194,000	22.5	24,450	45	48,900
49,000	243,000	25	36,700	50	73,400
56,000	299,000	27.5	52,100	55	104,200
The remainder		30		60	

7.35   Appendix — inheritance tax rates from 18 March 1986

Slice of cumulative chargeable transfers	*Cumulative total*	*% on slice*	*Cumulative total tax*
The first £71,000	£71,000	Nil	£Nil

The next			
24,000	95,000	30	7,200
34,000	129,000	35	19,100
35,000	164,000	40	33,100
42,000	206,000	45	52,000
51,000	257,000	50	77,500
60,000	317,000	55	110,500
The remainder		60	

from 17 March 1987 to 14 March 1988

The first			
£90,000	£90,000	Nil	£Nil
The next			
50,000	140,000	30	15,000
80,000	220,000	40	47,000
110,000	330,000	50	102,000
The remainder		60	

from 15 March 1988 to 5 April 1989

The first			
£110,000	£110,000	Nil	£Nil
The remainder		40	

from 6 April 1989 to 5 April 1990

The first			
£118,000	£118,000	Nil	£Nil
The remainder		40	

from 6 April 1990

The first			
£128,000	£128,000	Nil	£Nil
The remainder		40	

8 Inheritance tax — trusts

8.1 Settled property
(ITA Pt III, FA 1984 Ss102–104, FA 1986 Sch 19 & F2A 1987 S96 & Sch 7)

For further details concerning trusts and settled property reference should be made to Chapter 5 (CGT), Chapter 9 (income tax) and Chapter 12 (legal aspects).

The rules concerning IHT (and previously CTT) in relation to settled property are most detailed and the following are just a few guidelines:

(1)   Broadly, those settlements which are liable to IHT are charged at half the full rates (7.8.1). (Before 18 March 1986, CTT applied at the lifetime scale.) IHT applies to a trust's world-wide assets, if at the time it was made the settlor was domiciled in the UK. Otherwise, only assets situated in this country (7.26) are caught.

(2)   The settlement of any property after 26 March 1974 is itself treated as a chargeable transfer by the settlor. However, after 17 March 1986, settlements on accumulation and maintenance trusts (8.2) or for the disabled are classed as PETs (7.3). Thus property which you settle in this way only attracts IHT if you die within seven years.

(3)   If you have an interest in possession in any settled property for the time being (eg, you are entitled to receive any income as of right), the property itself is treated as yours for IHT (and CTT) purposes. Thus if your interest ends, you will be treated as making a chargeable transfer of the value of the property concerned. The tax is calculated on the basis of your cumulative transfers to that time. Since 5 April 1981, you can deduct your £3,000 annual exemption (7.15) and also marriage gifts allowance if applicable (FA 1981 S94).

(4)   From 17 March 1987, lifetime transactions involving *interest in*

possession settlements are classed at PETs. This treatment comprises setting them up, as well as transfers out of such settlements and changes in the beneficial interests.

(5)   No IHT (or CTT) is payable if you obtain an absolute interest in property in which you previously had a life interest (or other interest in possession). Similarly, tax normally is not payable on the reversion to you in your lifetime (or your spouse during your life or within two years of your death) of property which you previously settled. Regarding discretionary trusts, however, this rule does not usually apply after 8 March 1982.

(6)   Special rules apply to trusts where there is no interest in possession — particularly discretionary trusts, etc (8.3) and accumulation and maintenance settlements (8.2).

(7)   Quick succession relief is given if an interest in possession comes to an end within five years of a previous chargeable transfer of the settled property. The relief is given against the CTT or IHT on the later transfer. It is calculated, broadly, as a percentage of the tax on the *first* transfer. The percentage is 100%, 80%, 60%, 40%, or 20% where the interval is not more than one, two, three, four, or five years respectively.

(8)   Superannuation and other pension schemes and charitable trusts are normally exempted from IHT, as are those for employees, newspapers, certain 'protective trusts' and trusts for the mentally disabled (treated as having a life interest in property settled for them after 9 March 1981). Where property is held temporarily on such trusts, some relief is now given; the charge to IHT is proportionately reduced on a time basis (FA 1984 S102).

● *Consider making larger gifts in the form of settlements. If these are discretionary, however, the ten year charge (8.3.3) would normally apply at some future time, as well as the tax which you pay when you make the settlement and further tax when benefits are paid to the beneficiaries (but the rates will not be great at current levels). Accumulation and maintenance trusts (8.2) are useful for the benefit of any children and grandchildren aged under 25 when you set up the settlement. If the beneficiaries obtain fixed interests (at least in the income) to which they become entitled when they are no more than 25 years old, then no IHT is payable, even if the payment of the ultimate capital is deferred to an older age.*

● *Fixed trusts are also of use if you wish your grown-up children to have income but no capital until a stipulated time. Thus, if you settle money on your 26-year-old son giving him an entitlement to the annual income until he is 35 and then the capital, you are immediately divested of the*

*capital. You are treated as making a PET when you settle the money.
Your son eventually gets the capital at age 35 without any IHT being
paid (unless you die within seven years of making the settlement). Your
son is fully taxed on the income, however, and if his other income
becomes high as he matures, his income tax burden could be heavy.*

8.2   Accumulation and maintenance settlements

Accumulation and maintenance settlements without any interests in
possession for one or more beneficiaries up to an age not exceeding
25 are most favourably treated for IHT purposes. Such settlements
are not subject to the periodic charge (see below); nor will IHT be
charged on the capital distributions to those beneficiaries. This relief
covers, for example, a settlement under which your son obtains an
interest in possession at the age of 25 and at 35 gets the capital, the
income being accumulated up to 25 apart from various payments for
his maintenance. No IHT (or CTT) is payable during the currency of
the trust, nor when your son becomes entitled to the income at 25 nor
the capital at 35.

Special rules apply to settlements made after 15 April 1976. Relief
broadly only applies if either not more than 25 years have passed
since the original settlement date (or when it first became
accumulating); or if all beneficiaries are grandchildren of a common
grandparent (or their widows, widowers, etc).

Accumulation and maintenance settlements have a new feature after
17 March 1986. Any gifts into them are now PETs (7.3). Thus no IHT
is payable regarding their creation unless the settlor dies within seven
years.

- *Accumulation and maintenance settlements provide a very tax-effective
  means of passing on capital to your children and grandchildren. If the
  beneficiaries are your children, however, be careful they do not receive
  any benefit until age 18 (unless married) or an income tax charge on you
  is likely to result (9.3). You might also include similar trusts in your
  will. (This is one way of using your nil rate band if most of your
  remaining estate is left to your husband or wife.)*

*When you settle any funds an IHT charge may result if you die within
seven years, but may well not bite in any event, because of your annual
exemption (£3,000) and nil rate band (£128,000). Remember that your*

spouse will also be able to settle funds in this way with similar exclusions.

8.3   Discretionary trusts, etc

The following rules apply where there is no interest in possession in *all* or *part* of the *property*. Note that prior to 9 March 1982, very different rules operated. Fuller details are given in earlier editions of this book.

8.3.1   Rules applying before 9 March 1982

CTT was charged on distributions of capital to beneficiaries. If the settlement was made before 27 March 1974 it was charged to tax on its distributions as if it were a separate individual but without certain exemptions (7.15) (unless there was an interest in possession — 8.1).

For a settlement made after 26 March 1974, distributions of capital up to the original amount settled were charged at a special rate. This was the rate which would have been paid by the settlor on a gift of the amount of the original settlement at the time that it was made (revised in line with the rate changes on and after 26 March 1980). Excess distributions over and above the original capital fell into higher rate bands as further gifts by the settlor would have done (subject to subsequent rate changes). A ten year 'periodic charge' also applied.

If the trustees of the settlement were not UK resident, an annual charge was payable, starting with the anniversary of the settlement falling after 31 December 1975. The amount was 3% of the total CTT which would have been payable on a distribution of the entire trust capital. The annual charge has been removed from the subsequent rules, however; only the periodic charge applies.

Transitional relief was given for capital distributions before 1 April 1983 out of pre-27 March 1974 settlements. (This has been continued in the new system.) A percentage only of the full tax was charged on such reorganisations or capital distributions.

8.3.2   Breaking discretionary settlements

- *It is not generally advisable to break discretionary trusts for IHT saving purposes. There is only limited scope for tax savings in this way under the present structure. However, one situation where trust breaking might be worthwhile is prior to the tenth anniversary. In that case, the exit charge (8.3.3) is likely to be low, or even nil.*

8.3.3 Rules applying after 8 March 1982
(ITA Ss58–85)

The following notes apply to the system which operates from 9 March 1982. Major changes have been made which, in some cases, resulted in relaxations and reductions in the IHT and CTT payable. The effect of the changed rules coming into operation was that some of the original provisions, such as the periodic charge at first envisaged, did not take effect at all.

(1) As before, IHT is charged on *distributions* of capital to beneficiaries. Now, it is also charged on distributions to the settlor or his spouse (see below). Such charges are in anticipation of the next ten year charge (see below) and are known as 'exit charges'.

(2) A *charge* is made on the trust property on every *tenth anniversary* of the creation of the trust, ignoring any such anniversary occuring before 1 April 1983. The rate is, broadly, 30% of normal lifetime rates, adjusted as below. For IHT purposes, this means 30% of one half of the scale rates (7.8.1).

(3) The annual charge which previously applied to *non-resident trusts* was abolished from 1 January 1982 but they are now liable to the ten year charge. A credit is given for any annual charges not previously offset.

(4) Previously, tax was charged on the value of the trust property leaving the trust. However, after 8 March 1982 the charge is based on the *reduction in the value* of the trust property, which could be greater. Thus, discretionary trusts were put in the same position as individuals in that respect.

(5) The IHT (and CTT) charges fall on '*relevant property*'. This excludes property held on accumulation and maintenance trusts, employee and newspaper trusts, maintenance funds, charitable trusts, protective trusts and trade compensation funds. Also, relevant property is that in which there is no *qualifying interest in possession*. This, in turn, is broadly defined as an interest to which an individual (or a company, in certain circumstances) is beneficially entitled.

(6) In general, IHT is calculated on discretionary trusts in isolation from any others. However, *related settlements* must be taken into account. (Related settlements are those with a common settlor which commenced on the same day; but if one or both are exclusively charitable and without limit of time they are not related.)

(7) The *ten year charge* is made on the relevant property comprised in the settlement at the time. The rate of charge is 30% of the tax

at lifetime rates. (Now that for IHT purposes only one scale is used, 30% of half the normal rates is taken.) The tax is charged on a notional transfer comprising the value of the relevant and other property of the settlement. The latter is taken at its value when introduced into the settlement. Any transfers made by the settlor during the seven years up to the date of the settlement are cumulated to arrive at the starting point on the rate scale (7.11). For periodic charges prior to 18 March 1986, transfers by the settlor during the period of ten years prior to the date of settlement must be considered.

(8)   If any of the relevant property has been comprised in the trust for less than ten years, the proportion of the rate attributable to that property is reduced to N40ths. (N is the number of completed three month periods for which the property has been held on discretionary trusts during the current ten year period).

(9)   Where a substantial additional amount has been transferred to the settlement after its inception, simply using the settlor's cumulative position at the outset could save substantial tax. For that reason, if it gives a higher figure, it is necessary to include in the notional cumulative total the transfers by the settlor in the seven years prior to the subsequent addition to the settlement. (For pre-18 March 1986 charges this period was ten years.)

(10)   *Exit charges* are calculated on the same basis as the previous ten year charge (see above), using the same rate, adjusted for subsequent additions. Where there has been no previous ten year charge, the opening position of the trust and subsequent additions are normally used to calculate the rate. The effective IHT or CTT rate is calculated as shown and N40ths of this is charged on the relevant property comprised in the distribution. As before, N is the number of completed three month periods for which the property has been held on discretionary trusts during the current ten year period. Thus, suppose the effective rate is 20% and the trust was formed on 1 January 1986. If the distribution is made on 1 April 1991, the fraction is $^{21}/_{40}$ and so the rate becomes 10.5%.

(11)   Note that in the case of a settlement made before 27 March 1974, special rules apply regarding exit charges. In computing the effective rate, the settlor's chargeable transfers during the ten years prior to the start of the settlement should be ignored. However, additions to the settlement after 8 March 1982 must be taken into account. Exit charges are thus based on the cumulation of the current distribution from the trust with previous ones (if any) since 27 March 1974.

(12) *Transitional relief* applied for pre-27 March 1974 trusts regarding distributions prior to 1 April 1983 (or 1 April 1984 where Court proceedings were involved).In those cases, the rate was 20% instead of 30% of the full rate, subject to the various rules mentioned above. However, the reduction to N40ths did not apply.

(13) An *election* could be made in respect of pre-27 March 1974 trusts to have them dealt with under the old system until 31 March 1983 (or one year later if an application to the Court was required).

(14) Under the new rules, where settled property *reverts* to the settlor or his wife, this is no longer exempt. However, for pre-27 March 1974 settlements, no CTT applied to any such reversions taking place before 1 April 1983 (one year later where Court proceedings were involved).

(15) No exit charge applies when trust property becomes held for *charitable purposes,* etc, or by exempt bodies; also exempt maintenance funds, employee trusts, etc. There is a charge, however, when property ceases to be held on *temporary* charitable trusts, etc.

(16) If property becomes settled under a will or intestacy it is taken to enter the settlement at death. Any such property which is distributed within two years of death to a charity, employee trust, etc, is treated as if distributed at death; it is thus IHT-free.

(17) Any property which passes from one discretionary settlement directly into another is treated as remaining in the first, for the purposes of the rules. (After 14 March 1983 this does not apply to certain reversionary interests existing before 10 December 1981 — FA 1984 S104.)

(18) If the *settlor* or his wife initially has an *interest in possession* in trust property which then ceases, it is treated as a separate discretionary settlement, starting when that interest ceases. (This does not apply to pre-27 March 1974 interests.)

(19) Where the *settlor* was domiciled (and deemed domiciled) *outside the UK* when the settlement was made, non-UK property is normally treated as excluded (7.17) although non-domicile is also required at the transfer or interest cesser date in situations (17) and (18).

(20) Where the settlor has made PETs before setting up or adding to a discretionary settlement IHT is first calculated ignoring the PETs. However, if the settlor dies within seven years of any PET, the IHT relating to the settlement may need to be revised, because of PETs now being cumulated, for example, exit charges may need to be revised.

- *Discretionary settlements provide a very valuable estate planning tool in view of their flexibility and comparatively low IHT. (Note that at the current rate the maximum is 30% × 20% = 6% on the top slice for any ten year charge). Thus if you are unsure as to the exact distribution of your estate, discretionary settlements are very useful. But beware of future possible rate increases.*

- *Depending upon the exact circumstances, a number of smaller settlements can result in lower IHT than a single larger one, particularly for future years. This is because the property in the smaller settlements is likely to attract lower IHT rates.*

- *It is particularly beneficial if both spouses create smaller settlements since you may each have your nil rate band available.*

- *If you wish to set up a discretionary settlement and also one or more accumulation and maintenance settlements, also possibly making other gifts, establish the discretionary settlement first. This is because the other items are PETs (7.3) and will be ignored for IHT purposes unless you die within seven years. In that case, had the PETs pre-dated your discretionary settlement, the IHT related to it would normally need to be revised (see 20 above).*

8.3.4   Small discretionary settlements

- *Although large discretionary settlements may sometimes be of questionable IHT benefit, smaller trusts are useful. Subject to the cost of setting them up and administering them (12.2.2), worthwhile IHT savings can be produced.*

  You can establish a discretionary trust with up to £128,000 by your will, including your wife as a beneficiary so as to use your nil rate band. Your wife could then receive funds if necessary (10.18.1).

  Alternatively you could establish a discretionary settlement up to the extent of your nil rate band during your life. However, you should take care not to reserve any benefit (7.22). If your wife is able to benefit during your life you will be liable to income tax on the trust income. However, if she is able to benefit only after your death you will not be so liable.

  Provided the discretionary settlement is made within your nil rate band, little or no IHT is likely to arise either from the ten-year charge or on distributions. However, appreciations in the fund in excess of IHT indexation may result in future tax charges. If it is wished to control the situation, whilst providing some protection against inflation, the fund could be invested in index-linked Government Stock.

8.3.5 Example: Inheritance tax on discretionary settlements

Mr A settles property worth £200,000 on wholly discretionary trusts on 1 January 1987, having made £100,000 of chargeable transfers in the previous seven years.

On 1 August 1992, the trust makes a capital distribution of £50,000. Assuming no more distributions and that the trust property all remains relevant property throughout and using current tax rates, compute:

(1) the exit charge at 1 August 1992; and
(2) the ten-year charge at 1 January 1997, taking the value of the relevant property as £350,000.

(1) *Exit charge at 1 August 1992*

Value of relevant property when settled	£200,000	
Chargeable transfers made by settlor in seven years prior to commencement	£100,000	(A)
	£300,000	(B)

IHT on (B)

at full rates £128,000 at nil	—	
£172,000 at 40%	£68,800	
	£68,800	
lifetime IHT 50%	£34,400	
Less notional IHT on (A) £100,000 (7.8.1)	—	
	£34,400	

Effective rate $\dfrac{34{,}400}{200{,}000}$ = 17.2%

Completed three-month periods prior to distribution = 22

IHT on capital distribution of £50,000 is thus

$$30\% \times £50{,}000 \times 17.2\% \times {}^{22}/_{40} = £1{,}419$$

(2) *10-year charge at 1 January 1997*

Value of relevant property	£350,000	
Pre-settlement transfers	£100,000	(A)
	£450,000	(C)

IHT on (C) £128,000 at nil	—	
£322,000 at 40%	£128,800	
	£128,800	
lifetime IHT 50%	£64,400	
Less notional IHT on (A)	—	
	£64,400	
10-year charge 30% × £64,400	£19,320	

9 Income tax — trusts and estates

9.1 Trusts

A trust is brought into existence when a person (the settlor) transfers assets to trustees for the benefit of third parties (the beneficiaries). Another word for a trust is a settlement. A trust may also be created under a will when a person (the testator) sets aside the whole or a portion of his estate to be administered (by trustees) for the benefit of his heirs or other beneficiaries. Because trusts are important capital tax planning tools, their legal aspects are considered in Chapter 12 and their CGT aspects in Chapter 5. IHT aspects are dealt with in Chapter 8 and this chapter covers certain income tax points of which you should be aware, if considering creating a settlement.

9.2 Income tax rates

Income tax is chargeable at the basic and higher rate as shown in the Table below. The higher rate does not normally apply to trusts but the basic rate (25%) is so applicable. An additional rate of 10% applies to all the income of discretionary trusts and accumulation ones. The additional rate was 18% for 1987–88 and 16% for 1986–87. For 1985–86 and earlier years this rate was 15%.

The basic and higher rate bands for individuals for future years will be increased in line with the retail price index. The index comparison will be made for the previous December each year and the figures will be rounded up to the next 100. (Parliament has the power to modify the effects of indexing the income tax bands.)

9.2.1 Table: Basic and higher rates for 1990-91

Slice of income	Rate	Total income (after allowances)	Total tax
£20,700 (£0-20,700)	25%	£20,700	£5,175
Remainder	40%		

- *Since individuals are not liable to the additional rate, it is attractive to distribute income to them from discretionary settlements (9.5). The respective beneficiaries will be able to reclaim their share of the 10% additional rate suffered by the settlement (subject to any extra higher rate tax).*

9.2.2 Trusts where the settlor or testator is deceased

Where the settlor or testator has died, the taxation of trusts normally follows simple rules. The trust is assessed to basic rate income tax and sometimes additional rate (9.2) on its income. Some of this tax will have been deducted at the source (eg taxed interest). CGT is charged on any capital gains of the trust (5.2).

The tax assessments are normally made in the joint names of the trustees who pay the tax out of the trust funds.

No higher rate tax is paid by the trustees but when the income is distributed to any of the beneficiaries this income is added to the beneficiaries' total income for tax purposes. The income distributions are normally treated as being net of income tax at the basic rate (25%). Thus they carry a corresponding tax credit. In the case of discretionary trusts, etc (9.5), the additional rate (10%) further increases the tax credit. If part of the underlying income of the trust is building society interest, however, the appropriate portion of each income distribution must be allocated to this interest which will be taxed in the beneficiary's hands in the same way as any income on his own building society investments. Similar treatment applies to bank deposit interest taxed under the composite rate scheme. (This 'see-through' rule does not apply to any UK resident with an absolute interest in the residue of an estate who can reclaim tax on the entire income distributions.) When the composite rate system comes to an end after 5 April 1991, this rule will no longer apply.

For example, suppose A has a life interest in a trust and receives from it income for 1990-91 made up as follows:

	Total	Building society income	Other income
Gross	£1,375	£375	£1,000
Income tax at 25% (tax credit)	£250	—	£250
Actual payment to A	£1,125	£375	£750

A will include in his total income £1,500 (ie, £1,000 distribution from other income plus £375 × 100/75 grossed equivalent of building society income). If A is able to make an income tax repayment claim he will have £250 income tax credit from the trust available for repayment (but not the notional £125 in relation to the building society interest which might have been available if A had an absolute interest in the residue).

The trustees should issue with each payment a form R185E which sets out the amount paid and the relevant tax credit.

9.3 Trusts where the settlor is still living
(ICTA 1988 Ss 660–685)

The taxation of trusts where the settlor is still living follows the general rules outlined above except that in certain circumstances the settlor himself will be assessed to tax on the income of the trust. This can be avoided by observing various rules, including the following:

(1) *Period (ICTA 1988 S660)*
The settlement must be set up for a period which is capable of exceeding six years.

(2) *The settlor must not have an interest (ICTA 1988 Ss673, 674A, 683 & 685)*
In the event that the settlor has retained an interest in the income or assets of the trust, he will be assessed to income tax on the income of the settlement to the extent that it remains undistributed. (The settlor has retained an interest in the trust if he or his wife can obtain some benefit from it.) Furthermore, if the income is distributed to others, subject to certain exceptions, the settlor and not the recipient will be charged to the excess of higher rate tax over the basic rate on the distribution. With some exceptions, for trusts made after 13 March 1989, in which the settlor retains an interest, he or she is

taxed on all of the income at the basic and higher rates. (This applies to the income from existing settlements arising from 6 April 1990.)

For 1990–91 and subsequent years, simple outright gifts and pension allocations between husband and wife are not to be treated as settlements for the purposes of these rules. However, this does not apply to gifts of property which do not carry a right to all of the income or where a right to income alone is given.

(3)   *The settlement must be irrevocable (ICTA 1988 Ss671 & 672)*
If the settlor or his wife has power to revoke the settlement or partially revoke it, he is assessed to income tax on all or part of its income.

(4)   *Discretionary settlements (ICTA 1988 S674)*
Discretionary settlements are those under which the application of the income and/or capital of the trust is left to the discretion of the trustees. Under such a trust the settlor or his wife must not be able to benefit from the income, or else he will be assessed to income tax on that income, whether or not any of it is actually paid to him. This does not apply if only the widow of the settlor may benefit.

(5)   *Settlements for benefit of own children (ICTA 1988 Ss663–670 & FA 1990 S82)*
Under a trust created by the settlor, his own unmarried minor children (under 18 years of age) must not receive any income nor must it be used for their upkeep or education. Otherwise the settlor will be assessed to income tax on such income. However, if the child's investment income in question is less than £5, the settlor will not be taxed on it. This figure increases to £100 for 1991–92 and subsequent years. The general rule does not apply to accumulation settlements, however (9.4), insofar as the income is in fact accumulated.

(6)   *Capital sums paid to settlor (ICTA 1988 S677)*
Where 'capital sums' from a settlement (including loans and loan repayments) are paid to the settlor, he is assessable to income tax. The assessments are limited to the undistributed trust income and the balances carried forward for matching against future income. After 5 April 1981, the carry forward period is limited to 11 years from the 'capital sum' payment and

no income is assessable for any period subsequent to the repayment by the settlor of a loan from the settlement.

The rules extend to companies connected to the settlement (normally where the trustees are participators and the company is close). A 'capital payment' from the company to the settlor before 6 April 1981 gave rise to the assessment of trust income on the settlor. After 5 April 1981, this only applies if there is an associated capital payment or asset transfer within five years from the trust to the company.

Note: In all of the above cases there are rules to prevent the double taxation of the trust income so it will not be assessed both on the settlor and the beneficiaries. Usually, basic rate income tax is paid by the trust or it has already been deducted at the source as in the case of, for example, interest on government securities. Dividends received by the trust carry with them tax credits which are effectively transferred to beneficiaries who are given income distributions. Also, if the trust is subject to the additional rate correspondingly higher tax credits attach to income distributions to beneficiaries (see below).

(7)   *Deeds of covenant*
These used to provide an effective method of tax saving in certain circumstances. Unless made to charities, they needed to be capable of exceeding six annual payments and running for more than six years. They were not effective if made by you to your minor children (see (5) above). Another relative such as a grandparent or uncle could execute deeds of covenant in favour of your minor children; but note that the Revenue have powers to block the tax-effectiveness of reciprocal arrangements.

In order to be effective for tax purposes, a deed of covenant needs to have been entered into before 15 March 1988. A further condition is that an Inspector of Taxes received the deed by 30 June 1988. Otherwise, payments under the deed are disregarded for tax purposes. An exception is in the case of charitable covenants, which remain allowable for basic and higher rate purposes. If a non-charitable covenant was in existence before 15 March 1988, it is effective for tax purposes, subject to the rules.

The covenantor who makes the payments deducts basic rate income tax (25%) and pays the net amount to the beneficiary. If the latter is not liable for income tax because his income is less than his tax allowances, he reclaims the income tax deducted by the covenantor.

- *If you are making payments under pre-15 March 1988 covenants to individuals, they will continue to attract tax benefits and should generally be continued as long as possible.*

- *Payments under deed of covenant to approved charities are of benefit to them since they reclaim the basic rate income tax which you deduct on payment. Furthermore, from 6 April 1980 charitable covenants qualify if they are capable of exceeding three years; and after 5 April 1981 you obtain higher rate tax relief, subject to certain limits. After 5 April 1986, no general limit applies.*

- *The deed must be properly drawn up – most charities have prepared forms for covenanted donations – otherwise seek professional advice.*

9.4   Accumulation settlements for the benefit of the settlor's children

If you wish to create a trust for the benefit of your minor children without being assessed to income tax on its income (9.5) this can be done by means of an accumulation settlement. The income of the settlement should be accumulated for each child until at least the age of 18 and no payments should be made for their benefit until that age. (The trust deed normally states that the trustees are empowered to accumulate income.) If it is wished to distribute income to adult beneficiaries this can be done, but the income shares of the settlor's minor children must be accumulated, or else the settlor is liable to higher rate income tax on such income. When the income accumulations are paid to the beneficiary they are treated as capital in his hands and not subjected to higher rate income tax.

9.5   Income of discretionary trusts, etc
(ICTA 1988 Ss686-687 & 809)

After deducting certain expenses, the income of discretionary and accumulating trusts is subject to the additional rate (10%). Thus if a discretionary trust receives dividends of £750 during 1988-89 these will be imputed with £250 tax to make a total of £1,000 on which additional rate tax of £100 will be payable by the trustees. If, however, allowable expenses of say £200 are incurred then only £1,000 – £200 = £800 is liable to the additional rate tax and so £800 × 10% = £80 is payable.

The above applies to trusts where the income is accumulated or is payable at the discretion of the trustees but not where the income is treated for tax purposes as being that of the settlor; nor where a person is absolutely entitled to the income.

Where income distributions are made to beneficiaries, the amounts received by the latter are treated as being net of tax at 35% (25% basic rate plus 10% additional rate). The recipients can reclaim part or all of this tax if their incomes are low enough. For example, if a discretionary trust pays £325 to your child (or for his maintenance) and he has no other income, there is a tax credit of £325 × 35/65 = £175 which is all reclaimable (unless you are the settlor).

Beneficiaries can reclaim tax on distributions of income made to them after 5 April 1973 even if the trust received the income before that date and thus only paid tax on it at the standard rate of income tax (38.75% or previously 41.25%). If, however, the tax attributable to such distributions exceeds notional tax of two thirds of the total net accumulations at 5 April 1973, the balance is assessed on the trustees.

- *Trustees of discretionary settlements should consider the tax positions of potential recipients of income distributions. If their other income is low then substantial repayments of tax can result. On the other hand, distributions of income to higher rate income tax payers will result in a further 5% liability at current tax rates.*

9.6   Foreign trusts
(FA 1981 S80 & FA 1989 Ss110 & 111)

For capital gains tax purposes a trust is generally treated as being resident abroad if a majority of the trustees are so resident and its administration and management are carried out overseas. Such foreign trusts are exempt from CGT on realisations of assets in the UK and elsewhere, subject to the detailed rules and stringent anti-avoidance provisions (5.2.5). For income tax purposes, special rules apply, broadly from 6 April 1989 (5.2.5).

UK income of foreign trusts is charged to income tax here along roughly the same lines as non-resident individuals are so charged.

There is no higher rate liability, however, unless distributions are made to beneficiaries resident in this country or if the anti-avoidance provisions apply regarding transfers of assets abroad. In the latter event, in certain circumstances, the Revenue may charge any beneficiaries who are resident in this country with basic and higher rate income tax on the trust income.

- *In view of the tax advantages of foreign trusts, if you are concerned with a UK one, in appropriate circumstances you should consider exporting it. This is discussed in more detail later (12.9.5).*

9.7   Estates of deceased persons

9.7.1   The income tax liability of the deceased
(TMA 1970 Ss40, 74 & 77)

When a person dies, income tax and other taxes must be settled on all his income and capital gains, etc, up to the date of his death. Any of this tax that is not paid during his lifetime must be settled by his executors or administrators out of his estate.

If the deceased has not been assessed to tax on all his income prior to his death, the Revenue are allowed to make assessments on such income within three years after the end of the tax year in which death occurred. The Revenue may make assessments in this way in respect of any tax years ending within six years before the date of death in cases of fraud, wilful default or neglect of the deceased but no earlier years can be assessed.

9.7.2   Income tax during the administration period
(ICTA 1988 Ss695–720)

During the administration period of an estate, the executors or administrators pay any basic rate income tax assessments that arise on the income for that period. The tax paid by direct assessment or deduction at source is subtracted from the amounts of income paid to those entitled to the income of the estate. The latter include the income that they receive in their tax returns when the payments are made to them. They must return the gross equivalents allowing for income tax at the basic rate (25%). Once the total income payable to each beneficiary has been ascertained, it is allocated to the respective tax years for which it arose and they pay (if applicable) higher rate tax on that basis.

10 Drawing up your will

10.1 Why you should make a will

In England and Wales, unlike Scotland (13.3) and many other countries, there is no compulsory share to which a member of your family is entitled on your death. You are therefore completely free as to how you dispose of your estate subject only to the statutory rights which a former spouse, a surviving spouse, children and certain other persons might have if they were dependent on you (10.11). Otherwise, the Courts generally have no power to interfere with any of the dispositions in your will unless they are called upon to resolve a problem of construction or interpretation or lack of capacity (10.23).

It is therefore important to make a will, since it is the only means by which you can dispose of your property on your death in accordance with your wishes. In addition, a will enables you to give directions as to your funeral arrangements and the guardianship of your children. Also, depending on the wording of your will, and your personal circumstances, you will be able to take advantage of the various inheritance tax exemptions and reliefs which are available. Finally, and most important, by making a will you can avoid an intestacy and the application of statute law which would otherwise govern the disposition of your property. An intestacy is inevitably more costly and complicated (11.11.2).

If some of your property is of a personal nature, ie, a bank account or stocks and shares, and it is in the joint names of yourself and another, then, unless there is an agreement to the contrary, such property passes automatically to the survivor on your death. You will not be able to dispose of such property under your will.

In the case of immovable property (ie, land) which is acquired in joint names, this will pass on your death according to the manner in which it is held. If you acquired your house jointly with your wife as 'beneficial joint tenants' then on your death the title to the property passes automatically to your wife as surviving joint tenant. However, if your house is held by your wife and yourself as 'tenants in common' then each of you is entitled quite independently to your share of the proceeds of sale. You are therefore free to dispose of your share by will as it does not pass automatically to the survivor (10.15).

There are, of course, numerous other ways in which you can make provision for your family independently of the provisions of your will. If you are a member of a company pension scheme, its rules may provide for a discretionary lump sum payment by the trustees on your death. Such payments do not form part of your estate and are therefore free of inheritance tax. You may request that the trustees pay all or part of such a lump sum to your children. This may enable you to leave your entire personal estate to your wife. Another way is for you to declare trusts of any insurance policies on your life for the benefit of your wife or children, although there could be an inheritance tax charge when the policies are put into trust (see Chapter 14). On your death the trustees can pay the monies directly to the beneficiaries and they will not form part of your estate.

10.2   Who can make a will?
(WA S11; WSSA)

You can make a will provided you are over 18 years of age and have what is known as 'testamentary capacity'. This means that:

(1)   you must know what you are doing and be aware of the implications;
(2)   you must be aware of the extent of the property of which you are disposing; *and*
(3)   you must have regard for your legal and moral obligations to particular beneficiaries.

You must know and approve the contents of your will at the time you sign it, otherwise it may be contested after your death (10.23). If you later have cause to regret any particular provision, this will nevertheless remain valid until your will is revoked or amended by a codicil or a further will (10.22).

If you are a soldier on active service or a sailor on maritime service you can make a will even if you are under 18. In such circumstances you can also make a will orally without complying with the formalities for execution (below). You will also be able to revoke your will informally.

10.3 The basic requirements for a valid will
(WA S9; AJA S17)

An English or Welsh will must be in writing. No special form is required provided it is clear that the document was intended to be a will. It is always revocable. You must also comply with the formalities for execution, otherwise your will is invalid and of no effect. These formalities are:

(1) you should sign your will at the foot or end of the document, (another person may sign for you provided you are present and direct him to so do). Even if you have not signed your will at the end it will still be valid if it is apparent that you intended by your signature to give effect to the will;

(2) your signature must be made or acknowledged by you in the presence of two witnesses both present at the same time; *and*

(3) thereafter both witnesses should sign in your presence although it is no longer strictly necessary for a witness to do so. It is sufficient if he acknowledges his signature in your presence.

Both witnesses must be aware of what is happening and must be in the line of sight of the proceedings. A proper attestation clause is desirable and is incorporated in most wills.

10.4 Witnesses
(WA S15; WA 1968)

A beneficiary under your will should not be a witness to it. Such a person would be a competent witness but as an 'interested person' his or her gift would be invalidated unless there were two other independent witnesses. Neither should the husband or wife of a beneficiary witness your will as the gift would be similarly invalidated.

An executor appointed under your will does not lose his appointment by acting as a witness. However, he cannot also take any benefit if he does witness the will and if he is a professional person this would render invalid a professional charging clause in the will.

If a beneficiary under your will subsequently marries one of your witnesses the gift to him will still take effect. If a beneficiary does not witness your will but witnesses a codicil which confirms your will he will still take the gift.

10.5   Drafting your will

There are various ways in which a will may be worded. An infinite number and variety of clauses may be inserted, depending on your wishes and your personal circumstances. You should seek your solicitor's advice on the final draft. What follows is an outline of the main points which you should consider and the most important clauses which should be included.

10.6   Appointing executors and trustees

You will need to appoint executors to administer your estate. They will make application for a grant of Probate, collect in your assets, pay your debts and then distribute the remainder of your estate according to the terms of your will.

Usually two executors are appointed, although you may appoint up to four. One executor is normally a relative or responsible close friend. It is often advisable to appoint a professional person such as your solicitor or family accountant as your second executor. Deciding on your executors requires careful consideration as they will be responsible for all your assets after your death. The welfare of your family may well depend on their judgment.

To guard against one of your executors predeceasing you or for some other reason being unable or unwilling to act, you can appoint a substitute executor.

Your executors are usually also appointed to act as trustees if property has to be administered for minors or if you have set up a trust by your will. It is not necessary for the same executors and trustees to be appointed to act for your whole estate. You may appoint separate trustees of any part of your estate and this might be the best course where you intend your business to be carried on after your death. If there are to be trusts for your children, you should consider choosing trustees who are relatively young. This may reduce communication problems when your children come of age.

You may appoint a bank or trust company to administer your estate. The advantages of such an appointment are the experience and confidentiality which such organisations can offer. The main disadvantage is the extra cost involved. You may also prefer your estate to be administered by a close friend or relative rather than by a comparatively impersonal institution.

10.7   Funeral arrangements

If you wish to be cremated or buried in a particular place you can give directions for this in your will. You can also direct that parts of your body be given to a teaching hospital or be used for grafting or transplantation. If this is your wish it is advisable to leave separate instructions with your family or relatives so that they can give effect to your wishes as soon as possible after your death.

10.8   Guardianship of your children

If you have young children or children who are incapable of looking after themselves you will probably wish to appoint someone to look after them after the death of both yourself and your spouse. On your death your husband or wife will automatically become the guardian of your children unless you wish to provide otherwise. A close friend or relative may be appointed as guardian together with your spouse only in special circumstances.

You should, of course, discuss the question of guardianship at length with your friends and relatives and ensure that the persons you propose to appoint will be prepared to take on such a responsibility.

10.9   Legacies

Beneficiaries generally either receive specific gifts of property (legacies) or a share of your residuary estate (10.17).

Legacies may be either specific sums of cash or specific items of your property. You might wish to leave all your personal effects to one of your relatives or close friends. If you own a particularly valuable item, eg, jewellery, you should consider whether it should be included in such a general gift or left to someone who you feel might particularly appreciate it. The item should, of course, be accurately described to avoid any confusion when your estate is being distributed. You can give a specific gift of shares or the proceeds of an insurance policy provided you are the beneficial owner of such a policy.

You may wish to leave one or more of your personal employees specific legacies. If any of them would be entitled to a redundancy payment on your death you would probably wish this to be deducted from the amount of the legacy and, if this is the case, you should make specific provision for it in your will.

If you wish to leave a legacy to your executor you should state whether it is a condition of the gift that he accepts the office or not.

You may, of course, leave property to a charity or a number of charities. The charity should be accurately described and its current address given. You should check whether it is a registered charity otherwise tax relief may not be available. A receipt clause should be included discharging your executors from liability provided they pay the legacy to the treasurer or another officer of similar standing in the charity concerned. Charitable gifts do have substantial inheritance tax advantages (7.16.1).

● *In considering legacies you will need to decide whether or not the beneficiary is to pay any inheritance tax on the gift. It is common to express a legacy to be 'free of inheritance tax' and it is often the most favoured procedure. Any inheritance tax payable on such a legacy will be paid out of your residuary estate by your executors.*

10.10   Legacies to children

10.10.1   Vested legacies

A vested legacy is payable immediately on your death. If you wish to benefit a number of children there are three forms of gift open to you:

(1)   Individual gifts of a stated amount to named beneficiaries — eg, '£100 to my son David'.
(2)   Individual gifts of a stated amount to each member of a class — eg, '£100 to each of my children (or grandchildren)'.
(3)   You may provide for a specific sum to be divided equally between a class — eg, '£1,000 equally between the children of my sister'.

Which form you choose will depend largely on your own particular family circumstances. Reference to children in a will automatically includes reference to an adopted or illegitimate child even though such a child may have been adopted or legitimated after your death.

10.10.2 Contingent legacies

A contingent legacy is payable only on the happening of a particular event, such as marriage or the attainment of a particular age.

If you give one or more minor children a contingent legacy then, unless you are the child's parent or guardian or you specifically provide to the contrary, the income of such legacy will belong to your residuary beneficiaries. Your residuary beneficiaries will be regarded as having an 'interest in possession' in the legacy, meaning being entitled to the income (12.2.1). Their life interest will only come to an end when the legacy becomes vested when the children reach the specified age.

- *If you wish to give minor children contingent legacies you should ensure that the clause is properly drawn. You may provide that the legacy be set aside for the beneficiaries, possibly in the hands of separate trustees. The better course would be to stipulate that the legacy carry the intermediate income for the benefit of the beneficiary. This will prevent an inheritance tax charge on your residuary beneficiaries at the time when the legacy becomes vested.*

You would probably be best advised to make absolute gifts to minors, particularly if you are planning that they should have legacies on attaining 18. Although a minor cannot give your executors a valid receipt for the gift, it is usual practice to provide for your executors to be discharged if they pay the legacy to his or her parent or guardian. If you do not make such provision your executors can only obtain a discharge by appointing two trustees or a trust corporation to hold the legacy on trust for the minor until he or she reaches majority, ie, 18.

10.11 Legacies and family provision claims

In considering legacies you will need to have regard not only to your own personal wishes but also to your legal obligations to persons who might have a claim under the family provision legislation (11.10.7). If you are divorced, your former wife or husband may have a claim for reasonable financial provision out of your net estate. Any other persons who could show that they were financially dependent on you during your lifetime might also have a claim. It would therefore be prudent to consider making provision for a potential claimant, since a substantial pecuniary legacy given by your will may avert the unpleasantness of a claim after your death which may lead to court proceedings.

10.12   Conditional gifts

You should not attach any condition to a specific gift which is too harsh or unreasonable. If the Court felt that this were the case the beneficiary would be entitled to the gift free of the condition. Similarly, a condition may be void for uncertainty if it is held to be too vague to be clearly interpreted and implemented. A condition that is onerous or immoral might be held to be contrary to public policy.

The only exceptions to this rule are gifts to named charities which fail or are too vague to be implemented. In such cases the Court may direct that the subject matter of the gift be applied for purposes which are as near as possible to those which you originally intended.

10.13   Failure of gifts

10.13.1   Ademption
(WA S24)

If you give a specific legacy and the subject matter of the gift has been sold, destroyed, given away or stolen during your lifetime the gift will be void ('adeemed') and of no effect. This is because your will takes effect from the date of your death. For these purposes, it is construed as if you had signed it on the day you died.

You may, however, show an intention in your will that it be construed at a time other than the date of your death. If you refer in your will to 'my car' or 'my house in which I now live' these words may be interpreted as denoting the present time. If such a clause in your will is treated as taking effect at the time when it was made and the asset in question is sold or stolen, the gift will be adeemed. This will be so even if the asset is replaced by another which satisfies the description you have given in your will. If your will is confirmed by a later codicil (10.22) it will be construed as referring to the new asset.

In order to avoid such a situation, use wording in your will such as 'the house in which I reside at the time of my death'.

Similarly, if you wish to benefit an employee of yours in your will you might wish to stipulate that the gift is only to take effect if the beneficiary named is still in your employ at the date of your death.

A specific legacy is also adeemed if the property is subject to a binding contract for sale on your death. Note that if an asset which is the subject of a specific legacy is subject to an option for sale which you have created after execution of your will, the gift may be adeemed by the exercise of the option, even after your death.

10.13.2 Lapse
(WA S33; AJA S19)

If you benefit a person in your will and this person dies in your life-time the gift will be void and of no effect. If the gift is a specific gift the property in question will fall into, and form part of, your residuary estate (10.17). If the gift which lapses is a share of residue (10.17) it will pass according to the intestacy rules (11.2.2).

Specific gifts and gifts of residue may both be saved from lapse by the provisions of Section 19 Administration of Justice Act 1982. The Section provides that if you give property by will to your child or other descendant and the donee dies before you, leaving children of his own alive at your death, the gift does not lapse but passes to your deceased child's children regardless of the provisions in his will.

The Section will not apply if you make the gift determinable at or before the death of the donee, nor does it apply to property appointed under a special power of appointment (10.18). In addition, the operation of Section 19 may be excluded by any contrary intention which you express in your will.

Similarly, if you leave a fund of property to a class of persons (known as a 'class gift'), eg, 'to all or any of my children living at my death', and one of your children dies before you, his potential share will not lapse but will remain in the fund and be divided amongst those of his children who are living at your death. However, if a gift is subject to your children attaining a certain age and one of them survives you but does not reach that age, his share will remain in the fund and be divided among those of your children who do attain a vested interest.

10.14   Exercising powers of appointment
(WA S27)

You may have been given a power of appointment over a trust fund under the will of a relative or friend or under a settlement. Such a power may be either special, eg, in favour of a certain class of persons, or general, eg, in favour of anyone, and will probably be exercisable by will or by deed.

If you are the donee of a special power of appointment you will have to exercise this by means of a separate clause in your will. If you are the donee of a general power its exercise will probably be incorporated in the wording of the bequest of your residuary estate.

10.15   Dealing with the family home

If you are the sole owner of your house you can dispose of it under your will either by means of a specific gift or as part of residue.

If you and your spouse own your house as 'beneficial joint tenants' your share will pass automatically on your death to your spouse as surviving joint tenant. There is therefore no need to provide for a gift of your share in your will as the principle of survivorship operates quite independently of the provisions of any will.

If you both own the house as 'tenants in common' your share will not pass automatically to the survivor. It will fall into your general estate and pass under the terms of your will. If you do not intend to leave the residue of your estate to your spouse, you should clearly stipulate in your will that your spouse should receive your share. If you wish your share to pass to another person, note that, as a co-owner, your spouse would be entitled to occupy the whole of the property after your death. However, the other co-owner may be able to force a sale of the house since technically, it would be held by the co-owners on trust for sale (10.17).

- *By owning your house as a joint tenant with your wife her security is enhanced, whereas owning as tenants in common can have inheritance tax advantages (7.14.3) and generally offers greater flexibility. The joint tenancy may easily be 'severed' to become a tenancy in common. A simple document is all that will be necessary to effect this.*

You might wish that your house be retained after your death in order to provide a home for your wife and family. You could give your house to your executors and trustees on trusts permitting your wife to have the use of it during her lifetime provided she makes it her home. On her death or if she ceases to reside there the house will pass absolutely to another named beneficiary, most probably your children.

- *If your spouse is given the right to occupy your house this will be treated as an 'interest in possession', (10.10.2) for inheritance tax purposes. Tax will therefore be payable on your spouse's death as if he or she owned the property absolutely. The way to avoid this is for your executors to grant your spouse an informal licence to occupy the property which would not be enforceable by your spouse.*

You may wish to provide for the possibility that the house may be too large or expensive for your wife to run. You could authorise your executors to purchase another house for your wife to live in. You could also extend your executors' powers of investment in relation to your residuary estate by including the purchase or improvement of land in such powers.

10.16 Survivorship clauses

If you and your spouse die in a common accident (such as a car or plane crash) the law provides that the younger of the two of you is deemed to have survived the elder. If you have both made wills leaving your estates to each other and if your spouse is younger than you, he or she will be deemed to have received all your estate. However, since you will be deemed to have died before your spouse; the gift to you will lapse (10.13.2) and pass under the intestacy rules (11.2.2). This could have serious family and tax consequences; in particular, the nil rate band may be wasted.

You should therefore consider whether your will should specifically provide that if you and your spouse die as a result of a common accident your spouse is to be treated as having died before you.

It has become common to include what is known as a '30 day clause' in gifts between spouses. Thus, a gift under a will of a share in a property held as tenants in common (or, indeed, the whole estate) would be conditional on the survivor surviving for a period of 30 days. This would avoid your spouse's estate being substantially increased by the share in the house and thereby attracting an unnecessary inheritance tax charge.

A '30 day clause' should not be inserted without full consideration of its impact. For example, it might, in certain circumstances, be beneficial for your spouse to receive (if only for a short period) the amount of the nil rate band so that the latter is not wasted.

10.17   The residuary gift

The term 'residuary estate' comprises everything which is not otherwise specifically disposed of by your will. Whatever is left in your estate — 'the residue' — can (subject to payment by your executors of your debts, funeral expenses and any inheritance tax) either be:

(1)   left outright to one person (eg, your spouse) or a charity, or divided equally or in varying proportions between a number of persons or charities or both; *or*
(2)   left in trust for your family, relatives, or others.

Your residuary estate is usually given to your executors on trust for sale. Their primary duty will be to sell all your property but they will be given power to postpone sale. They will also have power to distribute assets forming part of your residuary estate in kind so that individual beneficiaries could take shares or land without your executors having to sell such property first.

The wording of the trust for sale clause usually requires your executors to convert all your property into cash and thereafter to pay debts, funeral and testamentary expenses and legacies. Inheritance tax on your personal property (ie, cash, stocks and shares and personal effects) and on tax-free legacies is payable out of your residuary estate as a testamentary expense. This is also true of land unless you otherwise direct.

A separate clause — called the 'main beneficial clause' — sets out the distribution of residue between the beneficiaries. You may see the word 'trust' used in this clause in your solicitor's draft even though you have no intention of putting your property into trust on your death. The word 'trust' used in this context does not mean that a formal or 'strict' trust will come into being on your death. It is used to show that your executors do not take your property themselves as beneficial owners and that they hold it as trustees for the beneficiaries you have named. The word 'absolutely' is usually inserted after the name of a beneficiary of full age and this shows that he or she is immediately and unreservedly entitled to the gift.

You can, of course, leave shares of residue directly to your children. If any of them is under the age of 18 your executors will administer the funds for them until they are of age. The income of a child's share can be used for its maintenance, education and benefit but otherwise will be accumulated (8.2). As with contingent legacies, you can postpone the date at which your child becomes entitled to the capital of its share beyond 18.

In considering the division of your estate between your spouse and children one of your main considerations will be to ensure that your spouse is adequately provided for. While you might wish to leave a substantial portion of your estate to your children in order to reduce the inheritance tax liability on your spouse's death, no advantage would be gained if this left him or her without adequate means. Also, if you give away too much to your children, the overall tax liability could be increased either because the additional tax on your death may outweigh the saving on your spouse's death or because your spouse may not have enough assets to use her nil rate band. There are a number of factors which you will need to take into account in deciding how much you should leave to your children, namely:

(1) your own age and that of your spouse;
(2) the size of your estate and the income produced;
(3) how much your spouse will need to live on, bearing inflation in mind; and
(4) how much tax will be saved by making a gift to your children if you die first.

If you direct an equal division between your spouse and children, your children may get less than their full one-half share. This is because your spouse's share will be exempt from inheritance tax and the children's share will therefore have to bear all the tax attributable to it as a non-exempt share of residue. This rule applies despite a contrary intention expressed in the will. (ITA S41.)

10.18 Setting up a trust by will

10.18.1 Your spouse's fund

Instead of giving your residuary estate to your spouse absolutely you may consider giving your spouse an entitlement only to the income from your residuary estate (or part of it) during his or her lifetime (a life interest). After your spouse's death the capital will pass to your children then living or to other persons or to charity.

There are a number of advantages in giving your spouse a life interest which is as flexible as possible. These are considered below. 'Flexible' in this context means granting your trustees wide powers of appointment of capital to your spouse absolutely. There should also be additional powers to terminate the life interest by appointing the capital (or part of it) to your children or grandchildren.

A life interest has merit in that you can ensure that a measure of capital reaches your children. For example, if you give your spouse a life interest you can direct that it is to terminate on remarriage. This would protect the interests of your children should your spouse remarry. Also, if you have a large estate you may feel that your spouse would not be able to manage your property satisfactorily, in which case you may prefer to have it managed by your trustees. Against these advantages must be set the costs of having to administer a continuing trust.

It is often the best solution to give your spouse a flexible life interest and at the same time give your trustees unrestricted powers for advances and loans. There is no inheritance tax advantage in lending capital as opposed to advancing it. The main advantage of a loan is that your trustees will know that the capital will be used in accordance with your wishes. This may not necessarily be the case if they were to advance capital direct to your spouse.

If you make your spouse's life interest terminable on remarriage such termination will be a transfer of value for inheritance tax purposes. There will also be a deemed disposal for capital gains tax purposes at the time when he or she remarries. However, if you give your trustees an overriding power of appointment this will ensure that they at least have a greater measure of control over the termination of the life interest.

- *Your trustees could be given power to terminate your spouse's life interest by appointing the capital on discretionary trusts under which your spouse would be one of the discretionary beneficiaries. This would not constitute a reservation of benefit (7.22) since your spouse would not have made the gift.*

- *Where the trustees of a life-interest trust dispose of trust assets, capital gains tax will normally be payable at the lowest rate (as opposed to the higher rates payable where trustees of a discretionary trust or an individual dispose of assets (5.2.4)).*

- *It is possible that future legislation will restrict the scope of post-death deeds of variation (10.24). A flexible life interest with wide powers of appointment will minimise the effects of any such restriction.*

10.18.2 Your children's fund

If you give your spouse a life interest in all or a substantial part of your estate you may provide that on your spouse's death or remarriage your children are to take the capital. Their interest will then be contingent on their surviving both your spouse and yourself. In addition you might wish to provide that they take their shares only on attaining a specified age, eg, 21 or 25 or even 30. If any one of your children fails to satisfy these conditions his or her share could then pass to his or her children in equal shares.

In addition to your spouse's fund, or if you are widowed or divorced, you might wish to set aside a separate fund for your children. You would be advised to consider setting up an accumulation and maintenance settlement for your children. The main characteristics of such a settlement are:

(1) One or more of your children must become entitled to the capital of the fund or to a life interest in the income of the fund on attaining a specified age not exceeding 25. Entitlement to the capital may be deferred to a later age if the life interest requirement is satisfied at age 25.

(2) While any child is under age the income of its share will be accumulated so far as it is not applied for the maintenance, education or benefit of that child.

(3) Not more than 25 years must have elapsed since the day on which you made the settlement or (if later) since the time when the settled property began to satisfy the requirements in (1) and (2) above *or* all the persons who are or have been beneficiaries are or were grandchildren of a common grandparent (or their widows, widowers, etc).

(4) There will be a disposal for capital gains tax purposes as and when each child becomes entitled to his share or when an advance of capital is made but holdover relief is available (4.7).

(5) Your trustees will be given a power of advancement or an overriding power of appointment or of revocation.

• *An accumulation and maintenance settlement has substantial inheritance tax advantages. A payment made to a beneficiary out of the settled property is not taxable. When a beneficiary becomes entitled to an interest in possession no tax is payable. Finally, the ten year charge (which would otherwise be levied on the property of a trust without an interest in possession) is not applicable to such a settlement (8.2).*

- *You may wish to consider setting up a trust of your children's share which includes a power to make loans to your spouse. This could produce inheritance tax benefits as the loans will be deductible debts from your spouse's estate (provided that there is nothing in the trust which is derived from your spouse).*

- *Whether your spouse is given an absolute interest or a life interest he or she will be able to make potentially exempt transfers to your children which will be tax free provided your spouse survives the transfer by seven years.*

10.19   Discretionary trusts in a limited form
(ITA S144)

- *You can provide for the rearrangement of the trusts of your will after your death without incurring inheritance tax disadvantages. The way this is done is to provide for the bulk of your estate to be subject to a discretionary trust (12.2.2) terminable by a power of appointment amongst a specified class of beneficiaries within two years. During the two year period the income of your estate may be distributed at the discretion of your trustees or accumulated. If the discretion is not exercised by your trustees within that period the other provisions of your will automatically take effect. These could provide for absolute interests, life interests in income or an accumulation and maintenance trust.*

The following are the advantages of such a provision:

(1)   It enables your executors and trustees to draft your will after your death when they will be able to take account of lifetime gifts and of recent changes in tax law.

(2)   The termination of the discretionary trust itself will not attract an inheritance tax charge.

(3)   The distribution or trusts decided upon by your executors and trustees are treated for inheritance tax purposes as having taken effect from your death.

There are, however, also a number of disadvantages:

(1)   An additional burden is placed on your executors and trustees to

decide on a course of action which you would have approved of. A letter of wishes will be necessary.

(2)   *If a beneficiary becomes entitled to part of your residuary estate as a result of the exercise of the power of appointment there may be a capital gains tax charge.*

(3)   *Inheritance tax will have to be paid in order to obtain the grant. This would have to be reclaimed if an appointment is subsequently made which would bring the estate within one of the exemptions.*

(4)   *An appointment cannot be made within three months of your death without triggering the original provisions of your will. Inheritance tax would then have to be charged on that basis.*

10.20   Precatory trusts
(ITA S143)

● *You may express a wish as to the manner in which property you have left to a beneficiary by will is to be distributed. Provided the legatee distributes the property within two years of your death, the transfer by him will not be a 'chargeable transfer' for inheritance tax. Instead, the property will be treated as if you had left it to the transferee directly by your will.*

10.21   Administrative clauses

Your will may include a number of technical or administrative clauses which extend the powers of your executors and trustees. The following clauses are usually inserted:

10.21.1   Maintenance and advancement
(TA 1925 Ss31 & 32)

Where there is a likelihood that your trustees will be administering funds for minors the statutory powers of maintenance out of income and advancement of capital will apply.

Under Section 31 your trustees have a discretion to pay income for or towards a minor's maintenance, education and benefit. They may pay only such part of the income as is reasonable having particular reference to other income available. If an interest is contingent on attaining an age greater than 18, once the child attains 18 your trustees *must* pay him the income until his interest vests. You may, as is often the case, wish to amend the terms of Section 31 by substituting age 21 for 18.

Under the power of advancement (Section 32) trustees have power to advance capital to an infant up to one half of his vested or presumptive share. Often the will provides for this statutory power to be modified to enable the trustees to advance the whole of a child's share.

10.21.2   Investment

You may find it convenient to give your trustees as wide a power of investment as possible. An investment clause may be included giving your trustees power to purchase freehold or leasehold property and to improve such property. The purchase of property for occupation by a beneficiary is not an investment and if you wish your trustees to have such a power you should specifically provide for it.

10.21.3   Borrowing

The statutory power of borrowing by trustees is restricted and it is often convenient to include a wider power of borrowing enabling trustees to borrow for investment purposes.

10.21.4   Nominees

Trustees have a duty to ensure that all of the trust property is brought under their control. If you wish your property to be held in the name of one trustee only or of a nominee for all of them you should make specific provision for this.

10.21.5   Carrying on a business

There is no general or statutory power for your trustees to carry on your business. If you would like your trustees to do so you should give them specific power. You may wish to appoint a separate set of trustees for this purpose.

10.21.6   Apportionments

It is usually convenient to exclude the legal apportionments required by the Apportionment Act 1870. This will apply not only on your death but at all other times. If this is not done, the Act requires that income due to your estate be considered as accruing from day to day with the result that so much of a payment relating to a period before your death will be apportioned to the capital of your estate. The exclusion of these apportionments eliminates the extra time and expense involved in making the necessary calculations which usually outweigh the advantages.

10.21.7 Appropriation

By Section 41 of the Administration of Estates Act 1925 your trustees are given wide powers to appropriate any part of your estate in order to satisfy any interest under your will. The power is only exercisable if the necessary consents have been obtained, usually from those adult persons who are absolutely entitled or from the person entitled to the income for life. It is therefore simpler to amend the terms of the Section by removing the need for consent.

10.21.8 Exporting trusts

If a beneficiary of a share of residue lives outside the UK you may wish to consider giving your trustees power to appoint separate trustees of that share in a foreign country. This will facilitate the administration of your estate particularly if the share of residue is substantial. This power should be combined with a general power enabling your trustees to carry on the administration of your estate outside the UK.

10.21.9 Charging clauses

If one of your executors and trustees is a professional person, eg, a solicitor or an accountant, a standard clause is often inserted authorising him to take fees for work done in his professional capacity in connection with the administration of your estate.

It is also usual to provide that if your trustee receives remuneration from companies in which your estate has invested he may keep this for his own benefit.

10.21.10 Protecting trustees

It is usual to include a clause absolving your executors and trustees from liability if they have acted honestly and in good faith in the administration of your estate.

10.22 Altering and revoking your will

Your will has no effect until your death. It is therefore merely a declaration of intention and until your death it may be altered or revoked entirely.

You may alter any part of the text of your will before you sign it. If there are erasures, additions or deletions they must be signed, by both you and your witnesses. Otherwise the alteration may be invalid.

If you wish to make alterations after you have signed your will you should draw up a codicil to your will. A codicil is a supplement to your will. It sets out the amendments or additions you wish to make and confirms those parts which you wish to leave unaltered. It therefore brings your will down to the date of the codicil. A codicil must be signed and witnessed in exactly the same manner as a will.

Your will (or parts of it) may be revoked in one of the following ways:

(1) *By destruction*

It is often customary to burn a will which it is intended to revoke. You do not, however, need to destroy your whole will in order for the revocation to take effect. If you tear off a sufficiently large or vital part of it (eg, the signatures) revocation will be effective. You must intend to revoke, as if you destroy your will by mistake it is not revoked. Someone other than yourself may destroy it on your instructions but you must be present while he does so and be aware of what he is doing.

(2) *By making a new will or codicil (WA S20)*

The later will must either expressly revoke the earlier one or deal with all your property in such a way that previous wills are revoked by implication. A will revokes an earlier one so far as the earlier one is inconsistent with it, even if it contains no express revocation clause. It is always advisable to include an express revocation clause if you intend to revoke an earlier will.

(3) *By your marriage (WA S18; AJA S18)*

If you marry your will is automatically revoked unless it is clear that you made your will contemplating your marriage to a particular person and that you intended your will not to be revoked by your marriage. In such a case your will is valid provided you marry that particular person. Marriage to anyone else will automatically revoke your will. If it is clear from your will that at the time when it was made you were intending to marry a particular person and that you intended that a particular gift should not be revoked by your marriage to that person, it is presumed that not only that gift, but all the other gifts are to take effect.

(4) *By your divorce (AJA S18)*

If after you have made your will, your marriage comes to an end, any appointment of your former spouse as executor will be void. Also any gift to your former spouse in the will shall be deemed to have lapsed. This rule gives way to any contrary intention which you express in your will.

10.23 Can a will be contested?

You should be satisfied with the contents of your will when you make it and ensure that its dispositions are in accordance with your wishes. Nevertheless it is possible that someone, eg, a relative or close friend, might contest your will after your death.

Your will might be contested on one of the following grounds:

(1) That you did not have testamentary capacity at the time when you signed your will. A will that appears rational will be presumed valid since sanity is presumed unless the contrary is shown. Although the relevant time for testing mental capacity is when the will is signed, if you were competent when giving instructions for the will (but not at the time you signed it) the will would still be valid if at the time you signed you were aware of having given instructions and believed the will to be in accordance with them.

(2) That you executed a later will which expressly or impliedly revoked the one it is intended to prove.

(3) That the formalities for execution have not been complied with.

(4) That unfair or improper pressure — 'undue influence' — was put upon you at the time when you made your will and it therefore does not reflect your true wishes. ('Undue influence' means that you were coerced into making a will you did not want to make eg, by fear, force or fraud.) The onus is on the person alleging undue influence, to prove it. In the first instance, the party seeking to establish the will must remove suspicion by proving that the testator knew what he was signing. Then the opponents or the will must prove fraud or undue influence.

(5) That, as a result of a clerical error or unsatisfactory drafting, it is difficult to interpret all or part of your will and there is doubt as to whether it carries out your true intentions. Although it is now possible to apply to the Court for rectification of a will, clear evidence that it fails to carry out the testator's intentions must be produced. As stated above, you should ensure that the wording of your will accurately reflects your intentions before signing it.

Generally, probate business is divided into 'common form' (where there is no dispute) and 'solemn form' (where there is a dispute). These are known respectively as non-contentious and contentious business and the first is dealt with by the Family Division of the High Court and the second by the Chancery Division.

10.24   Re-arranging your estate after your death

● *The terms of your will can effectively be rewritten after your death. Your beneficiaries can enter into a Deed of Variation altering the dispositions of your will. Provided such a deed is entered into within two years of your death, and the parties so elect by notice to the Revenue within six months, the variation is deemed to have been made by you and inheritance tax is charged on this basis. However, the fact that your will may be rewritten after your death should not be relied upon to excuse a poorly drafted will. Post-death variations can give rise to legal problems (particularly where children are involved) and income tax disadvantages, and will require co-operation and agreement between your heirs. It is preferable to ensure that your will is properly drafted to reflect your wishes in the first place.*

11 Administering the estate

11.1 Obtaining the grant

11.1.1 Why apply for a grant?

If a person dies leaving assets in the UK, a grant of representation must usually be obtained before his estate can be realised and distributed, unless his estate is very small.

The grant is a document issued by the Court and is the only formal authority from the Court that:

(1) in the case of a grant of Probate, the will is valid;
(2) the person or persons named in it are the persons entitled to administer the estate; *and*
(3) all the assets of the deceased have been vested in the person or persons so entitled to enable them to administer the estate.

Thus the issue of the grant of representation to those entitled to it eliminates the risk of fraud in dealing with the deceased's property. Only those persons appointed by the Court will be able to obtain payment of the deceased's assets.

In England and Wales, where the deceased left a will and you have been appointed an executor, you will be entitled to apply for a grant of Probate. If the deceased has not left a will and you are entitled in priority to administer the estate under the intestacy rules (11.11.2) you will be entitled to apply for a grant of Letters of Administration. In Scotland, where special rules apply, the grant is known as Confirmation (13.5).

A grant of representation, whether it be Probate, Letters of Administration or Confirmation, will enable you to collect in all the assets of the estate. It will have to be produced to banks, building societies, insurance companies and other bodies in order to secure the release of funds into your name. In the case of stocks and shares, the grant is essential in order to change the name of the registered holder.

As an executor, you derive your authority from the will itself and the grant of Probate confirms your title. You can, therefore, even before the grant is issued, do various acts which do not require proof of your authority, such as paying debts, putting a house on the market or starting a Court action. An administrator has no authority until it is given to him by the Court and is therefore less able to commence administration immediately.

11.1.2   Small estates

Where an estate is very small it is sometimes possible for individual small amounts to be obtained without the necessity for a grant. This applies mainly to assets held by the main clearing banks, the Department for National Savings, Trustee Savings Bank and Building Societies, provided the amount involved is under £5,000. The Bank of England also has power to transfer small amounts of Government stock on its books in the name of a deceased person without requiring sight of a grant. These bodies are not bound to make payment without production of a grant. They are entitled to ask for it, particularly if a complication should arise.

The above provisions do not normally apply to monies held by insurance companies, although they may sometimes be prepared to pay over small amounts without a grant. A grant is usually required in the case of company shares or stock. However, if the holding is very small and the total estate does not exceed £5,000 individual companies may be prepared to register a transfer without sight of a grant, but against a suitable indemnity.

The undertaking concerned may require a letter of confirmation from the Capital Taxes Office that no inheritance tax is payable. For this purpose Form 22 should be completed and forwarded to the Enquiries Section, Capital Taxes Office, Rockley Road, London, W14. (Form 44 is used in foreign domicile cases). Unless any queries arise the appropriate letter will be sent to you in due course.

11.2 Entitlement to a grant

11.2.1 Where there is a will
(NCPR 20 & 27)

If you are appointed sole executor you alone are primarily entitled to a grant of Probate. If you are one of two, three or four executors appointed you may apply for a grant on your own if the others are unavailable or undecided as to whether they wish to act. This is usually the best course if you wish administration to commence as soon as possible. Power will be reserved to grant what is known as 'double probate' to those executors who have not yet proved if they should wish to apply at a later stage. Executors not joining in an application for a grant must nevertheless be notified of the application unless the Registrar directs otherwise.

If the deceased left a will but did not appoint an executor, or if an executor has been appointed but is unable or unwilling to act, the priority of entitlement to a grant is as follows:

(1)   Trustees of the residuary estate.
(2)   Residuary beneficiaries (including a life-tenant of the residuary estate).
(3)   The personal representative of any residuary beneficiary (but not a life-tenant).
(4)   Specific legatees or any creditor of the deceased (vested legatees being preferred to contingent legatees).
(5)   The personal representative of any specific legatee or of any creditor of the deceased.

In such a case the grant is known as Letters of Administration 'with will annexed'.

11.2.2 Where there is no will (intestacy)
(NCPR 22)

If no will can be found amongst the deceased's papers and there is no evidence that he made one it will be presumed that he died intestate. You may be entitled to share in the estate and to be one of the administrators if you are one of the next of kin of the deceased. The order of priority is as follows:

(1)   Wife or husband.
(2)   Child, grandchild or great-grandchild.
(3)   Parents (equally if more than one).

(4)   Brothers or sisters (equally) or their children.
(5)   Half-brothers or half-sisters.
(6)   Grandparents (equally if more than one).
(7)   Uncles or aunts.
(8)   Nephews or nieces.

If there are a number of persons equally entitled the grant is usually issued to the first person to apply. A relative who is not within one of the above degrees of relationship is not entitled to any share of the estate. If no entitled relative can be found either in the UK or abroad the whole estate, after payment of debts, will pass to the Crown. In such a case the grant of Letters of Administration will be taken out by the Treasury Solicitor's office.

11.2.3   Application by a creditor

If all the executors (10.6) renounce Probate or no beneficiary wishes to apply for Letters of Administration, a grant may be issued to a creditor of the estate. This usually occurs when an estate is insolvent. The creditor will have to show in the oath that all persons beneficially entitled have either renounced or been cited (11.2.6). If an estate is insolvent the Court may grant Letters of Administration to any person it thinks fit.

11.2.4   Minors and persons under disability
(NCPR 32, 33, 34 & 35)

A minor can be appointed an executor but cannot act or take out a grant during his minority. If other adult executors have been appointed they can apply for Probate immediately. Power will then be reserved to the minor to prove the will when he reaches full age, at which time he obtains 'double probate'. If a minor has been appointed sole executor his parents may apply for a grant of Letters of Administration (with will annexed) for his use and benefit. When he reaches full age he may apply for what is known as 'cessate probate'. A cessate grant may be either of Probate or Letters of Administration and is, in effect, a renewal of the original grant.

The right of a minor who has been appointed executor to apply for a grant of Probate on attaining full age cannot be renounced by any person on his behalf. A minor's right to Letters of Administration may be renounced by a person appointed as his guardian by the registrar of the Court and authorised to renounce.

Where the person appointed in a will as executor is mentally incapable of managing his affairs a grant of Letters of Administration for his use and benefit may be issued in the following order of priority to:

(1)   the person authorised by the Court of Protection to apply;
(2)   if no one is so authorised the lawful attorney of the incapable person acting under a registered enduring power of attorney (12.5.5);
(3)   if there is no such attorney the person entitled to the residuary estate of the deceased.

Alternatively Letters of Administration may be granted to such two or more other persons as the Registrar may direct.

11.2.5   Foreign domicile
(NCPR 19 & 30)

If a person dies domiciled in a foreign country and his will is valid and is in English naming executors whose duties compare with those of an English executor Probate may issue to those executors immediately. Otherwise a foreign will which deals with property in the UK may be admitted to proof if it can be established:

(1)   that the deceased was domiciled in a particular foreign country; *and*
(2)   that either the foreign Court has adopted the will or that the will is valid by the law of that country.

Evidence as to validity of the will is usually provided in the form of an affidavit of law sworn by a lawyer who has been practising in the particular country. Application for the grant in the UK is normally made by a person or persons acting under a power of attorney from the administrators of the estate in the country concerned. If no such person has been appointed, or if the deceased died abroad intestate, the affidavit of law must state who is, or would be, entitled to administer the deceased's estate in that country. The Inland Revenue Account (Form IHT 201 — 11.4.1), statement of domicile (11.6) and Executor's or Administrator's Oath must be filed together with the affidavit of law.

A person may make two wills, one dealing with his foreign property and the other with his English property, the intention being that they should take effect separately. If this is the case then, in applying for the grant of Probate in the UK, an official copy of the foreign will must also be filed. The grant will, however, issue only in respect of the English will.

11.2.6 Renouncing your right to a grant
(NCPR 37)

You cannot be forced to act as an executor even if you have promised the deceased that you will act. Similarly, you cannot be forced to act as an administrator on an intestacy.

The right to a grant of Probate or Letters of Administration may be renounced by signing a document in standard form. The renunciation will not be final, however, until it has been filed at a Probate Registry.

11.2.7 Intermeddling

If you are thinking of renouncing your right to a grant of Probate you should decide as soon as possible. If you delay you risk becoming an 'executor de son tort' if you have 'intermeddled' with the estate. This means impliedly accepting the office of executor by your conduct, for example, describing yourself as executor, paying debts of the estate, or opening an executor's bank account. If you merely arrange the funeral or look after the deceased's pets, or even swear the executor's oath (11.8), this will not make you an '*executor de son tort*'.

Even if you have not been appointed an executor under the will, dealing with the deceased's assets or advertising for claims may make you an 'executor de son tort'. The distinction between an executor who accepts office by implication as a result of his conduct, and the non-executor who intermeddles with the estate, is an important one. If you are appointed an executor and are held to have accepted the office by your conduct you can be compelled to take out a grant. If you have not been appointed you cannot be forced to act but you will be liable to account to the extent of the assets you have actually handled. You may also be liable to the extent of the debts you have released.

The right to a grant of Letters of Administration (with will annexed) may be renounced even though by your conduct you have impliedly accepted the office of administrator. You can never be compelled to take out such a grant. If no other person with an immediate interest in the estate is able or willing to act, a solicitor or trust corporation such as a bank may be appointed to act as administrator.

11.2.8 The chain of representation
(AEA S7)

If you die while acting as the sole or last surviving executor of an estate, having proved the will, your executor will become executor of that estate together with your own estate. This is called the 'chain of representation'. So long as the chain remains unbroken the last executor in the chain is the executor of every preceding testator. If any executor in the chain dies intestate or fails to appoint an executor in his will or fails to prove the will the chain is broken.

A subsequent administrator cannot act as executor of a preceding testator's estate, neither does the office of an administrator pass to his executor or administrator. If there has been a break in the chain of representation a new grant has to be taken out limited to the un-administered part of the estate. This is known as a 'grant *de bonis non administratis*'.

As an intending executor you should be aware of the implications of being the last link in the chain of representation. If the person who has appointed you was an accountant, solicitor or other professional person it is quite possible that he may have been acting as an executor when he died. As an executor in the chain you will have exactly the same powers and duties over the estate that you inherit as the original executor would have had. Even if you inherit an estate that has been almost completely administered you will still have to deal with any claims which may arise later. As executor of a proving executor you cannot renounce Probate of the former will and only take Probate of the one which specifically appoints you as executor.

11.2.9 Revocation of grants
(AEA Ss27 & 37 & NCPR 41)

A grant of Probate may be revoked by the Court if it has been obtained by fraud or if a later will is discovered. It may also be revoked if you become incapable of acting.

A grant of Letters of Administration may be revoked if a valid will is found. It may also be revoked if it has been granted to the wrong person, ie, where someone entitled in priority to the grantee is discovered later.

In general, acts made in good faith prior to revocation are protected so that conveyances or other transactions will not be rendered invalid. A purchaser from a personal representative is not therefore affected by a subsequent revocation of the grant.

11.2.10   Can the issue of a grant be stopped?
(NCPR 43, 44, 46 & 47)

If a person wishes to stop the issue of a grant (ie because he wishes to dispute a will) he may enter what is known as a '*caveat*' in either the Principal or any District Probate Registry. Such a person then becomes the 'caveator'.

A *caveat* is a stop-notice which prevents a grant of representation being issued without notice to the caveator. Once it has been entered, as executor you will have to issue a warning (this may only be done from the Leeds District Probate Registry) to the caveator. The warning requests the caveator to indicate within eight days if he wishes to continue to oppose the issue of the grant. If he does so, he will have to enter an appearance in the Leeds District Probate Registry and you will have to prove the validity of the will in Court. If not, you may remove the *caveat* by filing an affidavit of service of the warning in the Leeds District Probate Registry. A grant will then issue to you. A *caveat* expires automatically after six months unless renewed by the caveator.

A facility known as a 'standing search' is also available at the Principal Probate Registry only. The applicant for such a search will automatically be sent an official copy of any grant which complies with the details given in the application. Any such grant issued either not more than 12 months before the date of application or within six months thereafter will be sent to the applicant.

A citation is often used to deal with someone with a prior right to a grant. If the person cited does not enter an appearance to the citation he loses his rights to the grant. The person who issues the citation may then obtain a grant of Letters of Administration (with will annexed) or Letters of Administration if a simple intestacy is involved. Before a citation is issued a *caveat* must usually be entered.

11.3   How to obtain a grant in England and Wales

11.3.1   Personal application
(NCPR 5)

You may make a personal application for a grant if you do not wish to instruct a solicitor. Personal applications may be made to the Personal Application Department of the Probate Registry or Sub-

Registry. You will have to attend for an interview at a Registry or Sub-Registry or at a Probate Office. You may choose the most convenient place. A list of Probate Offices together with the relevant forms may be obtained from Probate Personal Application Department, 2nd Floor, Somerset House, Strand, London WC2R 1LP. There is no time limit within which an application must be made.

The following documents are required to be submitted:

(1)   The Probate application form.
(2)   Death certificate.
(3)   The will (if appropriate).
(4)   Return of the whole estate for inheritance tax.

The Probate application form asks for details of the deceased, the will, the deceased's relatives and the applicant.

The return for inheritance tax is known as Cap Form 44. In this form you are required to give full particulars of the whole of the deceased's property and debts owed by him at the date of death. This means assets of any description such as cash, goods, investments, and arrears of salary as well as freehold and leasehold property. You are also required to answer questions in order that the Capital Taxes Office may determine whether inheritance tax is payable on the deceased's death in respect of property other than his own. In particular you will need to know:

(1)   whether the deceased at the time of his death was entitled to an interest in any settled property whether as beneficiary or otherwise and whether he ceased to be entitled within seven years of his death;
(2)   whether the deceased made any gift or settlement within seven years of his death (details of the date of each gift, the name and address of the donee and the value of the property involved must be given);
(3)   whether an annuity or any other sum of money becomes payable on the deceased's death under a superannuation scheme; and
(4)   whether the deceased held any property jointly with any other person (full details of the name of the other joint owner and the date of purchase, investment or deposit must be given).

The Cap Form 44 duly completed may be incorporated by the Registry in a more formal Inland Revenue Account which you will also have to sign. In this Account you have to declare the truth and accuracy of the statements made and of the details provided in the form. Generally, in the case of small estates, the need for such an account is waived. If this is the case, the completed Cap Form 44 will be returned to you to keep.

When you attend for interview you will also have to swear (or affirm) as to the exact value of the estate and that the information you have given is true to the best of your knowledge.

A personal application fee (normally £1 per £1,000) is payable and also Probate Court fees, as follows:

Net value of estate	*Probate Court fee*
Not exceeding £10,000	Nil
£10,001–25,000	£40
£25,001–40,000	£80
£40,001–70,000	£150
£70,001–100,000	£215
£100,001–200,000	£300
£200,001–300,000	£350
over £300,000	£400 and for every additional £100,000 or part thereof a further £50

Separate fees are payable for office copies of the grant. A fee of 25p per page is payable for copies requested on application for the grant. On a subsequent application for a copy of the grant a fee of £2 is payable for the first such copy. Additional copies cost 25p each. Inheritance tax may be payable and all or part of this must be paid before a grant can be issued. After the grant has been issued the Capital Taxes Office will examine the account of the deceased's property. Enquiries may be sent to you and adjustments in value may be proposed. Depending on the values finally agreed additional inheritance tax may be payable.

The Registrar has power to refuse to accept a personal application, particularly if there is a dispute or the case presents special difficulties. Once a grant has been issued, the Probate Registry normally has no further involvement in the administration of the estate.

11.4 Application by a solicitor

You may wish to instruct a solicitor to prepare and submit the papers in application for the grant on your behalf, particularly if the estate is large and complicated. Depending on the type of grant required and the value of the estate your solicitor will need to lodge the following documents at a Probate Registry.

11.4.1 Inland Revenue Account

If a person is domiciled in the UK at the time of his death all of his assets wherever they may be situated form part of the gross value of his estate for inheritance tax purposes. In the Inland Revenue Account you are required to provide a detailed inventory of all the assets and liabilities of the deceased's estate, the values being those at the date of death.

Excepted estates

An Inland Revenue Account is not required to be delivered in the estate (called an 'excepted estate') of any person who dies on or after 1 April 1990 where:

(1) the total value of the estate is £115,000 or less;
(2) the estate consists only of property which has passed under the deceased's will or intestacy or by nomination or survivorship;
(3) not more than £10,000 consists of property situated outside the UK; *and*
(4) the deceased died domiciled in the UK and has made no gifts within seven years of death chargeable to inheritance tax on his death.

Unless within 35 days of the grant the Inland Revenue issue a notice requiring completion of an account, you will at the end of that time automatically be discharged from any liability to inheritance tax. If you obtain a grant without delivery of an account and later discover that the estate is not an 'excepted estate' you must then deliver an account of all the property in the estate. The account must be delivered within six months of the time when you discover that the estate is not an 'excepted estate'.

Non-excepted estates

In all other cases an Inland Revenue Account must be completed and, once signed by you, be delivered to the Capital Taxes Office. There are two forms in current use — Form IHT 202 and Form IHT 200.

11.4.2   Form IHT 202

Form IHT 202 is a short form of account. It is for use where:

(1)   the deceased died on or after 18 March 1986 domiciled in the UK;

(2)   the estate consists only of property which has passed under the deceased's will or intestacy or by nomination or beneficially by survivorship (10.15);

(3)   the whole of the deceased's property is situated in the UK and its total net value after deducting any exemptions and reliefs claimed does not exceed the threshold above which inheritance tax is payable at the date of death (7.20).

11.4.3   Form IHT 200

The full account Form IHT 200 is used in all other cases. This is a 12 page form and is divided into three sections. In addition, on page 3 of the form you are required to answer a number of questions in order that the Capital Taxes Office may determine whether tax is payable on the deceased's death in respect of property other than his own. These questions are similar to those asked in the return (CAP Form 44) to be completed in personal application cases (11.3.1).

The three sections of the Form 200 are as follows:

Sections 1A and 1B

In Section 1A you must account for all movable property including stocks and shares, bank and building society accounts, premium savings bonds, pensions, life policies and personal effects. Liabilities incurred by the deceased are deductible from the gross value of the property in Section 1A. Household liabilities which are settled on a monthly or quarterly basis, eg, rates, gas and electricity, may have to be apportioned to the date of death. Reasonable funeral expenses are deductible, including the cost of a tombstone or gravestone.

A full list of stocks and shares (both quoted and unquoted) and their corresponding market values should be scheduled in Form 40 which accompanies the Inland Revenue Account.

Section 1A property is known as 'non-instalment option' property. This means that you are required to pay any inheritance tax on the net value of such property in full on delivery of the Inland Revenue Account.

In Section 1B you must account for the deceased's immovable

property, such as freehold or leasehold property, held in his sole name or as tenant in common with another (10.15), business interests and shares in private companies. If there are liabilities relative to Section 1B property, such as a mortgage, these are deductible in computing the net value for inheritance tax purposes. Further details of freehold or leasehold property must be provided in Form 37 which accompanies the Inland Revenue Account.

Section 1B property is known as 'instalment option' property for the purpose of inheritance tax. Tax on the net value of such property, after taking into account business and other reliefs, may be elected to be paid by ten annual instalments. The first instalment (or the full amount of the tax) is due and payable six months following the month in which the death occurred. There is no harm in electing to pay by instalments at this stage. In the case of land or other income-producing assets there may be particularly good reasons for doing so. However, interest on unpaid inheritance tax now runs at 11% and it may be better in the long run not to involve the estate in an extra liability. If at a later stage it is clear that there will be alternative finance available all the outstanding tax can be paid off at any time.

Section 2
In this section you must account for all other property of the deceased (whether or not subject to the instalment option) for which you are liable to pay inheritance tax. This includes foreign property and jointly owned property which passes by survivorship (10.15). Liabilities due to persons outside the UK are normally allowed against the value of foreign property.

Section 3
Details of all other property (whether or not subject to the instalment option) in which the deceased had or is treated as having a beneficial interest immediately before his death are inserted in this section. This includes any gifts made by the deceased prior to his death where he retained a benefit for himself (7.22). If the deceased had a life interest in a will trust or settlement such an interest will terminate on his death. The capital value of the trust fund must be shown in Section 3 and will be added to the deceased's free estate in order to ascertain the rate of inheritance tax payable. The proportion of the tax liability relative to the trust fund will, however, fall on the trustees of the will or settlement concerned.

Property in Section 3 should be segregated according to whether or not the instalment option is available and whether or not inheritance tax is to be paid on delivery of the account.

11.4.4   Providing valuations

In the Inland Revenue Account you must enter each item at its 'principal value'. This means the estimated price which it would fetch if sold at the date of the deceased's death.

Stocks and shares should be entered at the price at which they were quoted on the Stock Exchange at the date of death. For probate purposes, quoted securities are valued at one quarter up from the lower to the higher limit of quotation. Most stockbrokers provide valuations for probate purposes and their charges are based on a fee scale. If the deceased had only a few holdings you may wish to value the securities yourself by reference to the Stock Exchange Daily Official List. Note that if a security is quoted 'ex dividend' the whole of the net dividend (or interest payment) should be entered separately.

You should take steps to establish the open market value of any freehold or leasehold property owned by the deceased at the date of death. Very often the deceased's family or relatives are able to provide you with a figure on the basis of discussions which they have had with local estate agents. In most cases where inheritance tax is payable the valuation (which either has been arrived at by agreement with the family or supplied by a professional valuer) will be passed to the District Valuer for his opinion after the grant has been issued.

If inheritance tax is payable on the estate and interest has started to run you would probably wish to obtain the grant as quickly as possible. Any reasonable estimate of the value of the deceased's house or other property can be provided, particularly if there is no time to obtain a more exact figure. There would be no particular advantage in inserting a low figure since this would be subject to agreement with the Capital Taxes Office in due course. While there might be an initial saving in terms of interest on any borrowing for inheritance tax this would be offset by further interest payable on the final figures in due course.

If the estate is not taxable, the Capital Taxes Office will not be too concerned with the valuations you have provided. In such a case, however, you should still avoid inserting a particularly low figure. The probate valuations that you provide will form the base cost in any future capital gains tax calculation on a sale and you would therefore wish to establish a reasonably high (but realistic) figure.

11.5 Raising inheritance tax

It is usual to finance the initial payment of tax by means of a bank loan although it is also possible to obtain a loan for this purpose from a building society. This enables the whole amount to be obtained quickly from one source. Once the grant has been obtained you can then give consideration to the best way in which the borrowing is to be repaid. Interest paid within one year of the loan is deductible for income tax purposes against estate income of the same year. There is no relief for interest paid on an ordinary overdraft and it will therefore be necessary to open an executor's loan account for this purpose.

There are other ways to finance payment of inheritance tax which could result in a substantial saving to the estate. If the estate includes a life policy the company concerned may be prepared to pay the proceeds direct to the Revenue without the necessity for sight of the grant. If there is a building society account the body concerned may be prepared to release the funds either if the balance is less than £5,000 or if payment is effected direct to the Inland Revenue. Also, if the deceased has set up a trust of a life policy, the trustees may have power to pay the inheritance tax bill for the benefit of the beneficiaries under the trust and the will.

A beneficiary may be prepared to lend money to the estate. If the deceased held a joint bank or building society account with a member of his family or a close relative, the survivor would be in a position to make cash available immediately to the estate. This would avoid borrowing from the bank and the consequent expense of high rates of interest. If the lender is in agreement the loan can be interest-free or at less than the market rate.

11.6 Foreign domicile

If the deceased was domiciled outside the UK Form IHT 201 should be used to account for the UK estate. This form is similar to the Form 200 except that the country of domicile must be stated. A short statement should be submitted with the Form 201 stating the circumstances relied upon to establish the foreign domicile and giving a brief history of the deceased's life movements. The completed form together with the statement of domicile should be sent to the Pregrant Section/Control, Capital Taxes Office, Minford House, Rockley Road, London W14 0DF, for assessment prior to submission to the Probate Registry.

11.7   Calculation of tax payable

The net values from each of the sections of the Form 200 (or 201) are carried to the section headed 'Exemptions and reliefs against capital' on page 10. Here you are required to give details of any exemptions or reliefs claimed against the property described in each section. The net values and the amounts of the exemptions claimed are both carried to the summary on page 11. A total figure for aggregate chargeable transfers on death is arrived at taking into account all transfers made prior to death.

The total amount of tax payable is calculated by reference to tables (see 7.38). Tax in respect of non-instalment option property is payable immediately and a formula is used to calculate the amount of tax referable to this property. A similar calculation is needed to arrive at the proportion of tax payable on instalment option property. If the tax on this property is to be paid by instalments the number of instalments and the amount of tax now to be paid must be inserted. If more than six months have elapsed since the end of the month in which the death occurred interest at the rate of 11% per annum must be calculated.

It is necessary to carry forward the totals for tax and interest to the further summary on page 12 of the Form 200 (or 201). The completed Account once signed by you, together with a cheque for the amount of tax immediately payable, ie, tax on non-instalment option property plus those instalments which have already become due plus interest (if applicable), should be sent to the Central Accounting Office (Cashier), Barrington Road, Worthing, West Sussex, BN12 4XH. The receipted account, once returned, must be lodged with the other documents mentioned below at a Probate Registry in application for the grant.

11.8   The Executors' Oath

If you have been appointed an executor under a will and you intend to prove that will then you must swear the Oath for Executors. In the Oath you recite:

(1)   that the document now produced to you is the true will of the deceased;

(2)   the full name and address and domicile of the deceased;

(3)   the date of death of the deceased;

(4)   that you are the sole executor or one of the executors or the surviving executor named in the will;

(5)   whether there is any land which was settled before the death (and not by the will) and remains settled notwithstanding the death;

(6)   the gross and net values of the estate (if the estate is an 'excepted estate' (11.4.1) you will be required to swear that the gross value does not exceed £115,000 and that, as the case may be, the net value (for the purposes of probate court fees) does not exceed £10,000 or £25,000 or £40,000 or £70,000 or £100,000 or £115,000);

(7)   an affirmation that you will duly collect and administer the estate according to the law and deliver up the grant to the High Court when required to do so;

(8)   where power is reserved to any other executor (11.2.1) the oath should contain a paragraph confirming that notice has been given to the other executor (or has been dispensed with in any particular circumstances).

11.8.1 The original will

The original will is an exhibit to the Oath and must be signed by you when you swear the Oath. At the same time it should be counter-signed by the solicitor who has taken the Oath. If the original will has been lost the Court may on application grant Probate of a will contained in a copy, but will want convincing that the original has not been revoked by destruction.

11.8.2 The Administrators' Oath

If you are an intending administrator under the intestacy rules you must swear the Oath for Administrators. In addition to general information about the deceased and the estate similar to that required by the Executor's Oath, the Administrators' Oath states:

(1)   that the deceased died intestate;

(2)   your relationship to the deceased, eg, lawful wife, son, brother, etc;

(3)   that all those with a prior right to a grant have been cleared off, ie, have either renounced or been cited; *and*

(4)   whether or not a minority or life interest arises under the intestacy.

11.8.3 Probate Court fees

These are payable on the net value of the estate (11.3.1). The amount payable must accompany the documentation in application for the grant. Application may be made to the Principal Probate Registry at Somerset House, Strand, London WC2R 1LP, or to any one of a number of district probate registries or sub-registries in England and Wales, whatever the value of the estate and the place of residence of the deceased.

11.9 Dealing with the assets

After you have established your title by obtaining a grant of representation your next duty is to collect in the assets of the estate, pay the debts and funeral expenses and thereafter distribute the estate to the beneficiaries.

11.9.1 Collecting the assets

Frequently the will includes a bequest of personal effects. If there are items of value they should be deposited with the bank or other agent for safekeeping. Clearly if it appears that the administration of the estate is going to be relatively simple personal effects can be released to the beneficiary entitled to them. A receipt should be obtained.

You will need to produce the grant to the deceased's bank, building society and life insurance company, among others, in order to obtain payment of monies due to the estate. Once the grant has been registered you will be sent a repayment claim form for signature. If the deceased had a life insurance or retirement annuity policy you will have to send the original policy to the company's claims department. In the case of building society or National Savings Bank accounts, if the money is not urgently required these may be left open until nearer the time of actual distribution.

If the deceased held stocks and shares the certificates are often held by the bank for safekeeping together with the title deeds for any land assets such as the family home. You will have to sign an authority to send all the securities or other documents held by the bank to you or your solicitor.

It will probably be convenient to open an executor's account in order to deal with the administration of the estate. You might already have opened such an account before the grant was obtained if there were urgent liabilities which required settlement. It is usually useful to open an executor's account as soon as possible after the grant has been obtained in order that cash, cheques and dividends can be paid in without delay. If this is not possible the bank may be prepared to accept dividends and cheques payable to the deceased for credit to the account in his name, even though all payments and direct debits will have been frozen at the date of death. Sometimes the bank is prepared to open a separate suspense account to accommodate dividends and other payments which are received prior to the grant.

Stocks and shares will continue to be registered in the name of the deceased until the grant has been received for registration. The certificates covering the deceased's holding should accompany the grant for endorsement into your name as executor or administrator. Once the grant has been registered with the company registrar dividends will be sent to you if you are sole, or first named, executor or administrator. These should continue to be paid into the estate account as income of the estate until all the liabilities (including administration expenses) have been settled.

11.9.2   Insurance

You should give attention to the question of insurance cover as soon as possible after death. Policies in the deceased's name should be endorsed with the names of the personal representatives and your interest noted. If the deceased possessed a car the insurers should be informed of the death as soon as possible. Unless the car is to be sold, new insurance cover should be obtained.

11.9.3   Dealing with land

If the deceased had a family then they will in all probability continue to occupy the family home, at least for the time being. If this is the case your administrative duties with regard to that property are minimal.

If the deceased's house or flat remains unoccupied and has not been specifically bequeathed by the will you should see that it is sufficiently secured pending sale. If possible a neighbour should be asked to keep an eye on the premises. There is nothing to prevent you putting the property on the market before the grant has been obtained, although you should bear in mind that the sale cannot be completed until the grant has been issued. It is as well to ensure that you take the advice of at least two estate agents in the area as to the most suitable asking price. The widest market should be aimed at since otherwise you may be open to criticism on the grounds that the property was insufficiently advertised or that the asking price was too low (or, indeed, too high). Once a suitable offer has been received there is no harm in consulting the principal residuary beneficiaries as to whether they feel it should be accepted. The ultimate decision however, is yours alone.

If the property is leasehold you will need to establish both outstanding and potential liabilities under the lease. When you come to distribute the estate you will need to be satisfied that all outstanding liabilities have been settled and that a sufficient fund has been set aside to answer any future claims under the lease. You will then be able to distribute the estate in due course without incurring any personal liability under the terms of the lease.

11.9.4   Carrying on a business

As personal representative you can only carry on the deceased's business if you are given express or implied authority in the deceased's will. Otherwise you may only do so for the purposes of sale or winding up or assenting to a beneficiary under the will. You can only use in the business those assets which the testator used at his death unless you have been given wider powers under the will.

You will be personally liable for any debts which you incur in carrying on the deceased's business. You will, however, be able to indemnify yourself from those assets which you have been authorised to use.

The deceased's business debts should be paid in priority to any debts which you incur in carrying on the business. If the deceased's creditors have formally consented to the carrying on of the business you have a right of indemnity against any debts which you incur out of the estate and not merely out of the business assets which you use.

11.9.5   Partnership
(PA 1890 Ss 33, 39, 42 & 43)

If the deceased was a partner in a firm or business you will need to consider the estate's interest in the business in the light of the partnership agreement. You should obtain a copy of the partnership agreement and the latest partnership accounts as soon as possible.

A partnership is dissolved by the death of one of the partners unless there is an agreement to the contrary. If the partnership agreement makes no provision for dealing with the death of a partner or if there is no such agreement then statute law applies.

As personal representative of a deceased partner you may apply to the Court to wind up the business. This would involve sale of the assets, payment of debts and distribution of any surplus assets among the surviving partners and the estate.

You should ensure that settlement of the deceased's share is completed within a reasonable time. When distribution does take place you are entitled to see the final partnership accounts, which should follow on from the last accounts. The deceased's estate is jointly liable with the surviving partners for the debts of the partnership outstanding at death. On distribution you should therefore ensure that all such debts have been paid, or obtain a suitable indemnity from the surviving partners. The share due to the estate of a deceased partner is deemed to be a debt due at the date of death or dissolution. If there is no final settlement of accounts then, unless otherwise agreed, you may claim either:

(1) such share of the profits made since the dissolution as is attributable to the use of the deceased partner's share of the assets; *or*
(2) interest at 5% per annum on that share.

You do not have this right if the continuing partners validly exercise an option to purchase the deceased's interest.

11.10 Dealing with the liabilities

11.10.1 The solvent estate
(AEA 1925 Sch 1, Part II)

Having obtained payment of sufficient of the estate's assets your next concern is to discharge all the liabilities as promptly as possible.

If the family home continues to be occupied early settlement of household expenses such as rates, gas and electricity is usually desirable. The family should be advised to settle such debts as soon as possible after death since reimbursement from the estate can be arranged later. Funeral expenses may also be paid straight away but if this would cause hardship they can be settled after the grant has been issued.

Once cash is available from the realisation of assets or the sale of shares you can give attention to discharging the major liabilities of the estate. The most important debt is usually the loan for inheritance tax and you may well be under some pressure to repay this as quickly as possible. If there are sufficient funds in the bank or building societies these may be used, otherwise you may need to sell securities. You will need to obtain expert advice before completing a sale, otherwise you may be open to criticism from beneficiaries and, possibly, even personal liability if it is made without guidance as to value. Besides stockbrokers, you may need to consult accountants or other professional advisers as there may be tax or other personal considerations to be borne in mind.

Normally all debts are payable within one year of death, but in practice you should settle them as soon as is convenient. As a rule, all the property in which the deceased had an interest which did not terminate on his death may be used for the payment of debts.

In practice, the will usually provides for all debts (including testamentary and administration expenses) to be paid out of the residuary estate. From the above it follows that on an intestacy all of the deceased's property may be used for the payment of debts.

11.10.2 Tax liabilities

Tax liabilities usually take some time to be finalised and if they are likely to be substantial a provisional figure may be given in the Inland Revenue Account. The Revenue usually wish to see a copy of the grant and, if appropriate, the probated will. If a tax assessment had been received by the deceased shortly before death and has not been paid this should be settled as soon as possible to avoid an interest charge. Generally, an assessment in respect of the deceased's tax liabilities is payable within 30 days of the date of issue of the grant.

As personal representative you will have to sign the tax return in respect of income and capital gains for the period prior to the date of death. You are also required to complete a tax return for the administration period covering the income and, if any, capital gains of the estate. An assessment will then be issued in your name.

11.10.3 Finalising the inheritance tax liability

When completing the Inland Revenue Account you may have submitted a provisional or estimated valuation of the deceased's house or personal effects. This value may have been estimated or arrived at by agreement with the beneficiaries and may not reflect the true market value of the particular asset. The Capital Taxes Office will examine the Inland Revenue Account and may raise observations and queries on particular values, particularly if the estate is taxable. The valuation which you return in respect of the deceased's house or any other freehold or leasehold property will usually be referred to the District Valuers Office. The District Valuer may raise queries but in most cases values are agreed without the need to engage a professional valuer. If agreement cannot be reached you may have to instruct an estate agent, chartered surveyor or other professional valuer to negotiate with the Revenue on your behalf. Note also that if quoted shares are sold at a loss within 12 months of death you may claim to reduce the inheritance tax bill by substituting the total of the sale prices for the probate values (7.24).

If your original estimate has to be corrected additional tax and interest may become payable. Such alterations in values, together with details of any other adjustments in the assets and liabilities of the estate, must be reported to the Capital Taxes Office in a form known as a Corrective Account (Form D3). This form is used to report any changes in the estate which have come to light since the papers in application for the grant were originally lodged. Once the completed form has been considered by the Capital Taxes Office a 'corrective assessment' may become necessary if additional tax is payable. Alternatively, a refund of inheritance tax may be due to the estate.

11.10.4 Your liability as personal representative

You are personally liable to an unpaid creditor or beneficiary but your liability is limited to the extent of the assets of the estate. However, if you have been guilty of wilful default or some other wrongful behaviour whereby a loss is caused to the estate by some neglect or mistake on your part you may be liable beyond the assets you have received.

11.10.5 Advertising for claims
(TA 1925 S27)

You are liable for all the outstanding debts of the deceased at the date of death. Even if you pay all known debts you remain at risk of a claim from an unknown creditor. The only way to protect yourself is to publish notices for claims in accordance with the provisions of Section 27 of the Trustee Act 1925. Provided that you delay distribution until the expiration of the period of the notices (at least two months) you will not be liable for later claims. If you have not protected yourself and are compelled to pay a debt personally you can seek an indemnity from the beneficiaries if you were not aware of the debt when you distributed the estate. You may also seek an indemnity if the debt was a contingent one, even if you did know of it.

Note that if you are an executor you can give notice under Section 27 before obtaining the grant. This is because you derive your authority from the will. If you are an administrator you cannot give notice until you have obtained Letters of Administration. This is because you derive your powers only from the grant.

11.10.6   The liability of a recipient of assets

A creditor or beneficiary has a personal claim for a refund from the recipient of wrongfully distributed assets, but only to the extent that he has no remedy against you personally. The claim does not carry interest.

11.10.7   Family provision claims
(IPFDA 1975; MFPA 1984)

Where a person dies domiciled in England and Wales certain persons may make application to the Court within six months of the date of the grant for reasonable financial provision out of the net estate. The following are entitled to apply:

(1)   A wife or husband of the deceased; persons whose marriages are dissolved or annulled overseas now also have the right to apply.
(2)   A former wife or husband who has not remarried; note, however, that under the Matrimonial and Family Proceedings Act 1984 restrictions may be imposed in divorce proceedings on any future application by either spouse for provision.
(3)   A child of the deceased (including an illegitimate or adopted child).
(4)   Any other person who has been treated as a child of the family.
(5)   Any person whom the deceased was maintaining immediately before his death.

If the Court is satisfied that the deceased's will does not make reasonable financial provision for the applicant it may order suitable provision, which may take any of the following forms:

(1)   Periodical payments.
(2)   Lump sum.
(3)   Transfer of property.

(4)   Acquisition of property out of the estate.
(5)   Variation of any ante or post nuptial settlement.

If such a claim is made against the estate, it does not mean that the validity of the will itself is being questioned. The claimant is maintaining only that he or she is entitled to financial provision out of the estate. Thus a claim may also be made where the deceased died intestate or partially intestate.

Once such a claim has been made you should adopt an impartial position between the beneficiaries and the claimant. Your duty is to see that the interests of children are properly represented. At the same time you must provide information about the estate when required to do so. If there are minor children involved any arrangement in settlement must be referred to the Court. Otherwise a compromise can be confirmed by deed without the necessity for Court proceedings.

Once you have been put on notice of a potential claim you cannot distribute the estate until it is settled. This is because you cannot be sure that the dispositions under the will will not be altered or varied.

11.10.8   The insolvent estate
(AEA 1925 S34)

If the assets of the estate are insufficient to meet all the liabilities then the estate is insolvent. If this is the case then debts must be paid in the following order, whether or not the estate is administered through the Court:

(1)   Funeral, testamentary and administration expenses.
(2)   Specially preferred debts, eg, money due to a Friendly Society or to a Savings Bank from its officer.
(3)   Preferred debts, eg, rates and taxes, and contributions payable by the deceased under the National Insurance Acts.
(4)   Ordinary debts.
(5)   Deferred debts, eg, a business loan by one spouse to another.

This order cannot be varied by will. The same rules apply in the case of an insolvent estate as in bankruptcy, particularly those with regard to secured creditors.

You need not continue with the administration of an insolvent estate if you do not wish to do so. You may apply to the Court for an administration order. Alternatively, any beneficiary or creditor may take proceedings to administer such an estate.

If you do continue to administer an insolvent estate you should take particular care to ensure that you do not become personally liable. If you pay a debt of a lower degree with full knowledge of the existence of a debt of a higher degree you could be held personally liable to make good the deficit. However, you will not be liable if you pay a debt in full in good faith without knowledge of the existence of creditors of equal degree and with no reason to believe that the estate is insolvent.

The rule is that if you are not certain whether the estate is going to be solvent or not you should only pay priority debts in full, ie, testamentary and administration expenses. Once the resources of the estate are fully known you will then be in a position to pay those debts of a lower priority which qualify.

If a bankruptcy order was made before the death of the deceased (so that the estate is being administered in bankruptcy) or if an insolvent administration order has been made subsequent to the date of death the estate must be administered by an authorised insolvency practitioner.

11.11   Distributing the estate

11.11.1   Paying legacies
(AEA 1925 S44)

A vested legacy (10.10.1) is normally payable one year from death, but there is nothing to prevent you paying such a legacy during this year if you consider it safe to do so. However, a legatee cannot require you to pay his legacy before the end of the year.

A contingent legacy (10.10.2) is payable at the time when the contingency occurs. In either case, interest at the rate of 6% per annum begins to run from the time when the legacy is payable.

Debts are paid in priority to legacies. If there are insufficient assets to pay all the debts and the legacies in full then specific legacies (such as gifts of personal chattels) must be dealt with first. Thereafter cash legacies diminish rateably according to their value — this is known as abatement. If there are a number of debts and it is uncertain whether there is likely to be any residue you should pay legacies with caution.

If you overpay a beneficiary you have no right of recovery unless you can show that you made the payment without knowledge of a subsequent claim against the estate.

Specific legacies (10.9) carry with them any income accrued since the testator's death. If there is a specific gift of land in the will the beneficiary will have to pay any administrative costs which may accrue. This would also be the case if there is a specific gift of valuables which have to be stored in a secure place such as a safe deposit.

If the will includes a legacy to a minor you will probably be given authority to pay the money to the child's parent or guardian and to get a good discharge for doing so. If you have no such authority it will be necessary for the legacy to be held for the child until he reaches 18, since he cannot give a valid receipt for it. You may, if you wish, appoint separate trustees of the legacy and you would then have no further responsibility for it. If a legacy to a child is contingent on his attaining a specific age you will have to set aside a fund from which the legacy can be paid when the contingency is satisfied. Once the administration of the estate has been completed it will be possible for new trustees of the legacy to be appointed.

11.11.2 Distribution on intestacy
(AEA 1925; IEA 1952; FPA 1966)

All the property of a person who dies intestate is held by his administrators upon trust for sale. There is power to postpone sale and the administrators may appropriate property in kind in satisfaction of a beneficiary's share. The rules for distributing an estate on an intestacy are as follows:

(1) *Where the deceased left a widow or widower and surviving children*
As widow or widower you take all the personal effects absolutely and a statutory legacy of £75,000. In addition you are entitled to the income for life from one half of the rest of the estate, which on your death reverts to your children. The other half of the residue passes to your children on what is known as the 'statutory trusts' (11.11.4). 'Children' includes illegitimate or adopted children.

(2) *Where the deceased left a widow or widower and no surviving children but also left parents or brothers and sisters*
As widow or widower you take all the personal effects, a statutory legacy of £125,000 and one half of the rest of the

estate. The other half goes to the deceased's parents or, if they have not survived, to the deceased's brothers or sisters on the statutory trusts (11.11.4).

(3)   *Where the deceased left a widow or widower but no children, no parents and no brothers or sisters*
As widow or widower you take the whole estate absolutely.

It follows that other more distant relatives only take an interest in the event of the deceased not being survived by a husband or wife, children, parents or brothers or sisters.

The terms of distribution provided for under the intestacy rules may be varied after death in the same way as the terms of a will (10.24).

11.11.3   The surviving spouse's rights
(AEA 1925 S47)

Capitalisation of a life interest
As surviving spouse you have the right to demand a capital sum in lieu of your life interest. You must exercise your right within 12 months of the date of the grant. The amount of the lump sum payable must be calculated in accordance with rules laid down by statute. If all the children are over 18 and of full capacity, agreement may be reached as to the capital sum to be distributed without the necessity for a calculation.

The family home
If you were living in the family home at the date of death and the house was owned by the deceased you have the right to demand that the house be appropriated towards all or part of any absolute interest you may have under the intestacy. Election to this effect must be made within 12 months of the grant. You do not have this right if the deceased's interest was a tenancy which would expire or could by notice be terminated within two years from death. The value at which appropriation takes effect is the value at the date of appropriation, not the value at the date of death.

11.11.4   The statutory trusts
(AEA 1925 S47(1); FLRA 1969 S3(2))

Where property passes on an intestacy to children, brothers or sisters or uncles or aunts it is held on the statutory trusts. This means that the property is held in trust in equal shares for those members of the class who attain 18 or marry before then. If any member dies before the deceased, leaving children living at the date of his or her death, those children take the share which their parent would have taken had he or she survived (provided they in turn attain 18 or marry).

11.11.5 Partial intestacy
(AEA 1925 S49)

If the deceased left a will but it only disposes of part of his property then a partial intestacy arises. If this is the case, any benefit which you receive as surviving spouse under the will must be brought into account against the statutory legacy of £75,000 or £125,000 as the case may be. Similarly, any gifts by will to children must be brought into account against their share.

11.11.6 Vesting assets in beneficiaries
(AEA 1925 S36)

Having settled the liabilities of the estate you are now in a position to distribute it by transferring property into the names of the beneficiaries. If the majority of actual and prospective liabilities are ascertained early in the course of administration interim distributions may be made. These will be shown in the administration accounts which set out the assets and liabilities of the estate and the transactions which have taken place since the grant was received.

Property is vested in a beneficiary by means of an assent. In the case of personalty, ie, cash or movable property, an assent can generally be informal. Stocks and shares are transferred by means of a standard share transfer form. A legal estate in land will not pass out of your hands as personal representative unless you execute a written assent in favour of a beneficiary. The assent must be signed by you and name the person in whose favour it is given. The significance of an assent is that until the property is transferred it remains at your disposal for administration purposes. You continue to be responsible for its security. Once the transfer has taken place the property belongs in law to the beneficiary and you are no longer responsible for it. You may, however, retain out of a legacy or a share of residue a debt due to the estate from the beneficiary.

11.11.7 Accounts

If the estate is relatively small, it is advisable to prepare a simple administration and distribution account on a single sheet of paper. If you are dealing with a complex estate you may wish to instruct accountants to prepare full and comprehensive accounts.

You are entitled to ask beneficiaries to approve the accounts. Until approval is received you may withhold final distribution of the residuary estate since you cannot be sure that there will be no further administration expenses.

If it is subsequently alleged that a loss to the estate has been caused by neglect or mistake on your part an administration action may follow. You would then be entitled to an indemnity from the estate in respect of proper expenses incurred in connection with such an action. These would fall to be included in the estate's administration expenses.

11.11.8   Discharge and trusteeship

Once the inheritance tax liability of the estate has been finalised you may apply for a certificate of discharge from the Capital Taxes Office. The certificate in Form 30, known as 'clearance', discharges you from any further claims for inheritance tax in respect of those assets which you have disclosed in the Inland Revenue Account and any subsequent Corrective Account. You are not, of course, covered by this certificate in respect of assets which come to light at a later stage. Usually, the date of the clearance certificate is taken as the date on which administration ceases. If a trust has been created by the will or if property is to be administered for a minor the duties of the trustees commence on this date.

The position of personal representatives is very similar to that of trustees and their rights and duties are, except where a contrary intention appears, governed by the same statute law. There are some important differences, however, as follows:

(1)   The primary function of personal representatives is to distribute the estate, while that of trustees is to hold it.

(2)   The authority of trustees is always joint, whereas that of personal representatives is joint and several (12.8.1) over personal property and joint in respect of land. Thus one of several personal representatives may validly dispose of personal property, but not land.

(3)   The provisions of the Trustee Act 1925 with regard to the retirement and appointment of new trustees do not apply to personal representatives (12.4.8).

(4)   The period of limitation in respect of actions against personal representatives by beneficiaries is 12 years where claims to the personal estate of a deceased person are concerned. The period in respect of actions against trustees is six years.

12 The legal aspects of trusts

12.1 What is a trust?

A trust is the relationship that is created when a person ('the settlor') transfers the legal ownership of assets ('the trust fund') to trustees, either for the benefit of third parties ('the beneficiaries') or for the benefit of some object, eg charity. The benefit of the trust assets is enjoyed by the beneficiaries or the charity, not the settlor or the trustees, although one of the beneficiaries may be the settlor himself or a trustee. Another word for a trust is a settlement.

A trust may be created by a settlor during his lifetime (a trust *'inter vivos'*) or incorporated in a will, in which case it will take effect only when the testator dies.

A trust (other than a charitable trust (12.2.7)) is void if under its terms trustees are bound to hold property beyond what is called 'the perpetuity period', usually 80 years. Income may be accumulated during the first 21 years but normally should be paid to the beneficiaries after that period has expired.

12.2 Types of trusts

Trusts may be classified according to the nature of the duties undertaken by the trustees, according to their purpose or according to the way in which they have been created. The following is merely a brief outline of the main types of trust.

12.2.1 'Strict' or fixed-interest trusts

In a strict trust one or more beneficiaries are entitled as of right to the income from the trust fund during their lifetime. These beneficiaries are said to enjoy a life interest in the trust fund and are referred to as life tenants. After their death the capital passes to some other person or persons (called 'the remainderman') or to charity. Such persons or bodies are said to have a 'reversionary interest' in the trust fund. The trustees are often given power to distribute all or part of the capital of the trust fund to the life tenant.

12.2.2   Discretionary trusts

In a discretionary trust the trustees are given power to distribute both capital and income amongst a class of beneficiaries as they, in their sole discretion, think fit. A trust period is usually defined, at the end of which there is an ultimate destination for capital or income not distributed. The trustees are therefore given a far greater element of judgement and initiative than in a strict trust. They also have the added responsibility of considering the competing interests of the members of the specified class.

12.2.3   The 'flexible trust'

Some discretionary trusts have tax disadvantages but it is still possible to give your trustees freedom of action (without the trust being a pure discretionary trust) by giving them a power to appoint the trust property amongst a wide class of beneficiaries. The ultimate beneficiaries enjoy an immediate interest in possession (8.3.3) in the trust property and take to the extent that the trustees do not use their power of appointment. This type of trust is often called a 'Flexible Trust' (14.4.5).

12.2.4   Protective trusts
(TA 1925 S33)

This type of trust is designed to protect a beneficiary from his own irresponsibility or the consequences of his own financial mismanagement. The terms of a protective trust are governed by statute law, although they may be modified by the terms of the trust deed itself. As a general rule, such trusts last for the life of a principal beneficiary until a particular event occurs which has the effect of depriving this beneficiary of his right to receive the income. Such a determining event may be the bankruptcy of the beneficiary or his conviction for a criminal offence or if he gives up his right to part of the income. Whether the beneficiary's interest has been terminated by the events which have happened is a question of construction of the relevant clause in the trust deed.

If the Court is satisfied that the principal beneficiary has forfeited his right to the income a discretionary trust will be held to arise automatically for the benefit of a class of beneficiaries usually comprising the principal beneficiary, his or her spouse and their children.

12.2.5 Accumulation and maintenance trusts

These trusts are intended for the benefit of a class of minors and are particularly useful as a way of providing for your children or grandchildren. The trust fund can be used for the maintenance, education or benefit of your children but they do not have to be entitled to a share of the income until they are 25. Entitlement to the capital may be deferred to a later age. The advantages of this arrangement are more fully set out at 10.18.2.

12.2.6 Implied, resulting and constructive trusts

In some circumstances, where there is no trust as such, the law demands that a person becomes a trustee, and when this occurs, implied, resulting or constructive trusts are created.

Implied and resulting trusts

The law will imply a trust where it considers that it was intended by the parties to a particular transaction. As an example, where two persons agree to make wills in a certain form and put this into effect, on the death of the first person, the survivor, if he accepts the benefits given to him under the deceased's will, is bound by an implied trust to give effect to their agreement.

Nearly all implied trusts are also resulting trusts in that the beneficial interest goes back or 'results' to the settlor. The most common examples are where trusts fail or are only partially achieved in which case the trust property, or the surplus reverts to the settlor.

Another example of an implied and resulting trust is where a purchaser buys property in the name of another. The nominal purchaser is regarded as holding the property on trust for the true purchaser. However if the true purchaser is the father, husband or fiance of the nominal purchaser the presumption is that the purchase in the other's name was intended to be a gift.

Constructive trusts

These arise independently of any express or presumed intention of the parties normally where there has been misconduct on the part of an existing trustee, or interference by an outsider with trust property. Some examples are:

(1)   A trustee who makes a profit from his trust becomes a

constructive trustee of the benefit received for his beneficiaries (12.8.2).

(2)   If a stranger acquires trust property, knowing (or later discovering) its transfer to be in breach of trust, he becomes a constructive trustee of that property for the existing beneficiaries. However, a bona fide purchaser will not become a constructive trustee even if he discovers the true nature of his property.

(3)   A vendor of land becomes a constructive trustee of the property for the purchaser from the date of exchange of contracts.

12.2.7   Charitable trusts

A trust can only be charitable if it is for certain specified purposes:

(1)   the relief of poverty,
(2)   the promotion of education,
(3)   the promotion of religion, or for
(4)   other purposes of benefit to the community.

Trusts for the promotion of education or religion must, in order to be charitable trusts, show an element of public benefit.

A trust is not charitable unless the objects are exclusively charitable, ie, the words 'for benevolent purposes' or 'charitable or benevolent purposes' will not do. Such phrases are too vague to imply an exclusively charitable trust.

Charitable trusts have numerous advantages, the principal ones being:

(1)   A charitable trust will not fail because the trust objects are uncertain, provided it is clear that the settlor intended the property to go to charity exclusively. (For a non-charitable trust to be valid the interest to be taken by the beneficiaries must be certain).

(2)   Charitable trusts enjoy freedom from income tax, investment income surcharge and CGT, provided that any profits from trade or any capital gains are applied solely for charitable purposes.

(3)   Inheritance tax does not apply to gifts to charities.
(4)   Charities obtain rate relief on land held by them.
(5)   The perpetuity period (12.1) does not apply to charitable trusts

so that the objects of a charity may last indefinitely without affecting its validity.

Charitable trusts are administered and supervised by the Charities Commission. In particular, the Commissioners maintain a register of charities and all charities with a permanent endowment are required to register. Promoters of new charities must submit details of their proposed objects for approval to the Charity Commissioners.

12.3 Setting up a trust

A trust may be created by anyone over the age of 18 with full capacity to manage his or her affairs. A minor can make a valid trust but this is voidable by him when he comes of age.

You may set up a trust either by means of a formal declaration of trust or by transferring property to your trustees.

Thus, for a trust to be validly constituted, you must ensure that not only are the required formalities with regard to writing or evidence in writing satisfied but that the trust property itself has been vested in the trustees.

12.3.1 The legal formalities
(LPA 1925 S53)

No particular form of documentation is required for a declaration of trust *inter vivos* of cash, stocks and shares and other movable assets. Such a trust may be declared orally or even inferred from conduct. Any words expressing the settlor's intention are sufficient, although, as a general rule, no conditions must attach to them. For such a trust to be completely constituted, however, the property must be transferred into the names of the trustees.

In general, in order to pass legal ownership to the trustees the forms of legal documentation necessary to transfer the particular type of property settled must be used. You will therefore have to sign a conveyance or transfer if freehold land is to be put into the trust, leasehold land must be assigned by deed and if stocks and shares are to be put into trust then the standard form of transfer must be signed and forwarded for registration.

A declaration of trust of land or of any interest in land must be in writing and must be signed by the settlor himself. Such writing need not take any particular form and a letter or memorandum is sufficient, provided all the requisite terms of the trust are set out.

A declaration of trust of any property, whether it be cash, shares or land, that is to come into existence on the donor's death must be set out in a will which complies with the formalities for execution (10.3).

A beneficiary under an existing trust may set up a further trust of his beneficial interest for the benefit of someone else. Such a trust must be in writing (not merely evidenced by writing) and must be signed by the person creating it or by his agent. If these requisites are not complied with the trust will be void.

A completely constituted trust can be enforced by any beneficiary whether or not he has given anything of value in return for the benefits he receives under the trust. In practice, most beneficiaries are 'volunteers' in the sense that they have not provided any value in return for their beneficial interests. If a beneficiary has given value for his interest it does not matter whether the trust is completely constituted. He can enforce the trust. If a trust is incompletely constituted it cannot be enforced by a volunteer.

In general, an ineffectual attempt to transfer property to trustees will not be construed as a declaration of trust. However, if you are able to show that you have done everything reasonably within your power to transfer ownership to trustees the trust will be effective. This will be the case even if the trustees still have to do something further to perfect their own legal title.

12.3.2   The costs

If you are planning to set up a trust you should be aware that the legal fees and disbursements incurred are your responsibility as settlor. You may, however, expressly authorise the trustees to take them out of the trust fund once the trust has been set up.

Besides solicitors' costs, stamp duty, CGT and inheritance tax may also be payable. You are primarily responsible for tax liabilities but if you do not pay them the Revenue may call upon the trustees to do so. Your trustees may therefore ask for confirmation that all the tax liabilities arising on the creation of the trust have been assessed and paid before they accept the trusts.

12.4 Trustees

12.4.1 Who may act?

Anyone over 18 years of age may act as a trustee. The appointment of a minor as trustee is void but another person can be appointed to act instead. A minor may, however, hold property on an implied, resulting or constructive trust.

12.4.2 Trust corporations

Certain companies may act either as a sole or a co-trustee. They are known as trust corporations, and are usually subsidiary companies of banks or insurance companies, charging a fee for their services. They must be authorised to act as trustee and apart from companies incorporated by special Act or Royal Charter, they must have very substantial issued share capital. This of course means that in practice only the larger companies can act in this capacity, thus offering an effective guarantee that, in the event of any improper conduct, the corporation will be of sufficient substance to reimburse the beneficiaries for any loss.

The position of a trust corporation is largely the same as that of private trustees, except that whereas two trustees must act together in transactions involving land which forms part of the trust fund, a trust corporation can act on its own.

The conditions under which a bank or insurance company will accept trusteeship are published in booklets available from them and always include the requirement that a charging clause (ensuring payment to the corporation for its services) be included in the will or trust deed.

12.4.3 The Public Trustee
(PTA 1906)

The Public Trustee is a trust corporation and was established by statute at the beginning of this century. The Public Trustee himself is appointed by the Lord Chancellor.

The Public Trustee is authorised to charge for acting as executor, administrator or trustee. He cannot act for a charitable trust, although he has a discretion as to whether to accept any other particular trusteeship but he may not refuse to undertake any work merely because the value involved is too low. He may act as a Custodian Trustee (below).

Generally, the Public Trustee does not have any particular status over and above ordinary trustees. He is authorised to obtain professional advice particularly on legal matters and his powers to manage a business which forms part of a trust are limited.

12.4.4   Custodian Trustees
(S4 PTA 1906)

The office of Custodian Trustee was also created by statute law. The Public Trustee, other trust corporations and various other bodies may act as Custodian Trustees. The settlor himself may appoint a Custodian Trustee or such an appointment may be made by order of the Court.

If a Custodian Trustee does act, the exercise of the administration of the trust is placed in the hands of managing trustees. The trust property is transferred into the name of the Custodian Trustee who has custody of all securities and documents of title.

The main advantage of appointing a Custodian Trustee is that changes in the managing trustees can take place without the need to transfer the trust property into the names of the new trustees. The Custodian Trustee arrangement has never been popular. It does however form the basis of many pension funds where a corporate trustee holds the trust fund while individual trustees manage the fund itself.

12.4.5   Number

If the trust fund consists entirely of assets other than freehold or leasehold land (cash or stocks and shares are the most common) only one trustee is necessary although it is usually desirable to appoint at least two. There is no maximum to the number that may be appointed.

If the trust fund comprises or includes land at least two trustees must be appointed, unless a trust corporation is acting as sole trustee. Otherwise a sole trustee cannot give a valid receipt for the proceeds of sale of property, even if so authorised by the trust instrument. The number of trustees must not exceed four and if more than four are appointed only the first four able and willing to act may do so. This restriction does not apply to charitable trustees.

12.4.6   Accepting trusteeship

If you are setting up a trust you will need to inform your prospective trustees of your intentions and of the terms of the intended trust. If one of your trustees is a professional person he will probably wish to see a copy of the draft trust deed. A prospective trustee would wish to ensure that the proposed trusts are capable of implementation and that the wording of the deed is clear and unambiguous.

No one can be compelled to act as trustee if he does not wish to do so. Acceptance is usually evidenced by the trustee signing the trust deed. A trustee need not accept the office and may disclaim before he does any act which shows that he has assumed the office. Disclaimer of office may be in any form. It may be inferred from a trustee's conduct, eg, by not acting as trustee for a long period. If a trustee does not expressly accept the trust acceptance may be presumed by his subsequent conduct and even small acts may be construed as acceptance.

12.4.7   The mechanics of appointment and retirement

As settlor, you usually appoint the original trustees on creation of the trust. Once the trust is in existence you cannot appoint new trustees unless you have reserved such a power for yourself in the trust deed. Subsequent trustees may be appointed under powers given by the trust deed, by statute law or, in certain circumstances, by the Court. In the case of charitable trusts the Charity Commissioners have the power to appoint new trustees if the circumstances warrant it.

12.4.8   Appointment under the statutory power
(TA 1925 Ss36 & 37)

Statute law authorises the appointment of a new trustee in a number of circumstances:
(1)   on the death of a trustee;
(2)   on the retirement of a trustee;
(3)   if a trustee refuses to act or is unfit or incapable of acting; or
(4)   if a trusteee remains out of the country for more than 12 months (in which case he can be removed against his wishes).

The appointment may be made by:
(1)   the persons nominated in the will or trust instrument or, if none,
(2)   the surviving or continuing trustees or, if none,
(3)   the personal representatives of the last surviving or continuing trustee; or

(4)   if none of these methods is possible, the Court.

There is also power to appoint an additional trustee provided that a trust corporation is not acting and the number of trustees is not increased above four. Separate trustees up to a maximum of four may be appointed of any part of the trust property to be held on trusts separate from those of the rest of the trust property.

12.4.9   Appointment by the Court
(TA 1925 S41)

The Court may appoint a new or additional trustee on the application of a trustee or beneficiary if it would be difficult to do so by any other method. The Court does not have power to appoint a new trustee against the wishes of a sole trustee who intends to exercise his statutory power of appointment. Neither will the Court normally interfere if a trustee has been appointed under the statutory power, even though it feels that some other appointment may have been more suitable.

12.4.10   Retirement
(TA 1925 S39)

Once accepted, trusteeship cannot be disclaimed. A trustee may retire by deed provided the following conditions are fulfilled:

(1)   a trust corporation or at least two individual trustees should remain to carry out the terms of the trust;
(2)   the continuing trustees and the person entitled to appoint new trustees consent; and
(3)   the retiring trustee has done everything necessary to vest the trust property in any new trustee and the continuing trustees.

Usually the retiring trustee and the continuing trustees are made parties to the deed of retirement. A declaration vesting the trust property in a new trustee appointed by the same deed may be included but is not strictly necessary. Trust assets may, however, have to be transferred into the name of the new trustee (12.5.2).

A retiring trustee would normally wish to ensure that all debts incurred prior to his retirement are settled before it becomes effective. He may seek an indemnity from the continuing trustees but is only entitled to one for costs and expenses properly incurred. A former trustee cannot be held liable for taxation or other liabilities which have been incurred after his retirement.

12.4.11   Removal of trustees
(TA 1925 S36)

As settlor it is possible for you to give yourself a power to remove trustees in the trust deed. Since such a provision gives the settlor considerable control over the trust, it may be strictly construed by the Court.

A trustee may be removed by the Court in the following circumstances:

(1)   if he remains out of the country for more than 12 months;
(2)   if he refuses to act;
(3)   if he is unfit to act; or
(4)   if he is incapable of acting.

In addition, the Court has a general power to remove a trustee and appoint a new one if the circumstances warrant it.

12.4.12   Remuneration and indemnity
(TA 1925 S30)

A trustee is not entitled to any remuneration for his duties unless such a power is given in the trust instrument. On the whole, such clauses are strictly construed by the Courts.

If a professional person is acting as trustee it is usual to include a professional charging clause. Such charges must be reasonable. A power to charge must be widely drawn if a professional person is to be permitted to charge for services that do not require professional expertise.

Trustees may come to a separate agreement with the beneficiaries on the question of payment, provided the latter are all of full age and absolutely entitled to the trust fund. The Court may authorise remuneration of trustees in special circumstances where the trust has become particularly difficult to administer.

If a trust corporation is appointed (12.4.2), a power to charge is usually given in the trust deed. The Public Trustee (12.4.3) and a Custodian Trustee (12.4.4) may also charge.

Trustees may, however, reimburse themselves in respect of their out of pocket expenses from the trust fund. Reimbursement comes primarily from the capital of the trust fund but is a charge on all of the trust property, both capital and income.

12.5   The duties and powers of trustees

12.5.1   The distinction between duties, powers and discretions

A trustee's duty obliges him to do something. A trustee's power gives him the authority to do something. A trustee's discretion requires him to exercise his judgement and initiative in relation to a specific power.

Trustees have general duties which derive from trust law. These are principally to comply with the terms of the trust and to act in the best interests of the beneficiaries. They also have specific duties which derive both from trust law and from the trust deed. Their powers and discretions are set out only in the trust deed.

12.5.2   Securing control over the trust fund
(TA 1925 S40)

Trustees have a duty to ensure that they have full control over the trust assets by having them transferred into their names as soon as possible. However, a deed of appointment of new trustees is deemed to include a vesting declaration whereby the trust property is automatically placed in the names of the new trustees. Nevertheless, in the case of the following forms of property such an implied vesting declaration will not operate:

(1)   mortgages of land;
(2)   stocks and shares (which should be transferred and re-registered); and
(3)   leasehold property (where a transfer into the names of new trustees would be a breach of the covenant against assignment in the lease).

On taking up his appointment a trustee should familiarise himself with the terms of the trust and the nature and extent of the trust property. If, in the course of his enquiries, he discovers that a breach of trust has been committed in the past it is his duty to correct the situation. An examination of the trust accounts should reveal the changes which have taken place in the trust assets. If accounts are not available a new trustee will have to study the trust's documents in order to satisfy himself as to its history.

12.5.3 Accounts
(TA 1925 S22)

Trustees are under a duty to keep accounts and produce them to any beneficiary when required to do so. Trust accounts should be audited by an independent accountant not more than once every three years unless the nature of the trust necessitates a more frequent audit.

Trustees must provide beneficiaries with reasonable information as to the manner in which they have dealt with the trust property. Beneficiaries should be given an opportunity to inspect title deeds and any other documents relating to the trust fund.

12.5.4 Delegation
(TA 1925 Ss23 & 30)

Where a number of trustees are appointed the trust assets should be placed under the joint control of all the trustees. However, they are sometimes given power under the trust deed to act by a majority. The trust deed may authorise one trustee to have sole control of certain assets and in certain circumstances during the course of administration (such as the signing of trust tax returns) only one trustee need act. As a general rule, however, trustees have a duty to act jointly and they should keep records in the form of minutes or resolutions of the joint decisions which they have taken.

Trustees have a duty to act personally. They are expected to take basic decisions themselves and to administer the trust fund themselves.

The trust instrument may, however, include an express power of delegation. Most modern trust deeds include a power to delegate investment management and to place investments in the names of nominees.

Trustees may employ the services of professional agents, such as solicitors and accountants, to deal with routine administration of the trust. In the absence of an express authority in the trust deed, agents may only carry out the decisions of the trustees. They cannot take decisions themselves.

Trustees are not liable for the negligence of an agent provided he was employed in good faith. They are also not liable for any loss to the trust estate unless this was caused through their own 'wilful default'.

Nevertheless, trustees should exercise care over the choice of their agents and should supervise them where necessary. Professional trustees, in particular, have a higher duty of care. Trustees should not allow funds to be left in the hands of an agent for longer than is necessary. They will be accountable if an agent with whom trust money or securities are deposited defaults as a result of their own negligence or neglect.

12.5.5   Special delegation
(TA 1925 S25; PAA 1971 S9 & EPAA 1985)

A trustee may, by Power of Attorney, delegate for a maximum period of 12 months all his powers and duties as trustee. The donee of the Power of Attorney may be a trust corporation but not the donor's only other co-trustee. Within seven days of the appointment the donor must give written notice to the persons having power to appoint new trustees and to the other trustees. The donor of the power is liable for the acts and defaults of the donee as if they were his own.

The Enduring Powers of Attorney Act 1985 provides that an enduring power of attorney which complies with the requirements of the Act is not revoked by the subsequent mental incapacity of the donor. The attorney must register the power with the Court of Protection once the donor has become incapable. The Act provides that an enduring power of attorney does cover the exercise of the donor's functions as trustee but in practical terms the circumstances in which such delegation would be possible may be very limited. In particular, the power of attorney is likely to be useless after the donor's incapacity because he can be removed as a trustee (12.4.11). You should seek your solicitor's advice if you are considering delegating your functions as trustee by enduring power of attorney.

12.5.6   Investment of trust funds

Trustees have a duty to invest the trust fund. They may only invest the trust property in those investments which are authorised by the terms of the trust deed or by law.

In most modern trusts very wide powers of investment are given to the trustees. These are called 'beneficial owner' powers since they give trustees the same powers of investment as those which a person who beneficially owned the property might have. As trustees cannot invest in land unless they are specifically authorised to do so, the investment clause should include power to buy land and buildings and to improve them. It is also useful to give trustees power to invest in foreign assets.

Trustees are bound to exercise a higher standard of care in relation to the investment of trust funds. They should seek professional advice where necessary. Although they may appoint investment managers (if authorised by the trust deed) they must continue to control investment policy and monitor its progress by establishing effective reporting procedures.

- *If the trust deed does give trustees power to invest in land, the investment must yield income. For example, a power to invest in land does not allow trustees to purchase a house for a beneficiary to live in. This is because part of the purchase price is paid for vacant possession and is not laid out in an income-producing asset. Therefore, it is useful to include a power both to invest in non-income-producing assets and for beneficiaries to occupy land or buildings rent-free.*

12.5.7 Trustee Investments Act 1961

This Act applies to all trusts (including those arising under a will or on an intestacy) which grant investment powers less than those conferred by the Act itself. Thus the powers contained in the Act are in addition to the powers set out in the trust deed. The trust deed may narrow or broaden the scope of the Act and it is usual for the latter to be done. The application of the Act has therefore become somewhat limited.

The Act lays down general guidelines on the appropriateness and diversification of investments (S6). These principles are intended to apply to all trusts regardless of whether the other provisions of the Act are applicable to them or not.

Trustees are under a duty to have regard for the need to diversify the investments of the trust 'insofar as is appropriate to the circumstances of the trust'. The suitability of an investment to the trust itself, rather than merely for its own sake, is emphasised.

When considering an investment trustees must have regard to the particular requirements of the beneficiaries. Thus if the trust is a fixed-interest trust the rival claims of the life-tenant and the person ultimately entitled to capital (the remainderman, 12.2.1) have to be considered. Trustees must ensure that they maintain a balance between capital growth and possible loss of income which would be to the detriment of the life-tenant.

12.5.8 Mortgages
(TA 1925 S8)

Trustees may lend money on mortgage subject to the following conditions:

(1) the security mortgaged must be either freehold property or leasehold property where the lease has not less than 60 years to run;

(2) the loan must not exceed two-thirds of the value of the property; and

(3) the property must be valued by a surveyor believed to be competent by the trustees.

Provided that the surveyor states the value and advises the loan to be made and the above conditions are complied with, the trustees cannot be held liable on the grounds that they have lent too much. If trustees do lend too much on a security which is authorised (as above) they will be liable only for the excess over the proper amount. If the security is unauthorised they will be liable for the whole loss.

12.6   Maintenance and advancement

12.6.1   Maintenance out of income
(TA 1925 S31)

Where property is held by trustees in trust for any person who is a minor (or is under a disability) then subject to any prior interests in the property, the trustees can use any part of the income towards that person's maintenance, education or benefit during his or her minority. The statutory power applies regardless of whether the interest is dependent on the beneficiary attaining a particular age or on the happening of a particular event, but it must carry the right to intermediate income.

The power of maintenance may be expressly excluded or varied in the trust deed or may not apply at all if a contrary intention is shown. If a minor's interest is contingent on his attaining the age of majority, and there is a direction that the income be accumulated, then there is no power to maintain.

If an interest is contingent on attaining a greater age than that of majority (ie, more than 18 years of age) and it does carry the right to intermediate income then the trustees may maintain the beneficiary out of income during his minority. However, once he attains 18 he must be paid the income until he either attains a vested interest and becomes entitled to capital or he dies.

Where there is surplus income after the power has been exercised this is added to capital and invested. However, at any time during a beneficiary's minority the trustees may use such accumulations as income.

12.6.2 Advancement of capital
(TA 1925 S32)

Trustees have the power to use the capital of the trust fund for the 'advancement or benefit' of both infant and adult beneficiaries. Advancement means helping a beneficiary to establish himself at an early stage in his life or his career. It does not cover merely casual payments to him or paying his debts.

Benefit has a wide meaning and covers a payment to a parent or guardian on behalf of a beneficiary as well as a payment direct to the beneficiary himself. It may also cover a loan to set up a beneficiary's husband or wife in business or payments to a beneficiary's dependants who are in financial need. Most trust deeds specify that the receipt of a beneficiary's parent or guardian will be a good discharge to the trustees.

The power applies even though the beneficiary's interest may be dependent on the happening of a particular event and despite the fact that the size of his or her share may be reduced by an increase in the class of beneficiaries of which he or she is a member. The statutory power may be varied or excluded by an express provision for advancement given in the trust instrument. Many modern trust deeds expressly extend the scope of the power. It may also be excluded by implication if a power has been granted to accumulate the income of capital during the settlor's lifetime.

There are a number of limits on the statutory power, as follows:

(1) the maximum that can be advanced is one half of the beneficiary's vested or presumed share;
(2) the owners of prior interests in the property must be alive, of full age and give their written consent; and

(3)   if the beneficiary becomes absolutely entitled to trust property at any time after an advance of capital has been made, the advance already received must be accounted for as part of his or her total share.

12.6.3   The effect of the power

The effect of the exercise of the power in most cases is that money is taken out of the trust fund and handed to the beneficiary. However, it is sometimes possible for the power to be exercised so as to create new trusts quite independent of the original trust. The original trustees may continue as trustees of the new trust or they may retire in favour of new trustees. Such an appointment may however have capital gains tax consequences (5.2.4).

12.7   Insurance
(TA 1925 S19)

Trustees may insure up to three-quarters of the value of the property insured. Premiums are payable out of the income of the property insured or of the other property held on the same trusts.

Trustees may not insure trust property for its full value unless specifically authorised to do so by the trust deed.

12.8   Breach of trust

Trustees must act impartially on behalf of the beneficiaries in accordance with the trust deed. Their relationship with the beneficiaries is based on 'utmost good faith'. They must preserve the trust fund and act honestly and fairly at all times. If they do not do so they may find themselves under a personal liability to make good any loss suffered.

12.8.1   Liability for acts of co-trustees

A trustee is personally liable for any breach of trust he commits. He is not liable for breaches by his co-trustees unless they acted with his knowledge in which case he may be liable as well.

Since trustees are under a duty to act jointly it follows that they are jointly and severally liable for a breach of trust. This means that if two or more trustees are liable each may be sued for the whole loss but if one trustee pays more than his share he can seek a contribution from the others since all trustees must bear liability for the breach in equal shares in the absence of any contrary agreement between themselves.

Trustees should ensure that the trust property is placed under the control of all of them. In particular, property should not be left in the sole control of one trustee for an unreasonable period of time. If this does happen and the trustee defaults all the trustees will be liable for any loss suffered.

A retiring trustee remains liable for breaches of trust committed while he was a trustee. He is not liable for a breach committed after his retirement unless he retired in order that a breach be committed.

12.8.2 Making a profit from the trust

A trustee must not take advantage of his position and his knowledge of the trust fund in order to obtain an advantage or profit for himself. If he does acquire a profit he is accountable as a constructive trustee (12.9) to the beneficiaries.

If a trustee uses the trust assets in a commercial venture or in his own business he is personally liable for any losses suffered. Any gain accrues to the beneficiaries.

A trustee must act with prudence. Trust assets should not be the subject of reckless speculation in land or shares.

12.8.3 Purchase of the trust property

If a trustee buys the trust property for himself the transaction may be set aside by the beneficiaries. It makes no difference that the sale was fair and honest and that a fair price was obtained. The trust deed may however authorise such a transaction.

A trustee cannot retire expressly in order to purchase trust property. If he does so the transaction is voidable unless it is shown that his retirement took place several years before the date of the transaction.

A sale by a trustee of trust property which he has purchased can be adopted by the beneficiaries. The trustee may be required to account for the profit he has made. If there has been no sale the Court may order the property to be offered for resale. If a greater price is offered than that paid by the trustee the sale to the trustee will be set aside.

In certain circumstances the Court may give permission for such a sale. Provided the beneficiaries do not object, the transaction will be valid.

12.8.4   Overpayment

If trustees by mistake overpay a beneficiary they are entitled to recover the excess by adjusting future payments. If the wrong person is paid the trustee is personally liable to the beneficiary entitled to the payment. He can however claim against the person wrongly paid.

It may happen that after the trust fund has been distributed a claim is made against it of which the trustees had no previous knowledge. They can then ask the beneficiaries to refund the property to the extent necessary to satisfy the claim.

12.8.5   Tracing

If by mistake trust property is handed to the wrong person then the beneficiary who is entitled to the property may try to trace his property to the recipient and reclaim it. The recipient, being a stranger to the trust, becomes a constructive trustee of the property he has received for the true beneficiary (12.2.6). The property does not become part of the recipient's estate.

12.8.6   Unauthorised investments

A trustee who makes unauthorised investments (12.5.6) may be required to sell them and make good any loss suffered or account for any profit made. It is open to the adult beneficiaries to adopt an unauthorised investment.

Trustees have a duty to invest the trust fund and are absolutely liable for failure to carry out this duty. Thus if trustees do not invest at all they will be liable for loss of profit.

If trustees do make authorised investments and a loss occurs because they retain these investments they will not be liable if they have acted honestly and with reasonable prudence in the exercise of their discretion. However trustees must obtain advice before making investments and they must seek advice from time to time on the continuing suitability of their investments (12.5.6).

12.8.7 Remedies of beneficiaries

If beneficiaries discover that a breach of trust has been committed they may bring proceedings against the trustees personally. The measure of liability is the loss caused to the trust. Beneficiaries may claim any profit made by the trustees. If there have been several breaches a trustee cannot set off a loss against any profit made. If a trustee is required to replace trust money interest is payable at a rate determined by the Court.

Beneficiaries may follow trust property into the hands of a recipient and recover it provided the recipient was aware that it was trust property, even if he gave value for it.

If a trustee in breach of trust is also a beneficiary his interest may be impounded to make good the breach as far as is necessary.

If a beneficiary has in any way consented to a breach of trust he cannot complain of this breach unless he was under some disability at the time. Other beneficiaries who have not so agreed may compel a trustee to make good the breach. In such a case the Court may grant the trustee an indemnity against the beneficiary who has instigated the breach.

An adult beneficiary who is aware of the facts may preclude himself from further action against a trustee by giving a formal release. A trustee is not however entitled to a formal release as of right on the termination of his duties.

12.8.8 Release by the Court
(TA 1925 S61)

The Court may, at its discretion, relieve a trustee from liability if he has acted 'honestly and reasonably and ought fairly to be excused'.

A trustee who is seeking to escape liability must prove that he has acted in such a manner.

The Court has a discretion in such cases and is not bound to excuse a trustee.

Trustees should not view this provision as a general indemnity clause. They should at all times exercise a high degree of care in the execution of their duties. They may however only be prepared to accept office if the trust deed contains a blanket indemnity clause.

12.9 Changing the terms of a trust

12.9.1 Action by beneficiaries

Beneficiaries cannot interfere with the way a trustee administers the trust, although they can intervene to prevent a breach of trust.

If all the beneficiaries are of full age and capable of consenting they can reach agreement on a variation of the terms of the trust with the trustees without referring the matter to the Court. The arrangement will then be set out in a deed of family arrangement executed under seal by all the parties. The deed will contain an indemnity by the beneficiaries in favour of the trustees. The costs of the exercise are payable from the trust fund.

In a simple trust where all the beneficiaries are of full age, not under any disability and between them absolutely entitled to the trust property they may terminate the trust. They can ask the trustees to transfer the trust property to them or as they direct, regardless of the wishes of the settlor. This is known as 'the rule in *Saunders* v *Vautier*'.

Beneficiaries may be able to remodel or terminate a trust by a number of other methods. A life tenant (12.2.1) may surrender his life interest to the remainderman (12.2.1) bringing the trust to an end. An elderly person entitled to an interest in reversion (12.2.1) may assign all or part of his interest to younger relatives or to the life tenant. The trust property may be divided between the life tenant and the remainderman thereby also terminating the trust. A life interest may also be disclaimed.

All the above transactions are capital transactions and may involve a liability for inheritance tax and CGT. Reversionary interests may be assigned or surrendered without a charge to inheritance tax provided they are regarded as 'excluded property' (7.17). (Income tax may be involved under S 437 if the recipient is the minor child of the reversioner.)

12.9.2 Statutory provisions

In more complex situations trustees may need to obtain the Court's approval to any proposed change in the terms of the trust. There are a number of statutory provisions which can be used and in some circumstances trustees do not even have to make the application themselves. The following are two of the most important provisions.

12.9.3 Management and administration
(TA 1925 S57)

The Court has power to sanction a particular transaction which it considers to be 'expedient' in the management or administration of trust property. The Court can authorise specific dealings with trust property but cannot alter the beneficial interests under the trust. Trustees make the application and the costs of all the parties are usually met from the trust fund.

12.9.4 Variation of Trusts Act 1958

The Court has a general statutory power under the Variation of Trusts Act to vary trust terms on behalf of persons who lack the ability to do it themselves. Adult beneficiaries who are not under any disability must reach a decision on their own.

Where property is held on trusts arising before or after the passing of the Act and contained in a Will, settlement or other disposition the Court may at its discretion approve any arrangement which either:

(1) varies or revokes all or any of the trusts; or
(2) enlarges the powers of the trustees in relation to the trusts on behalf of the following persons:
   (*a*) a minor beneficiary or someone who is under a disability and therefore incapable of assenting;
   (*b*) persons who might become entitled to an interest at a future date;
   (*c*) unborn persons; and
   (*d*) persons who may be granted a benefit under a discretionary trust arising under the provisions of a protective trust where the interest of the principal beneficiary has not failed.

The consent of the trustees to the proposed arrangement is not required and the application is often made by the beneficiaries themselves. Application can also be made by the settlor who should in any case be consulted on the proposed variation and be given an opportunity to express his views. In practice proposals for a variation are usually discussed between trustees and beneficiaries although the details should be formulated by the beneficiaries themselves. Separate representation is usually insisted on by the Court.

The Court will not approve the proposed arrangement unless it is satisfied that it will be for the benefit of all interested persons. Neither will the Court override objections or a refusal of consent from an adult beneficiary no matter how unreasonable such objections might be.

The Act has frequently been used to vary investment clauses where the settlor's wishes limit the scope of the Trustee Investments Act (12.5.7) to the disadvantage of the trust interests. Many other applications have had as their object the avoidance of tax. This has been regarded as a legitimate use of the Act's powers provided it is clear that the arrangement is for the benefit of all interested persons under the trust.

12.9.5　The importance of a flexible trust deed

- *The general law and the statutory provisions outlined above provide a limited means of varying the terms of a trust. Application to the Court is both expensive and time consuming and inevitably involves delay. It is most important that the trust deed itself is made as flexible as possible. This will enable your trustees to take advantage of changes in tax law as well as your own and the beneficiaries' financial circumstances without recourse to the Court.*

If the trust deed contains an express power of variation it may be possible to effect a variation of the trust terms without the need for a formal deed. Alternatively there may be power to appoint the trust property on entirely new trusts. These powers may be exercisable with or without the consent of the settlor. Section 32 of the Trustee Act may also be used to release or resettle capital on entirely new trusts (12.6.2).

12.9.6　Discretionary trusts

Discretionary trusts, the majority of which were created before 1974 have suffered from numerous tax disadvantages (8.3.2). It has often been found desirable to terminate them altogether under an overriding power of appointment in the trust deed or to reconstruct them so that they cease to be discretionary in nature. Following the 1982 Finance Act, however, smaller discretionary settlements have become more popular.

Reconstruction of a discretionary trust is usually effected by means of a deed of appointment executed by the trustees. The deed is usually drafted so that the new settlement or trust is part of the old settlement which remains in existence. Many of the administrative provisions of the old trust are expressed to apply to the new sub-trust. This is to avoid a possible CGT charge. Such a charge may arise if it can be shown that the trustees of the new trust have become absolutely entitled to the trust assets as against the trustees of the old trust.

The main aim behind the reconstruction of a discretionary trust is to remove the trustees' discretion as to which beneficiaries are to benefit under the trust. To this end particular individuals are given the right to property or at least to the income of trust assets. Usually provision is made for those persons who were members of the 'specified' or 'appointed' class of beneficiaries in the old discretionary trust to receive a benefit. Frequently the reconstruction is designed to benefit the settlor's children or grandchildren. This is accomplished by means of the accumulation and maintenance trust (12.2.5) because of its tax advantages.

12.9.7 Exporting trusts

An English trust is a trust made in conformity with English law and where the trustees are subject to the jurisdiction of the English Courts. An overseas trust is one which is controlled and managed outside the UK. The UK does not include the Channel Islands or the Isle of Man which have their own trust and tax law.

Provisions can be inserted in an English trust whereby it can be removed to another country. This can be done by substituting for the English trust a new trust in another country and then transferring the trust fund to that new trust. It is desirable to appoint new foreign trustees at the same time.

If there is no power in the trust deed to export the trust, it may be necessary to apply to the Court under the Variation of Trusts Act.

Alternatively, UK trustees may merely retire in favour of foreign trustees. The trust will then become resident outside the UK as it will be controlled and managed abroad notwithstanding that the trust assets are situated here. This will have certain income tax consequences (9.6).

There is nothing in law to prevent the appointment of non-resident trustees although this should only be considered in exceptional circumstances. It seems that any such appointment against the wishes of a beneficiary is voidable by that beneficiary particularly if it would not be sanctioned by the Court. If all the beneficiaries approve a non-resident appointment it cannot later be set aside. It would appear that it is also unlikely that the Revenue could interfere with such an appointment. If all the beneficiaries of an English trust are resident in another country this would constitute 'exceptional circumstances' and the approval of the Court would not normally be necessary.

Indemnities will in all probability be required by the retiring trustees from the settlor and the new trustees, and possibly also from at least some of the adult beneficiaries. Trustees retiring in favour of non-residents will have to ensure that all liabilities to the date of retirement have been settled. It will be more difficult for creditors (and the Revenue) to recover debts in another country and the former trustees may well find themselves personally liable for them.

Exporting a trust could have CGT advantages although these would be limited where there are UK resident beneficiaries and the settlor was domiciled and resident or ordinarily resident in the UK either when he made the settlement or when the capital gain is made (5.7). Unless the settlor was domiciled abroad at the time when the settlement was made exporting a trust will not produce any inheritance tax advantage (8.1).

13 The law of wills, succession and trusts in Scotland

13.1 Introduction

The law of wills, succession and trusts in Scotland has developed separately from English law. The following is an outline of the main provisions of Scots law.

13.2 Wills

Any minor child (a girl over 12 or a boy over 14) can make a will. The rules for testamentary capacity (known as 'capacity to test') are broadly the same as those in England.

A will must be signed in the presence of two witnesses, although a will which is holograph (ie entirely in the testator's own handwriting) may be signed without witnesses. If the will is written on two or more sheets of paper or on both sides of the same sheet, the foot of each page, or each side of paper must be signed by the testator, although the witnesses need only sign the last page. Signature at the foot or end of the will is essential as anything written below the signature may be given no effect whatsoever. A proper attestation clause (known as a 'testing clause') is desirable.

It is not essential for the witnesses to be in the line of sight of the proceedings although this is, of course, desirable. It is sufficient if the testator acknowledges to the witnesses that the signature on the will itself is his signature.

A Scottish will is revoked by physical destruction or by making a new will. Unlike in England, it is not revoked by the subsequent marriage of the testator because the testator's spouse is provided for to some extent by other legal rights. However, if a Scotsman makes a will which does not mention children (because no such children have yet been born) and subsequently a child is born to the testator, there is a presumption (albeit rebuttable) that the will is automatically revoked.

For the purposes of succession, whether testate or intestate, reference to 'children' or 'descendants' (in legal jargon 'issue') includes adopted and illegitimate children, but excludes step-children. An adopted child is treated as a natural child of the adopting parents and has no relationship with its natural parents.

The rules for ademption and abatement of legacies are similar to those applicable in England (10.13.1).

The provisions of a Scottish will (and legal rights — see 13.3 below) can be altered within two years of the date of death (in the case of a will) by the beneficiaries of the will (or their executors if they die after the deceased) and by (in the case of legal rights) those entitled to legal rights. The requirements and procedure are the same as those applicable in England and Wales (10.24).

13.3   Legal rights

Under the common law of Scotland a deceased person's surviving spouse and children, and the descendants of predeceasing children, have certain legal rights which entitle them to claim a proportion of the estate. Such rights remain essentially common law rights but these have been expanded and clarified, particularly as regards representation in legitim (see below) by the Succession (Scotland) Act 1964 and take priority over the claims of other beneficiaries. These rights must be satisfied out of the deceased's movable estate (ie cash, stocks and shares and personal effects) and do not extend to what is known as 'the heritable estate' which includes land and buildings and fixtures together with any sums secured on such property.

Legal rights are classified into two categories which reflect the respective claims of the surviving spouse and children:

(1)   *Jus relictae* – being the right of a widow to one half of her husband's movable estate if there are no children, and to one third of that estate if there are children. (The equivalent right of a widower to the appropriate proportion of his wife's movable estate is known as *jus relicti*.)

(2) *Legitim* – being the right of the children to receive one third of their deceased parent's movable estate or, if the other parent is already dead, to receive one half of that estate.

Legitim extends not only to the deceased's children but also to the children or remoter issue of any child who has predeceased him. In such circumstances, the descendants would share in that part of the *legitim* which the deceased child would have taken. Adopted children are entitled to be included in the *legitim* fund, likewise illegitimate children (but not illegitimate remoter issue). The shares falling to the descendants depend on the number of surviving members of the class nearest in degree of relationship to the deceased (which will determine whether the division is *'per stirpes'* or *'per capita'*).

If a person is predeceased by a spouse, then the rights of succession which otherwise would have been enjoyed by such spouse on survival lapse and do not pass down to others as there is no representation of a spouse. A stepchild (or his issue) has no claim on his step parent's estate.

Legal rights and *'per stirpes'* division are best illustrated by the following example.

13.3.1 Example: legal rights and *per stirpes* division

Mr A dies, survived by his widow, a son (B), a daughter (C) and a stepson (D). Mr A was predeceased by another son (E) who had two children who both survived Mr A, and an adopted daughter (F) who had one child who survived Mr A. In his will Mr A left his entire estate, heritable and movable, to his brother, who also survived. Legal rights are claimed by one and all, and the result is:

Heritable estate:	Brother succeeds in total.
Movable estate:	After deduction of expenses, etc the net moveable estate is divided thus:
(1) Mrs A (widow))	$\frac{1}{3}$ share under *jus relictae.*
(2) The children	$\frac{1}{3}$ share under *legitim*, divided as follows: $\frac{1}{4}$ — Son B.
	$\frac{1}{4}$ — Daughter C.
(*per stirpes* division)	$\frac{1}{4}$ — Predeceased son E's two children—each taking a $\frac{1}{8}$ share — representing their father.
	$\frac{1}{4}$ — Predeceased adopted daughter F's child — taking the mother's $\frac{1}{4}$ share by representation.

(3) Brother   — takes the remaining $\frac{1}{3}$ share.

Note The stepson of Mr A, although surviving, has no right in his stepfather's estate even if Mrs A had predeceased Mr A, because there is no representation available of the spouse of the deceased.

It follows that a Scottish will may be rendered partially ineffective if a testator does not take account of legal rights which may be claimed despite the contents of the will. If a surviving spouse or surviving children or the descendants of predeceasing children decide to contest a will, only the balance of the estate (called the 'dead's part') after deducting legal rights will be available for the benefit of others in terms of the Will. Legal rights are not appropriate where the deceased is survived by neither spouse nor children or other descendants.

A claim to legal rights may be satisfied in whole or in part by the actions of the deceased during his lifetime or by the provisions of the will itself. For example, if a child of the deceased has received a gift from the deceased during his lifetime, then, unless the will shows a contrary intention, the gift may be taken into account in arriving at that child's share in *legitim*. Similarly, if the will already contains a gift in favour of a surviving spouse or children, then that gift must be treated, unless a contrary intention is shown, in satisfaction of legal rights. In such circumstances a legatee is normally required to choose between his legal rights and his rights under the will. If he chooses the latter, his legal rights are held to be satisfied as a result.

Equally legal rights can be claimed where a person dies intestate.

13.4 Intestacy
(SSA 1964 Ss2, 8 & 9)

Where a person dies domiciled in Scotland intestate special rules apply as follows.

The surviving spouse has 'prior rights' to the estate which are:

(1) The right to the deceased's interest in the matrimonial home up to the value of £65,000. If the value of the house exceeds £65,000 the surviving spouse is entitled to the sum of £65,000 in place of the house.

(2) The right to the furniture and contents of the house up to the

value of £12,000. This right exists quite independently of the right mentioned in (1) above.

(3) The sum of £21,000 if there are surviving children, or remoter issue, or the sum of £35,000 if there are no surviving children or remoter issue. In either case interest is payable at the rate of 7% per annum, from the date of death until payment.

After prior rights, legal rights must be calculated and the balance remaining (the 'free estate') is distributed amongst the surviving next of kin in the following order of priority:

(1) Children, grandchildren or great-grandchildren.
(2) Parents take one half (equally if both survive) and brothers and sisters, or their descendants, take the other half (again equally if more than one).
If neither parent survives then brothers and sisters, or their descendants, take everything. If no brothers and sisters or their descendants survive then the parents take everything.
(3) Wife or husband.
(4) Uncles and aunts or their descendants.
(5) Grandparents.
(6) Great uncles and great aunts or their descendants.
(7) Great-grandparents.
(8) The Crown.

13.5 Obtaining Confirmation
(SSA 1964 Ss14–15 & ESA)

The process of obtaining Probate in Scotland is referred to as obtaining Confirmation. Whether a person dies testate or intestate, Confirmation is the decree of the Court declaring that the appropriate persons are entitled as executors to administer the deceased's estate. The whole of the estate, both movable and heritable, vests in the executor by virtue of the decree which constitutes a valid title in the executor of the deceased's property.

Executors appointed expressly or impliedly in a will are known as 'executors-nominate'. If there is a will but no executor is expressly nominated in it the persons entitled to be confirmed as executors are the trustees of the residuary estate, failing whom any universal legatory or residuary beneficiary. If the deceased died intestate, executors are appointed by the Court and are referred to as 'executors-dative'.

The appointment of an executor in a will does not, in itself, authorise him to deal with the estate. He may, for example, sue for a debt due to the deceased before Confirmation but he cannot enforce payment until Confirmation has been obtained. He must therefore obtain Confirmation in order to obtain his authority which is essentially administrative in nature.

Applications for Confirmation should be submitted to the Sheriff Court within whose jurisdiction the deceased was domiciled at the time of his death. Such proceedings are known as Commissary Proceedings. The procedure is similar to that in England ie the estate must be valued, an inventory prepared and the inheritance tax liability assessed. Where the deceased was domiciled outside Scotland, application for Confirmation is made to the Commissary Clerk at Edinburgh Sheriff Court. There is, however, no personal application procedure similar to that available in England, although an executor may apply personally without professional guidance if he feels competent to be able to do so and there is a procedure for personal application in the case of small estates. (13.5.2).

If the deceased died intestate the normal procedure is for one (or more) of the persons entitled to succeed to the estate to apply to be appointed as executor(s)-dative. Such an application is made by initial writ to the Sheriff Court for the area in which the deceased was domiciled. The order of preference in making the appointment broadly follows the order of entitlement under the intestacy rules.

Where there is a surviving spouse and the estate is less than the amount which the spouse is entitled to receive under prior rights (13.4) he or she has the right in priority to be appointed executor-dative. All applicants with an equal right are entitled to be appointed to the office. It is usually necessary for an executor-dative to provide security for the performance of his office by way of Bond of Caution (pronounced 'Kayshun') which is issued by an insurance company, usually for a relatively small single premium.

13.5.1   The inventory

An executor (whether nominate or dative) is responsible for the preparation of an inventory of the estate. There are various forms of inventory to choose from depending on the value of the estate and on whether there have been life-time transfers. The inventory must be sworn before a notary public or Justice of the Peace or solicitor and then signed by the executor and the notary public or JP or solicitor. Where the executor is appointed under a will, the will itself is produced and signed by the deponing executor and the notary or JP or solicitor as relative to the inventory. Where the executor is appointed by the Court (executor-dative) details of the decree of Court by which he is appointed are disclosed on the inventory.

The inventory contains numerous questions about the deceased's estate in much the same form and content as the English Inland Revenue Account (11.4.1). Once the inventory has been completed and sworn any inheritance tax payable is calculated provisionally by the person completing the inventory and paid. Payment of inheritance tax on the heritable estate and on certain other items of estate can be postponed and paid by instalments (11.4.3). The inventory (duly receipted if tax is payable) is then lodged with the Sheriff Clerk with the request that the decree of Confirmation be issued. Confirmation dues (13.5.3) must be tendered to the Sheriff Clerk at this time.

Unlike Probate or Letters of Administration in England, the Decree of Confirmation usually contains a complete list of all the property forming part of the estate. Separate certificates of Confirmation, which relate to specific items of estate, can be applied for and such a certificate is as effective for that one item of estate as the Confirmation itself. Each certificate effectively constitutes an extract from the original Confirmation and may be exhibited to the person or undertaking concerned with that particular item of property. Usually, if there is heritable estate, such a separate certificate will be appropriate as it can be placed, as the executor's title, with the title deeds to the property. If one or more items of property have been omitted from the original inventory the executors may be required to submit not only to the Revenue but also to the Court a corrective inventory listing the additional items. The title of the executors to the additional assets is confirmed by the Court by a document known as 'an eik' (ie additional or supplementary Confirmation).

13.5.2 Small estates

Where the total value of the estate is less than £17,000 an application for Confirmation may be made personally to the Sheriff Clerk. This procedure is available whether the deceased left a will or died intestate. Confirmation is isssued to the applicant on payment of a small fee. Proof of kinship is required where appropriate.

13.5.3 Fees for commissary proceedings

A flat fee of £5 is payable when lodging the petition for the appointment of an executor-dative. A further fee (known as Confirmation dues and payable to the Sheriff Clerk) is payable for examining the inventory of the estate as follows:

Estate not exceeding £	Fee £
3,000	No fee
13,000	20.00
20,000	50.00

and for every additional £10,000 or any part thereof a further fee of £20.00 is payable. Additional and corrective inventories are also charged in accordance with the above table on the amount of the total estate. Individual certificates of Confirmation are charged at £2 each.

13.6 Administration and distribution of the estate
(SSA 1964 S15)

The process of registering Confirmation, collecting in the assets and discharging liabilities is very similar to that followed in England.

Confirmation constitutes the executors' title to the deceased's estate and in the case of land or buildings it may be used by the executors to transfer such property to the persons entitled either under the will or under the rules of intestacy. The transfer is effected by endorsing a statutory form of docket on the Confirmation itself or more usually on a separate certificate of Confirmation relating to the specific property in question. Where the executors dispose of land or buildings by way of conveyance, the Confirmation is the necessary link in title.

Unless there is a reason requiring delay, debts are normally paid as soon as funds are available, and the estate is distributed as soon as the administration is completed, even within six months of death.

13.7 Creditors

Creditors have a period of six months from the date of death to lodge claims against the estate. Sometimes executors advertise for claims, but advertisement is not essential. An executor is not therefore bound to pay any debts or distribute any part of the estate until six months have expired since the date of death. An executor will not be liable to creditors who claim later than six months after death. Certain priority debts ie funeral expenses, the wages of domestic and farm workers, taxes and rates must be paid as soon as possible after death.

A creditor may sue the executor who has obtained Confirmation to the debtor's estate but if there has been no Confirmation the creditor himself may apply and may be confirmed as executor-creditor. Other creditors may join in the application but a creditor is not required to confirm to more than the amount which will cover his own debt.

13.8 Executors and trustees
(ESA; TSA 1921 & TSA 1961)

The office of executor is distinct from that of trustee but both are governed by the same general principles. The executor's duty is to gather in the estate and distribute it among the beneficiaries; the trustee's duty is to hold the estate for the purpose of the trust. In wills, trustees are usually also nominated executors. Both executors-nominate and executors-dative are included in the definition of 'trustee' contained in the Trusts (Scotland) Acts 1921 and 1961. Thus the powers, duties and rights of trustees apply equally to executors with the exception that an executor-dative (13.5) does not have power to retire or to appoint new trustees.

13.9 Trusts
(TSA 1921 & TSA 1961)

A trust is created expressly by the delivery of property to trustees to be held by them on the terms of the trust or, in certain circumstances, it may be implied by law. No technical wording is necessary to create a trust.

13.9.1 Types of trusts

As in England, trusts are generally classed as testamentary (effective on the death of the settlor) or *inter vivos* (effective during the lifetime of the settlor).

In addition to implied, resulting and constructive trusts (12.2.6) Scots law recognizes the main types of *inter vivos* trust known in England namely the fixed-interest trust, the discretionary trust and the accumulation and maintenance settlement. Marriage contract trusts (both *ante-nuptial* and *post-nuptial*) entered into between spouses have become less common. *Ante-nuptial* contracts were a contractual means of avoiding, until 1964, the rights of *jus relictae* and *jus relicti* and were a means of discharging the right of *legitim* (13.3).

In a fixed-interest trust the entitlement of the income beneficiary is known as 'the right of liferent'. The interest of the remainderman is known as 'the right to the fee'. The law does not recognise an intermediate interest between those of liferent and fee. A minor can enjoy the right of liferent.

An 'alimentary liferent' is broadly equivalent to an English protective trust (12.2.4). Once the liferenter has entered into possession, an alimentary liferent may not be surrendered without the consent of the Court. Neither may it be assigned, except to the extent of any excess over a reasonable alimentary provision. An alimentary liferent is designed to protect the trust fund and the beneficiary but there is no equivalent of the forfeiture arrangements implied by English law.

A discretionary trust in Scotland may be varied by the creation of a liferent in favour of a beneficiary where the trust deed contains an express authority to this effect. Similarly, a discretionary trust may be converted into an accumulation and maintenance settlement.

Accumulation and maintenance settlements require careful drafting. The law prohibits accumulation of income beyond defined limits which differ for *inter vivos* deeds and for wills. It should be noted that there is no statutory equivalent of Ss31 and 32 of the English Trustee Act (12.6.1, 12.6.2) covering the maintenance of, and accumulation of income for, infant beneficiaries, and the advancement of capital. A contingent 'right to the fee' does not therefore automatically carry the right to intermediate income once a beneficiary has attained majority.

Charitable trusts are known under Scots law as 'Public Trusts'. The law does not define the expression 'charity', neither does it distinguish between gifts to charitable trusts and gifts for other 'useful' purposes. The overriding distinction is between private trusts and those for the benefit of the public or a section of the public. The general principles of trust administration are applicable to both public and private trusts. However, as under English law a charitable or public trust will not necessarily fail because the trust objects are uncertain, provided it is clear that the settlor intended the property to go to charity. (12.2.7).

13.9.2   The retirement, appointment and removal of trustees
   TSA Ss3, 19, 22 & 23)

A trustee cannot be compelled to accept office. Acceptance of trusteeship may be in any form, written or verbal, and may be inferred from conduct.

Although trust assets vest in the trustees jointly the law provides that a majority of the trustees for the time being shall form a quorum. The quorum (or a sole surviving trustee if appropriate) also has the power to appoint new trustees unless a contrary intention is expressed in the trust deed.

The law also includes a power for any trustee to resign his office. A sole trustee cannot retire unless he has first appointed new trustees. Where a sole trustee is incapable of acting the court has power to appoint a new trustee or trustees in his place.

Under common law the court has a general power to remove a trustee but this power is usually strictly construed. There is statutory provision for a trustee to be removed by the court where he is unfit or incapable of acting or has remained out of the UK for at least six months.

13.9.3   Powers and duties of trustees
   (TSA Ss4 & 5)

As under English law, trustees must administer the trust fund in accordance with the provisions of the trust deed, must act honestly and prudently and must not allow themselves to be in a position of conflict between duty and personal interest.

Scots trust law gives trustees certain general powers provided that these do not conflict with the terms of the trust deed. These are the powers of sale, exchange or granting leases of the heritable estate, borrowing money on the security of the trust assets and buying property as residential accommodation for occupation by any of the beneficiaries. These powers may be exercised by trustees unless the trust deed expresses a contrary intention. Where trustees wish to exercise powers authorised by law but which are contrary to the terms of the trust (or, in exceptional circumstances, they wish to do something outside both the terms of the trust deed and trust law) they may only do so with the authority of the Court. It should be noted that trustees have no general power to buy land (other than as residential accommodation as mentioned above) unless authorised by the trust deed.

13.9.4   Investment of trust funds
(TIA)

The Trustee Investments Act 1961 (12.5.7) applies in Scotland. As in England, the powers conferred on trustees by the Act are in addition to those conferred by the trust deed and its provisions may be expressly excluded by the terms of that deed.

13.9.5   Breach of trust
(TSA 1921 S3)

The majority of the principles of English law in relation to beneficiaries' remedies for breach of trust (12.8.7) and protection of trustees against liability (12.8.8) also apply under the law of Scotland.

Trustees are jointly and severally liable for breach of trust and any one or more of them may be sued. However, statutory provisions protect a trustee from liability for breaches of trust committed by his co-trustees unless they acted with his knowledge and consent or he negligently acquiesced in the breach.

13.9.6   The variation of trusts
(TSA 1921 S5 and TSA 1961 S1)

The Scottish courts have power to approve the variation of trusts on behalf of beneficiaries or prospective beneficiaries who are incapable of giving their own consent. These provisions mirror those powers available to the Court in England (12.9.2) except that they extend to the variation or revocation of alimentary provisions (13.9.1). The application is made by the presentation of a petition to the Court of Session by the trustees or any of the beneficiaries.

13.9.7 Judicial factors
(TSA 1921 S2 and TSA 1961 S4)

The Court may appoint a 'Judicial Factor' to manage and administer an estate or trust where this is necessary to protect the assets and the beneficiaries and there is no other legal remedy available. For example such an appointment may be made where there has been misconduct on the part of trustees, or for some reason administration of the trust cannot proceed.

A Judicial Factor is an officer of the Court whose duties are to conserve and manage the trust estate. He must file annual accounts and an inventory of the property under his control with the Accountant of Court. If appropriate he may exercise the general powers conferred on trustees by Ss4 and 5 of the Trusts (Scotland) Act 1921 (13.9.3). He is entitled to a formal discharge on conclusion of his administration.

14 Capital taxes and life assurance

by VINCE JERRARD

14.1 Introduction

In this chapter, the life assurance industry's products are dealt with in three categories:

(1) life assurance policies (whole life, endowment and term policies);
(2) purchased annuities (immediate and deferred); and
(3) pension policies (occupational pension schemes, retirement annuities and personal pensions).

In each of these categories the taxation of capital gains is considered from the viewpoint of the life company and the individual. The IHT implications of policies written in or out of trust are also considered in separate sub-sections.

For the stamp duty implications of policies and trusts see Chapter 15.

Life assurance policies

14.2 Life assurance — tax on capital gains

14.2.1 The life company's tax position
(TA 1988 Ss 76, 432 et seq, FA 1989 Ss 82–89 & Sch 8 & FA 1990 Ss41–48 & Sch 6)

In respect of their life assurance business, companies are generally taxed on the excess of their investment income and realised capital gains over management expenses. In June 1988 the Inland Revenue issued a Consultative Document on the taxation of the life assurance industry. The results of the consultations have now been enacted in the Finance Acts of 1989 and 1990.

The key changes applicable to life assurance business (which came into effect on 1 January 1990) are:

(1)   The erection of a 'ring fence' around pensions business.
(2)   A reduction in the tax rate charged on policyholders' income and gains. A new rate of 25% will apply, replacing the existing rates of 35% for income and 30% for gains. As life companies are generally able to defer realisations of assets for a long period, it is likely that they will pass on this benefit by making deductions for tax policyholders' gains at a rate lower than 25%, particularly in the case of unit-linked policies.
(3)   There is a new formula for determining the proportions of a company's income and gains which should be allocated respectively to policyholders and shareholders.
(4)   The expenses of acquiring new business, previously available for tax relief in full when they were incurred, are to be spread forward and allowed over a period of seven years. This spreading of relief over seven years will not come fully into force until 1994.
(5)   The introduction of new rules to tax unrealised gains in a life company's holding of unit trusts.

14.2.2   The policyholder's tax position
(CGTA 1979 Ss31 & 143)

In respect of life policies 'disposal' includes: payment of the sum assured; the transfer of investments or other assets to the policyowner in accordance with the policy; and the surrender of the policy. However, CGTA S143 provides that no chargeable gains will arise on the disposal of life assurance policies except where the person making the disposal:

(1)   is not the original owner of the policy, and
(2)   acquired it for money or money's worth (ie bought the policy).

In the past, when the top rate of income tax was 60% and the rate of CGT 30%, it was attractive for some people to buy what were known as 'second-hand bonds' in order for the gains to be taxed as capital gains and not income. Therefore, rules were introduced in FA 1983 to amend the income tax 'chargeable event' legislation to bring gains on many second-hand policies (in the main non-qualifying policies) into the income tax net. Where income tax is chargeable in respect of a policy gain, relief is available in respect of the possible additional charge to CGT (CGTA S31).

● *There remains a small specialist market for the sale of existing life assurance policies because, if the policy is maintained until the death of the life assured, usually the return will reflect a mortality profit.*

● *Because buying a policy can introduce a CGT liability on future disposal, it is important that a gift of a policy is not expressed to be in consideration of a nominal price of, eg £1. This would turn the gift into what is technically a sale, and could introduce a CGT liability on a subsequent disposal of the policy.*

14.3 Life assurance — inheritance tax
(See generally Chapter 7)

The 1986 Finance Act introduced radical changes to CTT and renamed it Inheritance Tax. While much of the CTT legislation remains, Inheritance Tax (IHT) re-introduces some features of the estate duty regime, such as the prospect of avoiding liability on lifetime gifts on survival for seven years, and rules on reservations of benefit out of lifetime gifts.

14.3.1 Domicile
(ITA 1984 Ss6 & 267)

The usual rules of domicile (and deemed domicile) apply.

If you are domiciled in the UK any life policies which you own (wherever effected) will be potentially liable to IHT. If you are domiciled elsewhere, and not deemed to be domiciled in the UK, you will only be liable to IHT if the policy is a UK asset.

● *Generally a policy will not be a UK asset if it:*

(1)   was issued abroad (by a foreign insurance company or an overseas branch of a UK company) and is expressed to be payable outside the UK; or

(2)   was issued under seal and physically kept out of the UK. Such a policy is a 'specialty debt' and is considered to be payable in the place where the policy is kept.

14.3.2   Policy valuation
(ITA 1984 Ss160 & 167)

The value of a policy for IHT purposes is, as with other assets, usually its market value. During the lifetime of the life assured this will often equate with its cash surrender value but, if the life assured is seriously ill, the market value could be significantly higher because of the expectation of a mortality profit on the life assured's death. At the death of the life assured the policy value will be the sum assured or the cash surrender value, if greater.

A further rule applies where a policy is valued other than on the death of the policy owner. In such cases the policy value is taken to be not less than the sum of the premiums paid under it (less the value of any payments made from the policy). This further rule does not apply to most term assurances.

14.3.3   Lives assured and policy owners

Clearly, the questions 'who is the life assured under the policy?' (or who are the lives assured under a joint-life policy?) and 'on what event is the sum assured payable?' are very important.

However, for IHT purposes the more important issues are who owns the policy and who is paying the premiums.

The greatest influence which the life assured has on the policy is in respect of the increase in policy value which will usually occur on the life assured's death. However, this does not, of itself, trigger any IHT liability, it will mean only that the value of the asset (the policy) is increased.

Policies may be:

(1)   on a single-life basis (one life assured);
(2)   on a joint-life basis (two lives assured) with the sum assured payable on the death of the first life to die (a 'joint-life, first-death' policy);
(3)   on a joint-life basis (two lives assured) with the sum assured payable on the death of the second life assured to die (a 'joint-life, second-death' or 'joint-life last survivor' policy).

As with other assets, policies may be owned by one person or by two or more jointly, either as tenants in common or joint tenants.

14.3.4 Own benefit policies

(a) Own life policies

If you pay premiums on a policy you own, no IHT implications arise in respect of payment of those premiums. On your death the sum assured will form part of your estate and will be potentially liable to IHT in the usual way.

If you make a gift of the policy during your lifetime this may be either a chargeable transfer or a 'potentially exempt transfer' depending on the nature of the gift (7.3)

(b) Life of another policies

If you own a policy on someone else's life payment of premiums will, again, not be a gift.

Payment to you of the sum assured on the death of the life assured will have no IHT implications, as you will merely be collecting the proceeds of an asset you already own.

If you die before the life assured, the market value of the policy will form part of your estate.

(c) Joint-life policies

If you are the sole owner of a joint life policy the rules will be very much the same as for own-life/own-benefit policies and life-of-another policies which you own. The existence of joint lives assured and the timing of the payment of the sum assured (ie on the first or second death) will merely influence the value of the policy at the relevant time.

14.3.5 Joint-ownership policies

If you are one of two joint owners of a policy and:

(1)   The other joint owner is your spouse; usually the exemption for transfers between spouses will mean that the death of the first spouse to die will have no IHT consequences (except where the owners hold the policy as tenants in common and the deceased's share does not pass to the surviving spouse). This will be the case whether the policy is a first or second death contract.

If the surviving spouse becomes the sole owner of a second-death policy on the death of the first spouse, the sum assured will form part of the surviving spouse's estate on his or her subsequent death.

Either spouse may pay the premiums but although part of each premium is, in effect, a gift to the other policy owner, the inter-spouse exemption will usually be available.

(2)   The other joint owner is not your spouse; on the death of the first owner to die, the deceased's share will pass to the surviving owner (if they owned as joint tenants) or according to the deceased's Will (if they were tenants in common).

In either case an IHT liability can result in respect of the value of the deceased's share. If it is a first-death policy and the deceased was a life assured, the value of that share will typically be a portion of the sum assured.

If you are the surviving owner of a second-death policy your share in the policy (which could be the whole policy, eg if you are the survivor of joint tenants) will form part of your estate.

If one person pays premiums under such a policy, part of each premium is, in effect, a gift to the other policyowner. The annual exemption may be available, as may the exemption for normal expenditure out of income (in the case of a regular premium policy).

(3)   The policies are not owned by the payer of premiums; generally, any premiums you pay on a policy you do not own will be transfers of value as if they were gifts to the policy owner. Usually they will be potentially exempt transfers but may be covered by the usual exemptions, in any event.

Thus, IHT liabilities in respect of joint-ownership policies could depend on:

(a)   whether the ownership is as sole beneficial owner, joint tenants or tenants in common;
(b)   who pays the premiums;
(c)   whose lives the policy is written;
(d)   whether the policy is a first-or second-death contract;
(e)   who dies first.

The permutations and IHT consequences can be complex, particularly where the joint owners are not husband and wife.

14.4   Trust policies

(See generally Chapter 8)

14.4.1   Introduction

Within the limits of trust law, you can set up a trust of a policy for any beneficiaries, and subject to whatever conditions, you choose. The effect of the trust will depend on the wording of the trust document, ie the way in which the gift is expressed and the powers which are given to the trustees.

Where the specific provisions of the trust are silent on any matter the general law of trusts will apply.

Policies may be made subject to a trust either from issue or subsequently.

If the policy is to be written in trust from issue the policy applicant will complete a 'letter of request' directing the life company to issue the policy subject to specific trust provisions.

An existing policy can be put in trust by the policy owner declaring a trust of it or by an assignment of the policy to an existing trust.

14.4.2   Purpose

A trust is, broadly speaking, a way of making a gift with the imposition of certain restrictions.

In most cases life policy trusts are used:

(1)   To avoid probate delay. If the sole owner of a policy dies, the proceeds will form part of his estate and will be 'frozen' until probate is granted.

- *If a policy is held in trust, any surviving trustees will be able to give the insurance company a good receipt for the policy proceeds, without the need to obtain probate.*

(2)   For IHT purposes.

- *A trust can remove the policy from the settlor's estate to reduce the IHT bill which would otherwise be charged on the estate on his death. In this way the proceeds can create an IHT-free 'legacy' for the beneficiaries, or can be used to pay any IHT on the settlor's remaining estate.*

Life assurance policies are particularly suitable for IHT planning because:

(1) Death is the main occasion of paying IHT and a life policy is the only savings vehicle guaranteed to provide the money when needed.

(2) Provision can be made to meet the IHT bill, from income. For example, a man aged 40, in good health and with an estate of approximately £300,000, can probably provide the sum he needs to meet the IHT bill on his death for in the region of 0.25% pa of his estate.

(3) When the policy is written in trust, future premiums paid by you are treated as gifts but will usually benefit from your available IHT exemptions (eg annual gifts exemption or exemption for normal expenditure out of income). On death the sum assured will be payable to the beneficiaries free of IHT. Thus, for relatively small regular gifts, a large capital sum can be transferred IHT-free.

● *Another specific use for life policies in the field of IHT is in covering the tax payable on death within seven years of a lifetime gift, eg by means of a seven year term assurance.*

14.4.3 Trustees

You will probably want to be a trustee of any trust you create but this is not a necessity.

● *It is wise to try to ensure that there are at least two trustees at any time to avoid the difficulties which can be caused where a sole, or sole surviving, trustee dies.*

● *However, you should not appoint more trustees than are necessary. The insurance company, usually, will act only on the instructions of all the trustees and too many trustees can make administration of the trust unwieldy.*

Some insurance companies can provide 'standard' trust document-ation, under which the policy owner(s) will be the original trustee(s). It is often convenient to appoint the policy owner's spouse as an additional trustee.

14.4.4 Trustees' powers

The powers which trustees are given automatically by law are quite restricted and it is usual to give trustees other specific powers when creating the trust. Typical additional powers would include:

(1) the ability to take specific actions in respect of the policy, eg make it paid-up, surrender it;

(2) a wider investment power to permit a greater scope for investment of the trust money, eg including non-income-producing assets such as single premium investment bonds and other life assurance policies;

(3) an extension of the statutory provisions in respect of payments for maintenance, education and benefit of minor beneficiaries.

Of course, a policyholder can instruct a solicitor to prepare a trust with other powers, if required.

14.4.5 Life policy trusts

The three main types of life policy trust are:

(1) *Absolute* trusts, eg, simple trusts in favour of one or more beneficiaries where the share given to each is specified and fixed at outset, for example 'for the absolute benefit of my children John and Joan in equal shares'.

● *If the beneficiaries are only your spouse and/or children, and the trust comes into existence immediately the policy is issued, the trust will take effect under the Married Woman's Property Act. Trusts under the MWPA enjoy greater protection against creditors if the settlor goes bankrupt.*

(2) *Class* trusts, eg, trusts in favour of named individuals who are members of a specified class, subject to certain contingencies. For example, 'for such of my children John and Joan and any other children of mine, whenever born, as survive me and attain the age of 25 years, and if more than one in equal shares and if none survive me and attain that age then for the benefit of the last to die'.

● *This sort of trust can be used where you are able to decide, at outset, who should benefit and in what shares. The most usual contingencies are survival beyond your death and attainment of a particular age. However, this is an area in which specialist advice is needed because imprecise wording can result in the trust not working as intended.*

(3)   *Flexible* trusts, eg, a trust which might be established by a gift 'for such of my children John, Joan, Janet and Jeremy as I appoint but to the extent that I make no appointment, for Janet'.

- *This type of trust is suitable where you are uncertain, at outset, as to who should benefit. You remain free to change the beneficiaries, or the shares they might have, at a later date. The class of potential beneficiaries can be very wide and can include you (the Settlor) and your spouse so that the trust can be 'dismantled' if the benefits are appointed back to you (but NB the possible IHT consequences).*

The power to appoint benefits between members of the class of potential beneficiares can pass to the trustees after your death.

Please note that these trusts can be complex and that the wording shown above is for illustration only.

Flexible trusts could be constructed, for IHT purposes, as 'discretionary trusts' (ie trusts without an interest in possession) or as trusts with an interest in possession in favour of the default beneficiary (8.3.3). The 1986 Finance Act has made far-reaching changes to the IHT consequences of some flexible trusts (8.3.3 and 14.4.11).

14.4.6   IHT implications of trust policies

Introduction
(ITA 1984 S48) (and see generally Chapter 8)
Trust assets will be excluded property for IHT purposes if:

(1)   the settlor was not domiciled, or deemed domiciled, in the UK when he made the settlement; and
(2)   the trust property is not UK property when the event in question occurs.

   If a policy trust is declared by a non UK domiciled settlor and the policy is written under seal and physically held out of the UK, it will be excluded property.

14.4.7   Creating the trust

(1)   From outset — if the policy is written in trust from issue, the initial transfer made on establising the trust will be the first premium paid.

(2) Existing policies — if a trust is declared of an existing policy, the value of the transfer will be the policy value at that time (14.3.2 and 14.9.3). In applying the 'sum of premiums paid' valuation rule (14.3.2), the gross premiums should be taken into account, even if they have been paid net of life assurance premium relief (LAPR).

14.4.8 Premiums

By paying a premium on a policy held in trust you make a transfer of value (unless you are the beneficiary under the trust).

Where life assurance premium relief (LAPR) is still available in respect of pre 14 March 1984 policies and premiums are paid net of relief, the gift will be the net premium. If you pay gross premiums, even if you are able to reclaim your premium relief later, the transfer is the gross premium.

In some cases the premium payment will be an immediately chargeable gift but may be exempt from tax by virtue of the annual exemption or the normal expenditure out of income exemption.

However, in the case of bare trusts the premiums will be potentially exempt transfers (PETs) (7.3). Most gifts to accumulation and maintenance trusts, some trusts for the disabled and interest in possession trusts (which are not bare trusts) will also be PETs, but it is possible that gifts by paying premiums on a policy held by such trusts may be chargeable transfers, to the extent that the value of the policy is not increased by the premium. To avoid any doubt, a donor could give cash to the trustees (which would be a PET) so that the trustees can pay the premiums. (For policies issued before 14 March 1984, life assurance premium relief, if available, could be lost if the trustees pay the premiums (see *Allied Dunbar Tax Guide 1990–91*, p 385).)

14.4.9 Proceeds

Payment of the policy proceeds to the trustees and then to the beneficiaries will not cause any IHT consequences provided those beneficiaries have the 'interest in possession' in the trust. A beneficiary with an interest in possession is treated as if he owns a relevant proportion of the trust property, so no chargeable transfer is made on distribution of his share to him.

If there is no interest in possession in the trust an IHT 'exit' charge can arise (8.3.3) unless the trust is favoured under the IHT rules, eg an accumulation and maintenance trust.

14.4.10   Changing beneficiaries/altering shares
(ITA 1984 Ss52 & 53)

If a beneficiary loses an interest in possession an IHT liability can arise (8.1).

For example, if your flexible trust was written to give your daughter Janet an interest in possession, any subsequent appointment of benefits to any other children would result in the loss, in whole or part, of Janet's interest.

If a subsequent appointment were made to share benefits equally between Janet and three other children, Janet's 100% interest would be reduced to a 25% interest and the 75% reduction would be treated as a transfer by her, for IHT purposes. Any IHT payable will be the primary liability of the trustees.

- *Such appointments of benefit should, if possible, be made during the lifetime of the life assured under the policy. In such cases it is the market value of the policy (or sum of premiums paid, if greater) and not the sum assured, which is the basis of any calculation of the value transferred.*

One major exception to the rules in respect of liability on switching benefits is that there is no liability if the appointment is in favour of the settlor of the trust or the settlor's spouse. The exemption extends for the benefit of the settlor's widow/widower for up to two years after the settlor's death.

The value of tax-free reversions to settlor must now be read in the light of the rules on reservation of benefit introduced in FA 1986 (14.4.11 and 14.4.12).

- *If you effect a policy on your own life to protect your wife and children in the event of your untimely death, you may consider writing that policy under a flexible trust with your children as the default beneficiaries (with interests in possession) and your wife as a member of the class of potential beneficiaries.*

On your death, if your widow needs the policy proceeds they can be appointed to her, free of IHT. If she does not need the proceeds they can be distributed to the children, again free of IHT.

- *If your wife had been given the interest in possession she could have enjoyed the proceeds free of tax but, if she had not needed the money, might have faced an IHT bill in passing it to the children.*

Under a trust without an interest in possession no IHT liabilities (other than periodic charges where appropriate) will arise until a beneficiary is given such an interest or the trust money is distributed. The usual rules for taxation of discretionary trusts will then apply (8.3)

14.4.11 Reservation of benefit — post 17 March 1986
(FA 1986 S102 & Sch 20)

Broadly speaking, if a donor (such as a settlor of a trust) retains some benefit from a gift made on or after 18 March 1986, the property gifted will be treated as if it still formed part of his estate for IHT purposes.

If a settlor is a member of the class of potential beneficiaries under a flexible trust or a true discretionary trust, he will be treated as having reserved a benefit and the objective of putting the policy out of his estate will be frustrated.

The settlor's spouse can be a potential beneficiary without the reservation-of-benefit rules being activated but settlors should be wary of any 'understanding' that they will be able to benefit from the trust by virtue of benefits being given to their spouse. Such an arrangement could be attacked under the associated operations rules (7.7).

14.4.12 Reservation of benefit — pre 18 March 1986

The rules on reserved benefits apply to gifts made on or after 18 March 1986. They do not apply to policy trusts made before that date unless the policy has been altered subsequently to increase its benefits or extend its term. This is an important exemption, as payment of premiums under the policy would otherwise have brought such trusts into the reservation-of-benefit rules.

If a settlor is paying contributions to a policy written in trust before 18 March 1986, he should consider carefully before deciding to make payments direct to the trustees in order to make those payment PETs. Not only could any LAPR be lost (see 14.4.8) but so too would the exemption referred to in the paragraph above.

A transitional relief existed to the effect that the reservation-of-benefit rules would not apply merely because an indexation option was exercised not later than 1 August 1986 on a pre-18 March 1986 policy, where the option would be lost after 1 August (FA 1986 S102(7)).

14.4.13   'Back-to-back' arrangements
(ITA 1984 Ss21, 263 & 268)

It was common during the estate duty era for estate holders to effect, at the same time, a whole-life policy in trust and a life annuity on their life. The payments under the annuity then funded the premiums on the whole-life policy, the proceeds of which were normally free of estate duty.

To avoid the Revenue invoking the estate duty 'associated operations' provisions it was necessary for the two contracts to be issued on independent terms, ie, it was not acceptable for the life policy to be issued at ordinary rates (in consideration of the purchase of the annuity) when your state of health was such that you would in the ordinary way have been charged an extra premium.

The 'associated operations' provisions were carried over into the CTT legislation and now into IHT (ITA 1984 S268). The position remains that the Revenue will not invoke these provisions against 'back-to-back' arrangements if the life policy is fully underwritten independently of the annuity, on the basis of the life company's standard rules for medical evidence.

However, the annuity instalments are normally 'dissected' for income tax purposes into capital and interest and the capital part is tax-free, only the interest part being taxable (ICTA 1988 S656). Only the (taxable) interest part of each instalment is eligible to be exempt as normal expenditure (7.15).

- *You can still set up a 'back-to-back' arrangement if you wish but if the life policy is substantial you may well have to use your £3,000 annual exemption (7.15) as well as the normal expenditure exemption in order to escape IHT on the payment of premiums.*

14.4.14   Investment bonds and IHT

Prior to the Budget in March 1986 many insurance companies marketed plans for mitigating CTT liability on investment capital by the use of single-premium investment bonds in trust.

14.4.15   Inheritance plans

There were basically two types of inheritance plans. With one version you would apply for a bond for a purchase price of £1,000, issued in a flexible trust, and then lend the trustees the balance of the sum to be invested, which sum they in turn invested in bonds, in small denominations for flexibility. The trustees then agreed to repay the loan, usually at 5% pa so as not to attract an immediate higher rate income tax charge on the bonds (see *Allied Dunbar Tax Guide,* Chapter 24).

The effect of this was to provide you with an 'income' (the loan repayments). Once the loan was repaid the trustees could provide further 'income' by cashing in a bond and appointing it back to you from time to time or, as a further refinement, making loans to you. The latter method had the advantage that on your death the outstanding loans were debts against your estate and, on the assumption that you did in fact spend the cash as it was lent to you, this reduced your estate for CTT purposes.

The second version was a plan which combined gifts from the settlor with the prospect of loans being made by the trustees, as briefly referred to above. A trust was established with a large initial gift, invested in bonds, usually to make use of the settlor's nil rate band. The trustees were empowered to make loans to any of the trust beneficiaries and, if they decided to exercise this power, used the withdrawal facility on the bonds to obtain the necessary cash.

Both types of inheritance plan ensured that the growth on the money transferred to the trust accrued outside the settlor's estate.

The second version also made use of the (then) ten-year cumulation rules and the fact that any loans made to a beneficiary (for example, the settlor) were debts against his or her estate.

Of course, larger gifts could be made by the settlor to take advantage of the lower lifetime rates of CTT and a combination of gifts and loans was also possible.

The introduction of IHT led to these plans being withdrawn. The provisions in the plans for benefit being given to the settlor would invoke the operation of the reservation-of-benefit rules for any such plans effected on or after 18 March 1986.

Plans established before that date will continue to be effective, save that loans made from such a trust to the settlor after 17 March 1986 will not be deductible debts for the purpose of reducing the settlor's estate (FA 1986 S103).

14.4.16   'Peta' plans (and discount gift schemes)

Under these schemes you would invest in a policy which was technically an endowment, but with a maturity date (commonly your 100th birthday) to which you were unlikely to survive.

The endowment usually had no value before maturity date (apart from the value of the permitted withdrawals at a pre-determined rate) but you would also effect, in a flexible trust, a term assurance running to the same term as the endowment and with a sum assured always equal to the value of the endowment, ie it reflected unit growth and any withdrawals made.

The result was that you obtained 'income' from the endowment by way of withdrawals, the capital passing to the beneficiary free of CTT on your death.

Setting up the arrangement was in itself a chargeable transfer of the difference between the capital invested and the actuarial value of the endowment. This actuarial value depended on your age, state of health and rate of withdrawals you chose.

The discounting inherent in this actuarial valuation meant that you could usually invest considerably more than the CTT nil-rate band with no CTT liability, eg, at age 65 investment of £100,000 could have given rise to a chargeable transfer of about £45,000.

There were further elaborations of this approach, involving artificial 'devices' designed to avoid any transfer of value on establishment of such a scheme.

Examples of the latter type of arrangement were challenged by the Revenue in 1985 and specific legislation was introduced in FA 1986 to counter both types of scheme. Plans effected prior to 18 March 1986 appear to remain effective, subject to possible further Revenue attack in specific cases.

Annuities

14.5 Annuities — tax on capital gains

14.5.1 The life company's tax position
(ICTA 1988 Ss436 & 437)

If the annuities paid by a life company to general annuitants exceed or equal the income and realised gains of the general annuity fund, the fund is not taxed in respect of such income and gains. Companies, therefore, endeavour to balance the fund's income and gains with the annuities they pay, which explains the special rates which may sometimes be offered for different classes or ages.

14.5.2 The policyholder's tax position
(CGTA 1979 Ss143 & 144)

Immediate annuities (those where income payments commence straight away) are exempt from CGT.

Deferred annuities are treated in the same way as life assurance policies and so do not give rise to any CGT liability in the hands of anyone who did not purchase them.

Annuities are not often sold 'second-hand' and gains realised from them will often attract an income tax charge under the 'chargeable event' rules (ICTA 1988 Part XIII Chapter II). (See *Allied Dunbar Tax Guide 1990–91.*)

14.6 Annuities — inheritance tax
(See generally Chapter 7)

An ordinary lifetime annuity will cease on your death. Accordingly there will be nothing to form part of your estate and no IHT liability.

If the annuity is guaranteed for a minimum period and you die during that period, the outstanding payments will form part of your estate (although in valuing those payments at market value some discount will be allowed if there is a delay before they become payable). The spouse exemption may, of course, be available in such circumstances.

A joint annuity will pay the income benefit until the death of the second annuitant to die. As with life policies, joint annuities may be owned by one individual, or by two or more people either as tenants in common or joint tenants. The IHT implications will depend on the ownership of the annuity, who provided the purchase money, who dies first and the relationship between the annuity owners.

Pension Policies

14.7   Pension policies — introduction

Recent years have seen considerable change in the structure of pension provision in the UK. For example; payment of lump sum benefits has, in some circumstances, been restricted; a new type of contract, the 'Free-Standing Additional Voluntary Contribution Scheme' has been introduced; S226 (ICTA 1970) Retirement Annuity Contracts and S226A term assurance policies have been replaced by Personal Pension Plans (although retirement annuity contracts and S226A term assurance policies effected prior to 1 July 1988 can continue as before); new ways of contracting-out of the State Earnings Related Pension Scheme (SERPS) have been made possible; and contracting-out has been made more attractive while at the same time the benefits payable to many people in the future under SERPS have been reduced.

Further details of the types of pension available and the benefits they can provide can be found in the *Allied Dunbar Tax Guide* 1990-91.

14.8   Pension policies — tax on capital gains

14.8.1   The life company's tax position
(ICTA 1988 S438)

No tax is charged on capital gains made by assurance companies' pension funds, either in respect of occupational pensions, retirement annuities or personal pensions.

14.8.2   The policyholder's tax position
(CGTA 1979 Ss143 & 144)

Annuities and capital sums payable out of superannuation funds or superannuation schemes do not give rise to chargeable gains on disposal but are, in any event, generally unassignable.

Annuities from retirement annuity contracts and personal pension plans are deferred anuities but are also unassignable so no CGT consequences arise. Since FA 1980 it has been possible to assign term assurances effected under S226A and the death benefit which a S226 annuity contract may provide on death before the annuity payments commence and these rules are continued under the legislation which introduced personal pension plans with effect from 1 July 1988 (14.9.2).

It is rare for anyone to purchase a S226A contract or S226 death benefit because the legislation prevents a purchaser from paying contributions to ensure the policy remains in force and because if the policyholder survives to the end of the term (in the case of a S226A policy), or to take his pension (in the case of a S226 death benefit), there will be no return to the purchaser. In general, the same will be true for personal pension plans.

14.9 Pension policies — inheritance tax
(See generally Chapter 7)

14.9.1 Occupational pension schemes
(ITA 1984 Ss12 & 151; SPs 20/1975 & 7/1976, IR Notes 7 May 1976)

Contributions
Usually the larger part of an occupational scheme contribution is paid by the employer and gives rise to no IHT consequences.

Employees' contributions are regarded as being for the provision of a pension and, in practice, are usually ignored for IHT purposes. Contributions made to provide death benefits are treated as incidental to the main pension purpose and also disregarded.

Benefits
Exempt approved schemes are almost invariably established under trust. Without special tax treatment a pensioner would be regarded

as entitled to an interest in possession in the scheme and so a liability would arise whenever a pensioner died.

Special rules do exist, however, and the death of a pensioner is not treated as the coming to an end of an interest in possession so that no IHT consequences will usually result.

Employees are often given an option, just before retirement, to use the accumulated fund to produce a smaller pension for themselves in exchange for a pension payable to the widow or a dependant.

If this option is elected, an IHT charge could arise at that time in respect of the notional gift of the funds to provide the other pension. If the pension is for the pensioner's widow the transfer will be exempt under the usual rules for transfers between spouses.

If the pension you take on retirement has a guaranteed payment period, the pension will continue after your death should you die during that period. In this case there may be an IHT liability (as with other guaranteed annuities).

The scheme may provide that the balance of any guaranteed pension payments are to be paid in a lump sum. In this case the normal rules for lump sum payments will apply.

Lump sum benefits on death

Schemes will usually provide for a lump sum payment on death before retirement. The maximum amount, under current regulations, is four times salary plus a return of any personal contributions.

Most schemes will provide that this lump sum will be paid at the discretion of the scheme's trustees, 'discretionary disposal'. The pensioner may indicate to whom he would like the benefits to be paid but, although the trustees will usually follow such an indication, they are not required to do so. They may pay to any of a wide range of possible beneficiaries including all of the pensioner's family.

- *The discretionary disposal ensures that the benefits are free of IHT thanks to specific rules exempting pension schemes from the usual discretionary trust IHT regime of periodic and exit charges. Note that:*

    (1)   These rules apply whether the lump sum comes from the fund which was accumulating to provide the pension or from a

specially arranged term assurance, subject to the limit of four
times salary.

(2) *A return of the pensioner's personal contributions may be made in
addition to the benefits in (1) above;*

(3) *The same rules apply if the balance of a guaranteed pension is
payable as a lump sum.*

(4) *On the face of it, the IHT rules on gifts with reservations of
benefit could override this exemption but the Revenue have
confirmed that this is not the case.*

(5) *The lump sum benefit on death will usually be paid direct to an
adult beneficiary. If it is paid to a trust (or held in trust by the
pension trustees where the rules permit) the normal IHT
legislation will apply.*

● *Funds are most often held in trust where there are minor beneficiaries in
which case the advantages of an accumulation and maintenance trust
may be available.*

14.9.2 Personal pension plans, retirement annuities and S226A policies
(ITA 1984 Ss12, 151 & 152)

Contributions
Contributions are treated in much the same way as for occupational
pension schemes.

Unlike the position with retirement annuity contracts and S226A
policies, an employer can pay contributions to the employees'
personal pension plans. It appears that any such contributions will
have no IHT consequences, again being treated in much the same
way as employer's contributions under occupational schemes.

Pension benefits
The consequences of annuity payments are also very much the same
as for pensions under occupational pension schemes in respect of
payments continuing after your death for your widow, or for any
remaining guaranteed payments. The same consequences also apply
if you exercise an option to take a smaller pension for yourself and
provide a pension for your widow.

Lump sum benefits on death
A term assurance can be effected under the personal pension
legislation to provide a sum assured on death before pension age.

Also, if the member dies before starting to draw a pension, his contributions, together with reasonable interest on them, (in a unit linked plan this is usually taken to be the fund value) can be paid as a lump sum death benefit.

Originally death benefits under retirement annuity contracts and S226A plans were non-assignable. A nomination could be made in which case a pension would be provided for the nominated beneficiary instead of a lump sum being paid to your estate. Nominations did not cause any CTT liability when made or on payment of the pension. However, as the nominated beneficiary would usually be the pensioner's spouse, it was better in most cases to use the CTT spouse exemption and leave the lump sum to the widow, thus giving greater flexibility in use of the money.

Since FA 1980 it has been possible to assign (eg write under trust) S226A policies and the death benefit under S226 contracts, and this also applies to the equivalent benefits under personal pensions providing the scheme rules and structure permit it and providing the scheme is not established under a 'master trust' (in which case discretionary disposal of death benefits will occur, as with occupational schemes).

14.9.3   Personal pensions, S226A policies and S226 death benefits in trust
(See generally Chapters 7 and 8)

Putting existing policies in trust
In respect of retirement annuity contracts and S226A plans, it was not possible to put such policies in trust until 1980 there are still many held out of trust. Similarly there may be members of personal pension schemes where benefits are assignable but no assignment has been made. Declaring a trust in these circumstances is a gift for IHT purposes, the value transferred being the market value of the death benefit or sum assured.

Usually, however, the value of this gift will be negligible and ignored for IHT purposes unless you die from natural causes within two years after the gift is made. In such cases the Revenue may treat the market value at the date of the gift as a discounted amount of the benefit received by the trust on the death.

● *If you have an existing S226 or S226A policy or a personal pension with assignable death benefits, not written in trust, you should consider declaring a trust of the appropriate benefits. If you do not, the value of the death benefits will fall into your estate and could cause an IHT charge unless they pass to your widow/widower. While it may not be possible to be sure of the exact value of the gift being made in creating the trust, in most cases you will have something to gain (IHT-free proceeds to the beneficiaries) and little to lose.*

- *If your policy has an existing nomination you should also consider if this is appropriate because it will mean that the benefits will be paid as a pension and not as a lump sum. Any IHT advantages of a nomination are usually available through use of a suitable trust.*

- *However, if you reach the age at which you can take your pension benefits, but decide to postpone taking them (eg because you are seriously ill and would want the pension fund to pass to beneficiaries free of IHT), the Revenue might attempt to argue that the failure to take the pension was a deliberate omission to exercise a right within the meaning of ITA 1984 S3(3).*

Contributions

Even where the 'return of fund' death benefit has been assigned, subsequent contributions to the pension plan are, in most cases, ignored for IHT purposes on the basis that they are primarily to provide for the pension benefits which are personal to the policyholder.

There may be IHT consequences in respect of contributions to the policy (especially large one-off contributions) made within two years of the policyholder's death from natural causes. In such cases the Revenue may take the view that these arrangements were intended to provide death benefits for the trust beneficiaries, rather than pension benefits for the policyholder, and so treat them as transfers of value.

If a term assurance is effected under the pensions legislation and assigned by the policyholder, subsequent contributions will usually be gifts for IHT purposes (although they will usually be exempt as normal expenditure out of income).

Proceeds on death

Different types of trust may be used but the most common types are:

(1) absolute trusts;
(2) flexible trusts; and
(3) discretionary trusts.

Payment of benefit to a beneficiary with an interest in possession will not cause any IHT consequences. In respect of discretionary trusts, the Revenue have confirmed also that no IHT will be chargeable where such benefits are paid out within two years of the policyholder's death.

It has also been confirmed that inclusion of the policyholder as a potential beneficiary will not bring the reservation-of-benefit rules into play in respect of such pension contracts.

Switching beneficiaries
(ITA 1984 Ss52 & 53)

If a flexible trust with an interest in possession is used, redirecting benefits between beneficiaries can cause an IHT charge as for life policy trusts. However, the special valuation rule for life policies (which, other than for transfers on death, means that the minimum policy value to be used for IHT purposes is the sum of the premiums paid) does not apply to personal pensions, retirement annuity death benefits or 226A policies.

The value of a transfer of benefit, therefore, is the notional market value. This value will be significant only where the appointment is made when the policyholder is in particularly poor health (ie, where there is a high expectation that the death benefit or sum assured will be payable in the near future).

Appointments made after the death of the policyholder affect the actual value of the trust (ie the whole sum assured or death benefit) and IHT may be payable. Exemptions might be available eg if the trust property were being appointed to the policyholder's widow/widower within two years of the death.

15 Stamp duty

15.1 Introduction

Stamp Duty is imposed by the Stamp Act 1891 (SA), as amended by subsequent Finance Acts, whilst the Stamp Duties Management Act 1891 gives many of the administration provisions. The detailed rules of Stamp Duty are very involved and the following is only a broad outline of particular points with which you may be concerned regarding your capital transactions.

There are two kinds of stamp duties, *fixed duties* and *ad valorem duties*. *Fixed duties* do not change, regardless of the money involved (eg, the duty of 50p on a declaration of trust). On the other hand, *ad valorem* duties are charged according to the value of the transaction (eg, the duty on the conveyance of a house).

The payment of Stamp Duty is normally confirmed by a stamp being impressed on the document. The stamps are impressed on the documents at the local stamp office. First a marking clerk indicates the duty and then, on payment, the stamp is impressed. It may be either necessary or desirable for the document first to be *adjudicated* by the stamp office, which involves supplying them with the necessary particulars. They will then determine the duty to be paid. This applies particularly to company reconstructions, for example.

15.2 Basic rules

The following are some general guide-lines:

(1) Stamp Duty is essentially a charge on instruments (documents): it is not charged on the transactions. An exception concerns stamp duty reserve tax (15.10).

• *If you carry out a transaction without documenting it, as when you make an oral contract, no duty will be chargeable. Of course, this may not be desirable commercially or always legally acceptable.*

(2)   Although the duty is charged on instruments, the exact category of the charge, and hence its amount, depends on the nature of the transaction, not only the form of the document.

(3)   No duty is chargeable on an instrument which is ineffective for the purpose for which it was executed.

(4)   No duty is chargeable regarding a transaction which is effected orally. This follows from (1) above, since stamp duty falls on instruments and not transactions.

● *If you later make a separate written record of an oral contract, this will not normally require stamp duty to be paid.*

(5)   If a document covers several different matters all ancillary to its main purpose it only bears duty according to the latter. However, if several separate instruments are embodied in one document, they are all individually stampable. This also normally applies to several distinct matters covered by one instrument (SA Ss3 & 4).

(6)   Under a contract, the sum finally payable may depend on future events; eg, the final price might depend on results. In these circumstances, the ad valorem duty on this instrument is calculated on the maximum possibly payable. However, if only the minimum can be calculated in advance, this must be used.

(7)   If more than one head of charge applies to an instrument duty can only be charged under one of them, but the Revenue can choose which.

(8)   Sometimes it is necessary for one transaction to be effected by two or more instruments. Provided it is at least 50p, *ad valorem* duty cannot be charged more than once in these circumstances.

15.3   Unstamped instruments

If you do not stamp a document, in general you will not be open to any action against you by the Revenue. However, whilst the instrument remains unstamped it will not be admitted in evidence and will generally be of no value. Exceptionally, the Revenue can recover by action in the High Court certain duties, including particularly capital duties on companies and loan capital duty. Note that when a document is presented for stamping out of time, in practice after 30 days from when the instruments are first executed, or brought into the UK, the Revenue may, at their discretion, charge penalties. These comprise £10 together with 5% per annum on the duty and also, for certain categories, the amount of the original duty in addition. The categories where more than twice the duty can become payable on late stamping include gifts (made before 19 March 1985), leases and conveyances on sale.

15.4   Overseas aspects
(SA S14(4) & FA 1984 S109)

Stamp duty applies to instruments executed anywhere within the UK and those, wherever executed, relating to any property in this country or anything being done here. Thus an instrument executed in the UK must be stamped, even if it takes effect abroad. Furthermore, there is normally no double taxation relief in respect of stamp duty suffered abroad, except in Ireland.

A reduced rate of *ad valorem* duty was applied on sales of shares, etc, to overseas residents. Broadly speaking, the rate was approximately 1% instead of 2%. However, instruments executed after 19 March 1984 only bore 1% duty (15.8.2) and this rate also applied to overseas residents. From 27 October 1986 the $\frac{1}{2}$% rate for share transfers applies equally to non-residents.

15.5   Exemptions

Certain documents are exempted from stamp duty by the Stamp Act 1891 and subsequent legislation. The following table lists some of the more important exemptions.

15.5.1   Table: Exemptions

Transfers of Government Stocks ('Gilts')
Transfers of short term loans (no more than five years)
Transfers of certain fixed rate non-convertible loan stocks
Transfers of bearer loan capital after 31 July 1986
Transfers of certain non-sterling loans raised by foreign governments or
  companies after 31 July 1986
Conveyances, transfers or leases to approved charities (FA 1982 S129)*
Conveyances, transfers or leases to the National Heritage Memorial Fund*
Transactions effected by the actual operation of law
Documents regarding transfers of ships (or interests in them)
Transfers brought about by wills (testaments and testamentary instruments)
Articles of apprenticeship and of clerkship
Customs bonds, etc
Certain legal aid documents
Contracts of employment
Certain National Savings documents
Deeds of Covenant and bonds
Policies of insurance and related documents (including life assurance after
  31 December 1989)
One life assurance policy which is substituted for another according to the rules
  (FA 1982 S130)
Transfers (and issue) of certain EEC Loan Stocks
Transfers of Treasury guaranteed stock
Property put into unit trusts ($\frac{1}{4}$% prior to 16 March 1988) (FA 1988 S140).
Agreement pursuant to Highways Acts
Appointment, procuration, revocation
Letter or power of attorney
Deeds not liable to other duties no longer liable to 50p duty
In Scotland, resignation, writ etc
Warrants to purchase Government stock etc (FA 1987 S50)
Transfers to a Minister of the Crown or the Treasury Solicitor (FA 1987 S55)

*Not treated as duly stamped unless having a stamp denoting not chargeable to
duty.

15.6   *Ad valorem* duties

The most important Stamp Duties with which you may be involved
are those which increase according to the consideration involved.
These are known as *ad valorem* duties. Normally, *ad valorem* duties
are charged at a fixed percentage but this is sometimes expressed in
bands, so that the $\frac{1}{2}$% charge on share transfers, etc, is 50p for every
100 or part thereof. Also, for some duties, sliding scales apply for

small transactions. The following table gives the basic percentage rates of various *ad valorem* duties, which were largely reduced from 2% to 1% for documents executed after 19 March 1984 (or executed after 12 March 1984 and stamped after 19 March 1984). For stock exchange securities, the 1% rate applied to transactions after 11 March 1984 for settlement after 12 March 1984 and before 27 October, 1986 from which date the rate is $\frac{1}{2}$%.

15.6.1 Table: *Ad Valorem* stamp duties

Rate

Capital duty (1% prior to 16 March 1988)	Nil
Conveyance or transfer on sale other than share transfer*	1%
Share transfers (including unit trusts)†	
before 27 October 1986	1%
from 27 October 1986	$\frac{1}{2}$%
Certain non-exempt loan transfers after 31 July 1986	$\frac{1}{2}$%
Exchanges or partitions of freehold land	1%
Inland bearer instruments (3% before 27 October 1986)**	$1\frac{1}{2}$%
Overseas bearer instruments (2% before 27 October 1986)**	$1\frac{1}{2}$%
Conversion of UK shares into depositary receipts (15.17)	$1\frac{1}{2}$%
Lease premiums	1%
Voluntary dispositions (gifts etc) — generally	Nil
(1% before 19 March 1985)	

Leases: *Ad valorem* **duty on rents (see 15.20)**

Life assurance policies—up to 31 December 1989	Amount assured:	
	Up to £50	Nil
	£50–£1,000	5p per £100 or part
	Over £1,000	50p per £1,000 or part
After 31 December 1989	Nil	

Superannuation annuity contract	5p per £10
or grant—up to 31 December 1989	annuity or part
After 31 December 1989	Nil

*Includes land, etc. For most categories including houses, no duty is payable if the value is certified at no more than £30,000.
**Bearer loan capital exempt.
†See 15.8.1 concerning abolition.

15.7   Capital duty

(FA 1973 Ss47 & 48 & Sch 19 & FA 1988 S141)

Prior to 16 March 1988 capital duty applied to 'chargeable transactions' (see below) carried out by 'capital companies' (see below). The companies covered were effectively managed in Great Britain; or managed outside the EEC with their registered office in Great Britain.

'Capital companies' include UK limited companies, limited partnerships (formed under Limited Partnerships Act 1907) and EEC companies. 'Chargeable transactions' which you should particularly note are the formation of a capital company and an increase in its capital by the contribution of assets, including the capitalisation of a debt. Other examples of chargeable transactions include the changing of a member's liability regarding his capital from unlimited to limited and certain transfers of the registered office or place of management back to the UK from abroad. Chargeable transactions carried out after 15 March 1988 are not subject to capital duty.

15.7.1   Rate of capital duty

Duty was charged at £1 on every £100 of the amount on which duty was chargeable. Parts of £100 counted as £100: thus if the amount was £101, the duty was £2. The amount on which duty was charged on the formation of a company or the increase of its capital was the consideration contributed by the members. This was normally cash but could be other assets taken at open market value. Where the registered office, etc, is transferred from abroad, the duty was charged on the net asset value of the company.

15.7.2   Exemptions from capital duty

The following transactions did not normally attract capital duty:

(1)   Capitalisation of reserves by bonus issues etc.
(2)   Company reconstructions, etc (15.9).
(3)   Increases in capital following reductions.
(4)   Company demergers (FA 1980 Sch 18) but transfer duty (15.8) was payable after 24 March 1986.
(5)   Share issues following preference share redemptions.

(Items (2), (3) and (4) above required adjudication — 15.1.)

15.8 Conveyance or transfer duty
(SA Ss54-61 & Sch 1 etc & FA 1984 Ss109 & 110 & FA 1986 Ss64-66)

In essence, duty is charged at £1 for every £100 (or part) of the value comprised in a conveyance or sale of any property, subject to an exempt portion for most assets (15.8.2). (Broadly, prior to 20 March 1984, the rate was 2%.) Certain *voluntary dispositions* were charged to full *ad valorem* duty. (There were various exclusions such as marriage settlements.) However, voluntary dispositions made after 18 March 1985 are in general now exempt. Other conveyances or transfers not subjected to the *ad valorem* duty bear a fixed 50p duty.

House purchases at discounted prices by public sector tenants and discounted sub-sales by housing associations carry duty on the discounted rather than the full market value.

Duty on share transfers was reduced from 1% to ½% from 27 October 1986. At the same time, purchases by a company of its own shares became liable to ½% transfer duty.

15.8.1 Abolition of stamp duty on shares
(FA 1990 Ss107-111)

All stamp duties on shares will be abolished from a date late in 1991–92, to be announced. This is to coincide as far as possible with the introduction of paperless dealing under the new Stock Exchange share transfer system.

The duties to be abolished include the ½% stamp duty on individual share transfers (15.8), 1.5% where UK shares are transferred into clearance services or converted into depositary receipts, stamp duty reserve tax (15.10), stamp duties on bearer shares and unit trust unit transfers. The 50p fixed duty on share transfers other than sales will also go.

15.8.2 Reduced rates of duty

Prior to (broadly) 20 March 1984, duty was charged at a reduced rate of only 50p for every £50 (or part) for transfers at full value of stock or marketable securities to a non-resident. Subsequently, however, no such relief is given from the general rate. An exemption applied for bearer securities. The duty before 27 October 1986 was 2% for overseas and 3% for British bearer securities. However, it is now 1½% in each case.

Prior to 20 March 1984, reduced rates applied where property other than stock and marketable securities was transferred (FA 1982 S128). In order to qualify, you included in the instrument a *Certificate of Value* that the transaction effected by the instrument did not form part of a larger transaction or series of transactions, in respect of which the amount or value of the consideration exceeded a stated limit. The limits were £25,000, £30,000, £35,000 or £40,000 which respectively reduced your duty rate to nil, 25p, 50p and 75p for every £50 (or part). (Below £300, special rates applied.) From broadly 20 March 1984, the relief has been simplified so that transactions not exceeding £30,000 are free of duty (apart from stock, etc) and others carry 1%.

15.9   Reliefs on company reconstructions and amalgamations, etc

Provided certain conditions are satisfied, company reconstructions and amalgamations are afforded relief from duty on conveyance or transfer (and before 16 March 1988, from capital duty). Also, transfers of assets between associated companies are relieved from duty on conveyance or transfer, provided one company owns at least 90% of the issued share capital of the other or both are owned to the same extent by a third company (FA 1930 S42).

15.9.1   Relief from capital duty
(FA 1973 Sch 19; & FA 1976 S128)

Prior to 16 March 1988, relief from capital duty (15.7) applied where an existing capital company, or one being formed, acquired share capital of another capital company so that it owned 75% of it. Relief also applied if the whole or part of one capital company's undertaking was acquired by another.

In order to obtain the relief, the consideration must have consisted of no more than 10% cash and the rest of shares in the acquiring company. The relief was normally lost if within five years the shareholding in the acquired company fell below 75%.

15.9.2   Relief from conveyance or transfer duty
(FA 1927 S55; FA 1928 S31, FA 1985 Ss78 & 81 & FA 1986 S75)

Similar relief applies from *ad valorem* stamp duty up to 24 March 1986. The exemption applied where a company issued shares, etc, in exchange for those of another company, in the course of obtaining control. It also applied if the first company already had control. Relief normally remains, however, where there is a company reconstruction with no real change in ownership. A once popular device for saving stamp duty on takeovers is known as the 'pref trick'. This has been broadly countered from 1 August 1985.

15.10 Stamp duty reserve tax
(FA 1986 Ss86–99)

Stamp duty reserve tax applies at $\frac{1}{2}\%$ on certain transactions in securities otherwise not liable to stamp duty. The charge broadly operates from 27 October 1986 but does not apply to securities exempt from sale duty (eg gilts) or traded options, etc. The stamp duty reserve tax is being abolished during 1991–92 (15.8.2).

Examples of when the tax applies are renounceable letters of allotment and sometimes where there is no transfer document (eg closing transactions within Stock Exchange accounts). A special rate of $1\frac{1}{2}\%$ applies to the conversion of UK shares into depositary receipts after 18 March 1986.

A specific case where $\frac{1}{2}\%$ stamp duty reserve tax applies is 'bed and breakfast' transactions, where shares are sold and repurchased within the same stock exchange account. Before 27 October 1986, no *ad valorem* duty arose.

15.11 Leases
(SA Sch 1; FA 1974 Sch 11; FA 1980 S95; FA 1982 S128; & FA 1984 S111)

Stamp duty at the 1% *ad valorem* rate applies to premiums on leases. The special scale in the following table applies to the rent element in a lease of land and buildings but not chattels, etc. Also excluded are licences.

15.11.1   Table: Leases — *ad valorem* duty on rents

Term	Annual Rent	Duty for every £50 or part thereof
Not exceeding 7 years or indefinite	not exceeding £500 exceeding £500	Nil 50p
7–35 years	—	£1
35–100 years	—	£6
over 100 years	—	£12

(Where the rent does not exceed £500, a sliding scale applies.)

From 20 March 1984 an *agreement for a lease* is subjected to stamp duty as if it were a lease. This blocks a previous avoidance device.

15.12   Fixed duties

These duties are paid at the same rate regardless of the size of the consideration involved in the transaction. The rate of duty is normally 50p which applies, for example, to miscellaneous conveyances or transfers not covered by *ad valorem* duty, declarations of trust, and surrenders. Many are now exempt under the Stamp Duty (Exempt Instruments) Regulations. A rate of £1 applies to leases of small furnished lettings and £2 to miscellaneous leases (eg, leases with uncertain rent or none at all).

16 Capital tax planning signposts

16.1 Introduction

Tax planning points have been interspersed throughout this book and generally appear in italics to distinguish them. Thus, CGT planning regarding your main residence appears in the section of the book which deals with that subject. However, other facets of capital tax planning regarding your home appear elsewhere in the book, such as joint ownership with your wife for IHT purposes. The purpose of this chapter is to group together references to the various tax planning points under different headings and circumstances. Thus, references are given together to various different planning points concerning houses.

As a general point, you should remember that, as with all other tax planning, capital tax planning should under no circumstances involve tax evasion. Evasion is completely illegal and could result in your paying substantially more to the Inland Revenue, including penalties and interest.

Tax avoidance, on the other hand, is completely legal and consists of arranging your affairs in such a way that they attract the lowest possible tax charge. It must be said, however, that very comprehensive anti-avoidance provisions are to be found in the Taxes Acts, some of which are described in outline in this Guide. In addition, a number of case decisions have been decided in favour of the Inland Revenue which increase their powers, with regard to blocking artificial tax avoidance schemes.

For example there was a far-reaching decision in the House of Lords early in 1981 in two jointly considered CGT avoidance cases (*W T Ramsay* v *IRC* and *Eilbeck* v *Rawling*). This decided, among other things, that the effect of an artificial tax avoidance scheme had to be considered as a whole if it had no commercial result other than the saving of tax. Subsequently, *Furniss* v *Dawson* has held this to mean that stages in a chain can be disregarded if they have no effect but to save tax.

The tax planning points throughout this Guide are not of an artificial nature. On the whole, they indicate various ways in which advantage can be taken of the legislation without exploiting it.

Put in a nutshell, capital tax planning consists of the art of maximising your wealth, for the enjoyment of your spouse, yourself and your children. Enjoyment is one of the key factors and if the measures which you have to take, such as going abroad to a country which you do not like, detract from your quality of life then the tax advantages probably would not justify the upheaval. Similarly, the gain of tax advantages at the risk of leaving your spouse insufficient to live on is not to be recommended.

A particular point to remember regarding capital tax planning is that, especially regarding IHT, the projected savings are not likely to take place for many years. Within that period of time, the law could be completely altered and so it is most desirable to have a degree of flexibility in your arrangements. However, capital tax rates are in general comparatively moderate at the present time, so that timely action is advisable, in case a future government makes adverse changes.

Remember that the following 'signposts' usually only relate to the planning points in the text and so it will normally be advisable also to refer to the basic rules shown nearby. Furthermore, the 'signposts' are not exhaustive and so reference to the contents and index may be necessary. The main headings are as follows:

	Reference
Business assets	16.2
Buying and selling assets in general (including shares)	16.3
Buying, selling and developing land	16.4
Buying your home	16.5
Charitable gifts	16.6
Coming to live in the UK	16.7
IHT on death – mitigation	16.8
Drawing up your will	16.9
Family company planning	16.10
Farming	16.11
Getting married and subsequent planning	16.12

16.2 Business assets

16.3 Buying and selling assets in general (including shares)

16.4   Buying, selling and developing land

16.5   Buying your home

16.6   Charitable gifts

16.7   Coming to live in the UK

16.8   IHT on death – mitigation

16.9   Drawing up your will

16.10   Family company planning

16.11   Farming

16.12   Getting married and subsequent planning

16.13   Gifts

16.14 Going to live abroad

16.15 Groups of companies and reorganisations

16.16 Life assurance planning

16.17   Providing for your children

16.18   Providing for your grandchildren

16.19   Providing for your retirement

16.20   Stamp duty saving

16.21   Tax-favoured investments

16.22   Trusts in planning

16.23   Working abroad

16.24   Year-end planning – reliefs, etc, to consider each tax year

CGT – annual exemption	2.5.4
bed & breakfast	2.14.1
IHT – annual exemption	7.15
Small gifts relief	7.15

Index